ANALYZING CRIMINAL MINDS

ANALYZING
CRIMINAL MINDS

Forensic Investigative Science
for the 21st Century

Don Jacobs

Brain, Behavior, and Evolution
Patrick McNamara, Series Editor

 PRAEGER

AN IMPRINT OF ABC-CLIO, LLC
Santa Barbara, California • Denver, Colorado • Oxford, England

Library of Congress Cataloging-in-Publication Data

Jacobs, Don (Don E.)
   Analyzing criminal minds : forensic investigative science for the 21st century /
Don Jacobs.
      p. cm. — (Brain, behavior, and evolution)
   Includes bibliographical references and index.
   ISBN 978-0-313-39699-1 (hardcopy : alk. paper) —
ISBN 978-0-313-39700-4 (ebook)
   1. Criminal psychology. 2. Forensic sciences. I. Title. II. Series.
   HV6080.J33   2011
   363.25—dc22   2010051242

ISBN: 978-0-313-39699-1
EISBN: 978-0-313-39700-4

15   14   13   12   11   1   2   3   4   5

This book is also available on the World Wide Web as an eBook.
Visit www.abc-clio.com for details.

Praeger
An Imprint of ABC-CLIO, LLC

ABC-CLIO, LLC
130 Cremona Drive, P.O. Box 1911
Santa Barbara, California 93116-1911

This book is printed on acid-free paper ∞

Manufactured in the United States of America

676729143

Discovery consists of seeing what everyone has seen
and thinking what nobody else has thought.
—Albert Szent-Gyorgi, Nobel Prize–Winning Chemist
(Good, Mayne, & Maynard Smith, 1963, p. 15)

Contents

Series Foreword

Beginning in the 1990s, behavioral scientists—that is, people who study mind, brain, and behavior—began to take the theory of evolution seriously. They began to borrow techniques developed by the evolutionary biologists and apply them to problems in mind, brain, and behavior. Now, of course, virtually all behavioral scientists up to that time had claimed to endorse evolutionary theory, but few used it to study the problems they were interested in. All that changed in the 1990s. Since that pivotal decade, breakthroughs in the behavioral and brain sciences have been constant, rapid, and unremitting. The purpose of the Brain, Behavior, and Evolution series of titles published by ABC-CLIO is to bring these new breakthroughs in the behavioral sciences to the attention of the general public.

In the past decade, some of these scientific breakthroughs have come to inform the clinical and biomedical disciplines. That means that people suffering from all kinds of diseases and disorders, particularly brain and behavioral disorders, will benefit from these new therapies. That is exciting news indeed, and the general public needs to learn about these breakthrough findings and treatments. A whole new field called evolutionary medicine has begun to transform the way medicine is practiced and has led to new treatments and new approaches to diseases, like the dementias, sleep disorders, psychiatric diseases, and developmental disorders that seemed intractable to previous efforts. The series of books in the Brain, Behavior, and Evolution series seeks both to contribute to this new evolutionary approach to brain and behavior and to bring the insights emerging from the new evolutionary approaches to psychology, medicine, and anthropology to the general public.

The Brain, Behavior, and Evolution series was inspired by and brought to fruition with the help of Debora Carvalko at ABC-CLIO. The series editor,

Dr. Patrick McNamara, is the director of the Evolutionary Neurobehavior Laboratory in the Department of Neurology at Boston University School of Medicine. He has devoted most of his scientific work to development of an evolutionary approach to problems of sleep medicine and to neuro-degenerative diseases. Titles in the series will focus on applied and clinical implications of evolutionary approaches to the whole range of brain and behavioral disorders. Contributions are solicited from leading figures in the fields of interest to the series. Each volume will cover the basics, define the terms, and analyze the full range of issues and findings relevant to the clinical disorder or topic that is the focus of the volume. Each volume will demonstrate how the application of evolutionary modes of analysis leads to new insights on causes of disorder and functional breakdowns in brain and behavior relationships. Each volume, furthermore, will be aimed at both popular and professional audiences and will be written in a style appropriate for the general reader, the local and university libraries, and graduate and undergraduate students. The publications that become part of this series will therefore bring the gold discovered by scientists using evolutionary methods to understand brain and behavior to the attention of the general public, and ultimately, it is hoped, to those families and individuals currently suffering from those most intractable of disorders—the brain and behavioral disorders.

Acknowledgments

To my colleagues in forensic investigative sciences: With your remarkable contributions as interdisciplinary-trained forensic investigative scientists, forensic science has become without question the most important of all applied sciences of the 21st century.

Thanks to my students for permission to use your excellent essays appearing at the end of each of the four parts of the book. Even though you will remain anonymous, your insightful essays provided moments of truth for my Brainmarks Paradigm. Thanks to Kate Garrett in the early stages of the manuscript for your review and helpful suggestions.

To all my students across three decades: I can never repay you for sharing with me the significance of your life in peer tribes, and through the years—25 and counting—to appreciate the workings of your brilliant sapient brains. You have taught me the real challenge for parents: *listen* more, *learn* more, and *trust* more.

That's quite an assignment.

Part I

Forensic Investigative Science

fur-**ren**-sik   the use of science, technology, and expert testimony in the investigation and verification of evidence presented in criminal court proceedings

in-**ves**-ti-g*uh*-tiv   systematically examine crimes or deaths to discover facts and truths

sahy-*uh* ns   branch of knowledge dealing with theory and facts derived from observation and research showing general laws that affect judicial verdicts and sentencing

Introduction to Part I: Scientists Who Seek to Capture Criminal Minds

From crime labs to crime scenes working to solve the twisted puzzle of criminal minds, a new descriptive title recently has emerged to describe the *interdisciplinary training* required for 21st-century forensic science careers. Forensic scientists are *forensic investigative scientists.* Each word has relevance in the evolution of 21st-century version of forensic science.

- *Forensic*—evidence must be processed and analyzed to a certainty in forensic labs and presented in a systematic way to sway juries in criminal cases;
- *Investigative*—careful examination of evidence is required and, in the age of diminished capacity and neurolaw, *additional psychological insights* into the perpetrator's state of mind during the commission of the crime is required; and
- *Scientist*—a high standard of training, knowledge, expertise, and *ability to communicate across disciplines* is necessary for reliable criminal minds' capture and to prove criminal cases beyond reasonable doubts using advanced technology such as neuroscans and brain fingerprinting.

In the 21st century, training in the classroom and in the field has become a pedagogical priority. In this regard, references appended at the end of chapters and included in the book's bibliography have guided my perspectives over years of *pedagogical development*—how best to present the wondrous workings of sapient brains to college students pursuing degrees in the behavioral sciences and now, forensic investigative sciences. (I will persist in using "sapient brains" throughout the book to define the ability of our species—*Homo sapiens*—to act eventually with purposive, self-reflective judgments, and as a benchmark of the "reasonable man standard" in legal jurisprudence.)

Is there a quantifiable process to explain how violent criminal minds emerge from sapient brains—the same brains with the potential to nurture offspring and to be law-abiding citizens? For compelling answers that square with cognitive neuroscience and evolutionary psychology, we must turn to the study of *spectrum psychopathy which will comprise, directly or indirectly, the subject matter of all twelve chapters.* In the meantime, as students prepare for forensic science careers, optimal preparation suggests interdisciplinary training in the classroom. What has transpired in this perspective represents the new tools and improved products described in Part I, Forensic Investigative Science.

In Part II, The Brainmarks Paradigm for Adaptive Neuropsychopathy, Chapters 4–7 define and describe my paradigmatic shift into a lifelong *adaptive version of psychopathy—a beneficial and restorative version*—referred to as neuropsychopathy. Peer-reviewers are not surprised at my conclusions based upon what we all see every day from sapient brains. Part II describes my cutting-edge paradigm of spectrum psychopathy, sure to kindle lively debate. The Brainmarks Paradigm is simply the next step in the understanding of this brain condition. Certainly, Robert Hare or Martin Kantor will not, in the least, be surprised by my conclusions.

From synergistic research alone, it is easy to document the contributions of brilliant colleagues, such as Hare and Kantor; they and numerous others are responsible for the evolution of spectrum psychopathy. Likewise, from student autobiographical essays that finally hit me "like a ton of bricks" in early 2010, the essays suggested elements of this paradigmatic shift as well. Four of these lightly edited autobiographies are included at the end of each of the four parts of this book. You soon will meet and discover facts about the lives of Rachel, Sabrina, Lauren, and Cassidy—all survivors of highly disruptive childhoods and adolescences who are now pursuing college degrees.

The time has come for the Brainmarks Paradigm. If this paradigm is perceived to be no more than a good idea that follows logically from what we already know about psychopathy, that is fine too. To quote Hungarian Nobel Prize–winning chemist Albert Szent-Gyorgyi, "Discovery consists of seeing what everyone has seen and thinking what nobody else has thought" (Good, Mayne, & Maynard Smith, 1963, p. 15). My conclusions already have been reflected on countless times; they simply have not been systematically presented and defended until now.

The existence and essence of an *adaptive version of ultramild psychopathy* (or my preferred term, "adaptive neuropsychopathy") as a natural brain condition will not be shocking, however, especially to scientists. To deny the ability of our sapient brains to survive and thrive would be to ignore on-the-fly adaptability inherent in the neuroanatomy and neurochemistry of our 2.5 pounds of cortical tissue. Sapient brains powered by awesome neurochemistry provide the launch pad to human behavior and social interactions for members of societies around the world. The same chemistry is responsible for the ability of sapient brains to fend off crushing despair thanks to nature's protective brain condition, and in contrast, across the continuum, this same chemistry is responsible for identifying the irreversible and violent psychopathic personality disorder.

In Part III, Order Becoming Disorder, Chapters 8–10 address the once widely embraced perspective of how criminality could be "parented-in" to offspring from "toxic" parenting and other damaging influences from peer and social milieus. Also, existing conditions of what now should be "parented-out" by informed parents are presented. The neurochemical basis of psychopathy is explored for both the adaptive version and the violent version, well-documented as psychopathic personality disorder. Chapter 10 begins by addressing a message in the famous poem "Richard Cory," and soon thereafter reveals aspects of the shocking murder and suicide of a mayor and her soon-to-be college-bound daughter in Coppell, Texas. At the end of Part III we meet Lauren, who is "tortured by tears."

Part IV, Truly, Honestly, Deceptively, includes the final two chapters. Chapter 11 presents two compelling essays, *Gender Differences among Psychopathic Serial Murderers* and *The Sexually Motivated Male Serial Killer: An Interdisciplinary Monster,* both written by my top student Ashleigh Portales, now a crime scene investigator in Wise County, Decatur, Texas. Chapter 12 concludes with a prescient look into 23rd-century forensic neuropsychology and the concept of "internal cortical prisons" created by brain chip technology. Will these technologies lead to the cessation of criminal minds, or will a new set of nightmares and challenges require new tools and improved products?

REFERENCE

Good, I. J., Mayne, A. J., & Maynard Smith, J. (Eds.). (1963). *The scientist speculates.* New York: Basic Books.

Chapter 1

 **Becoming a Forensic Investigative Scientist**

Forensic science is best described as an applied amalgam of both the physical and behavioral sciences. Approaches, tools, and techniques of case resolution become truly interdisciplinary. It is this eclectic and novel nature of the practice of forensic science that gives it such tremendous utility, and also appeals to the intellectual curiosity of those drawn to the profession.

—Michael A. Lytle, *res ipsa* observation, director, Forensic Investigation Program, University of Texas at Brownsville and Texas Southmost College, and founding faculty member, Forensic Science Program, Marymount University

The crime scene has its cast of participants: the perpetrator brings deception and violence, his or her victim brings life and likely losses it, and forensic investigative scientists bring skill, academic preparation, and interdisciplinary training. *Forensic investigate science is the science of crime scenes.*

—Don Jacobs (2010), *res ipsa* observation, author and creator of the FORS rubric of forensic science labs

GROWTH OF A SCIENCE

Since 2004, as a professor of psychology, I have been immersed in the voluminous literature related to our modern understanding of *spectrum psychopathy*. When I applied elements of modern evolutionary development from genetics (collectively known as Evo-Devo) to advances in evolutionary psychology, characteristics of my new paradigm begin to fit modern forensic investigative science like a glove. Authoring several textbooks related to forensic psychology helped to fill in the gaps that would go beyond the creation of three forensic science labs to insights that would become my Brainmarks Paradigm of Adaptive Neuropsychopathy soon to be addressed. In addition to making various conference presentations, often as keynote speaker, I authored numerous college textbooks as well as the widely popular FORS rubric of academic transfer courses. Three forensic science labs of the FORS rubric—FORS 2440, FORS 2450, and FORS 2460—offer college students a science-based and technology-rich interdisciplinary curricula with seamless academic transfer leading to bachelor's, master's, and doctoral degrees in university studies. It is my hope that students receive 21st-century training through *interdisciplinary forensic investigative sciences*—the focus of this book.

In the 21st century, students seeking careers in forensic science now may enter academic emphasis programs as freshmen and sophomores; this is possible because of three interdisciplinary labs—crime scene investigation (CSI) training and analysis (FORS 2440), forensic psychology (FORS 2450), and forensic chemistry or criminalistics (FORS 2460). From 2004 to the present, I assembled college curricula with a variety of interdisciplinary courses beyond the FORS rubric, some with the PSYC rubric (psychology), others with the CRIJ rubric (criminal justice), and still others with the ANTH rubric (anthropology)—all assisting students early in their academic preparation for optimal cross-disciplinary training. I cannot overemphasize the importance of multiple courses comingling and merging when educating 21st-century forensic investigative scientists.

I am honored to unveil the 10 pillars—the new tools and improved products—of interdisciplinary *forensic investigative sciences* for 21st-century analysis of criminal minds. Who knows how many more tools and products will be forthcoming? For now, the following 10 tools and products are united as part of multidisciplinary and interdisciplinary preparation:

- Criminal psychology
- Forensic psychology
- Forensic neuropsychology
- *Psychopathy Checklist–Revised*
- Neuroscans
- Neurolaw
- Adolescent neurobiology
- Criminal profiling
- Brain fingerprinting
- Brainmarks Paradigm of Adaptive Neuropsychopathy

These tools and products can be used to educate forensic investigative scientists who are eager to communicate with colleagues across disciplines. With the inclusion of different academic disciplines in curricula that are interacting and merging to solve the real problems of forensic investigation, *neuroscience* increasingly will be at the center of solving cases and identifying and apprehending perpetrators.

Neuroscience includes the scientific study of the central nervous system, and tangentially, its peripheral aspects in the endocrine system of glands that produce an array of powerful hormones. In the 21st century, neuroscience has evolved into an interdisciplinary science, including biology, psychology, physics, medicine, pharmacology, computer science, mathematics, and philosophy. Hence, neuropsychology—the science of psychology at the tissue level—has become a powerful and effective tool in studying molecular, evolutionary, structural, functional, and medico-legal aspects of the brain.

MODEL PROGRAMS

A salient example of the importance placed on interdisciplinary academic preparation is found in cutting-edge university programs that require a double major when studying for the bachelor's degree in forensic science. Roger Webb, president of the University of Central Oklahoma (UCO) in Edmond, recently stated, "We have no idea where science and technology will take us in the future. We do know that the criminals and terrorists will be there." His prescient remarks were made at the official opening of the school's new $12 million Forensic Science Institute in March 2010. The Institute's director is Dwight Adams, PhD, an alumnus of UCO, and former head of the Federal Bureau of Investigation (FBI) laboratory in Quantico, Virginia—the largest and best equipped forensics laboratory in the world.

Similarly, across the state from the FBI Lab, Marymount University in Arlington, Virginia, affords students six hours of graduate work concentrated in forensic science in the master's degree in forensic psychology. This program allows aspiring psychologists, who have no criminal investigative coursework, to experience criminal case preparation from the criminal justice perspective. Professor Michael Lytle, now of the University of Texas, Brownsville, developed this crossover component that opened doors into vital internships at multiple public and private agencies. For example, The Cold Case Unit at the Naval Criminal Investigative Service (NCIS) and the FBI's Behavioral Science Unit (BSU) cooperated in the program, offering cutting-edge internships. Professor Lytle recounts the story of one of his best students who is now an international corporate lawyer in London.

> I tell current students she was just like them—a sophomore psychology major and criminal justice minor—sitting in Principles of Forensic Science dressed in jeans and a T-shirt. She turned to the girl next to her—that girl later became a senior staffer at the Center of Missing and Exploited Children—and said, "Let's work together and make an A." She is now 32 years old and earns $250,000 a year.

When colleagues working as CSIs, medico-legal death investigators, laboratory criminalists, criminal attorneys, forensic anthropologists, forensic psychologists, and criminal profilers share a common link to the new technologies available across disciplines, solving tough cases posed by smart criminals can depend on this interdisciplinary knowledge. In embracing new technologies, 21st-century forensic investigative scientists are more likely to see commonalities and patterns in perpetrators and achieve the common goal of extracting violent criminals from society like a bad tooth.

TEN PRODUCTS OF MODERN CRIMINAL MINDS CAPTURE

Analysis of forensic evidence and criminal mind analyses drives 100 percent of criminal investigation and criminal prosecution. The four parts of this text, including 12 chapters, address the 10 products of modern criminal minds capture, plus a new paradigm of spectrum psychopathy.

Solving riddles at crime scenes is a focused adventure in problem solving. As novelist Thomas Harris (1988) stated, sapient brains appear to have a knack for it. We are inherently curious; we want to know *who* and *why*?

The oldest tool surviving into modern times asking "who and why?" is *criminal psychology*—the first product. From 19th- and 20th-century police psychology, criminal justice protocols, a long history of autopsy reports, rigorous FBI research into *known offender characteristics* (KOC) from the 1970s, and mainstream literary culture—specifically from the fictional novels of Sir Arthur Conan Doyle—criminal psychology has evolved as a viable tool of the investigative sciences. It has come so far that the stereotypical "clue-hungry" detective is now considered old school. In the 21st century, the field of criminal psychology has evolved in courtroom proceedings as forensic psychology.

The bar for conviction in criminal cases is beyond a reasonable doubt or more than 90 percent certainty of guilt. This benchmark of evidentiary proof, along with insights into the perpetrator's state of mind, produced the well known pronouncement from judges to "Prove your case." Scientists did just that as the labs of forensic science were born. DNA (deoxyribonucleic acid) analysis alone has become revolutionary in winning cases and, alternatively, freeing hundreds of wrongly convicted inmates as observed in the *Innocents Projects* created by attorneys Barry Scheck and Peter Neufeld. DNA evidence connects the accused to crime scenes. The 10 new tools and improved products of forensic investigative sciences explain *why* the perpetrator "authored" the "handy work" of crime scenes.

As mentioned earlier, criminal psychology found another pathway for expression in *forensic psychology*—the second new product. Applicable in criminal proceedings in the guise of expert witness testimony, forensic psychology includes a plethora of specific agendas, such as determining *competency to stand trial,* and procedural strategies in which practitioners are forensic *amicus curiae* (that is, "friends of the court in forensic matters"). Advances in high-resolution brain scanning technology (henceforth, *neuroscans*) have been highly influential in this regard, launching the third product—*forensic neuropsychology*—which progressively has found a niche in criminal cases carrying the death penalty. Neuroscans show juries cortical regions in high definition and in colorful images indicating increased or decreased blood flow. Triers of fact must decide whether the neuroscans are merely descriptive or clinically diagnostic. Expert forensic scientists can argue either way as "hired guns." Still, neuroscans are becoming commonplace in cases featuring "diminished capacity" defenses. This new subspecialty merging psychology and neurology with legal standards dates back decades earlier to advances in *general neuropsychology*, which stimulated advances in medical technologies.

Forensic neuroscientists have made compelling progress in criminal minds analysis featuring the startling science of *neuroscans*—the fourth new product. This merging of neuroscience and medical technology provides evidence of a "diminished mind" owing to cortical lesions and cerebral traumas. Although an infant science, neuroscans provide grist to scientists debating descriptive analysis: what are the scans describing occurring deep in cortices of the brain? Do neuroscans show the workings of criminal minds in real time? These neuroscans are on the rise as a new scientific ace up the sleeve of criminal attorneys. Always eager for new technology, this rising star in technology has hatched a neuroscience of criminal minds with the new legal component of *neurolaw*—the fifth new tool—addressed in Chapter 7.

Improvement by revision highlights the venerable sixth improved product—Robert Hare's psychometric indicator of psychopathy, *The Psychopathy Checklist–Revised* (2003). His PCL-R instrument will be discussed in more detail in Chapter 3. Hare's test has become the universal standard for *measuring reliably and validly psychopathic traits* worldwide.

Yet another rising star among new tools of 21st-century brain analysis comes from *adolescent neurobiology*—the seventh new product. The adolescent brain, young and developing, is a sapient brain typified by a *dangerous paradox*. Is the adolescent brain the breezeway to juvenile crime? Paradoxically, neuroscience tells us that young sapient brains are intent upon *cerebral bingeing,* observed in rapid proliferation of tissue, offset by the "pruning" back of seldom-used neurons in later adolescence. Also, young brains seek to squash boredom of routine with new stimuli as a priority almost whimsically as though *entitled to do so.* Is this a normal brain condition?

The adolescent brain is associated with a 200 percent to 300 percent increase in illness and violent death during that explosive pubescent growth phase. Also, producing bigger and stronger bodies accompanied by "amoral tunnel vision," the adolescent stage often becomes a behavioral nightmare for parenting. Yet, with insights from interdisciplinary training in 21st-century technologies of adolescent brain analysis, perhaps high-risk behavior resulting from minimally performing prefrontal regulatory control can be more effectively addressed, along with the knowledge of "what's really going on" in adolescent sapient brains. Directly from my acknowledgment page, "to *listen* more, *learn* more, and *trust* more" takes considerable courage and perhaps faith—a tall order for parents who must realize how important their influences are in providing yet another supportive layer of guidance over nature's gift of adaptive neuropsychopathy.

Largely because of the FBI's involvement in violent predator analysis and apprehension, the evolving art of *criminal profiling*—the eighth improved product—is inching closer to a higher bar required by the *inductive logic* of science—the "prove it" factor. The Atlanta child murders provided a national forum for FBI agents John Douglas and Roy Hazelwood to showcase this once highly controversial tool. In the 21st century, criminal profiling is used worldwide with increased accuracy.

Brain fingerprinting—the ninth new technological tool—is an applied product of electroencephalography (EEG) technology. Dr. Larry Farwell, the Harvard-trained scientist behind this applied technology, teaches technicians how to read brain "fingerprints." The goal is "deception detection" deeply embedded as *hypothalamic-encoded memories* in cortices of the brain. Recognition of memories can be objictified in a P3 wave MERMER (**m**emory- and **e**ncoding-related **m**ultifaceted **EEG** **r**esponse) addressed in Chapter 2. In the technology of brain fingerprinting, lies cannot hide within a guilty brain.

It is now clear that an impressive move is under way for forensic investigative scientists to understand *pathological psychopathy* evidenced by violence mixed with perverted sexuality. The move is *away* from traditional diagnostic criteria in psychopathology from DSM (*Diagnostic and Statistical Manual of Mental Disorders*) pedigrees in clinical psychology and *toward* paradigms of pathological psychopathy verified by *clinical forensic neuropsychologists* as a brain condition already known to underlie violent, cold-blooded criminality. I address a monumental shift in the reconceptualization of psychopathy within the Brainmarks Paradigm of Adaptive Neuropsychopathy—presented in Chapters 4–7 as the 10th and final new tool—sure to cause lively debate in academic circles. In the 21st century, deception detection and the realization of "what's really going on" in sapient brains have never been more important.

As evidence of biological predispositions from genetics continues to fill pages in neuropsychology journals, how much, legitimately, can be attributed to evidences of horrific parenting (identified herein as *predatory [toxic] parenting*) and discussed in Chapter 7?

- Is bad parenting enough by itself to produce antisocial (garden-variety criminals) and cold-blooded psychopathic monsters?
- Must effective parenting require a "parenting-out" of more moderate psychopathic brain conditions, in the middle zone of the psychopathy continuum, as well as "parenting-in" socially acceptable values or allegiance to ecclesiastical canons or personal ethics?

Lastly, what psychological conditions and behavioral manifestations might we expect to ensue from a brain marked by liberated ("high gain") dopamine (DA) and liberated Norepinephrine (NE) chemistry as powerful endogenous chemical neurotransmitters within the brain—what we refer to as "DANE" brain shenanigans of Chapter 9?

- Might this brain, characterized by two powerful catecholamines—DA and NE—translate as a brain "chemically fit" to thrive and survive?
- Might other endogenous hormones enhance this condition, especially high-gain testosterone and high-gain phenylethylamine (PEA)?

- Does the DANE brain "turbo boosted" by testosterone present the model mandated by evolutionary development (Evo-Devo) to configure the brain most likely to survive almost any catastrophic and debilitating social condition of humiliation and bullying across millennia?

Have we become obsessed by criminal minds in a society saturated by a "culture of sexually violent crime," in which archetypical bogymen invade our dreams as nightmarish creatures? How much danger is really out there in everyday life?

LITERARY MISANTHROPES AS ARCHETYPICAL BOGYMEN

From academic classrooms to the labs of neuroscience to field investigation, and from crime labs to criminal courtrooms, forensic investigative scientists seek the same result—a safer society in which to live, work, and raise psychologically healthy children soon to be young adults and destined to become tomorrow's leaders.

Before recorded history, misanthropic bogymen saturated our culture as malevolent archetypes. In the 21st century, forensic investigative scientists seek to know whether victims first trusted them as "engaging" individuals who, through deceptive practices, later exposed them to their violent and sexualized "dirty tricks," creating horrific crime scenes. Perhaps the scariest part of this archetypical imagination is the fact that *violent predators hide in plain sight as the majority of them do not look menacing.*

- Will investigators know what potentially lies behind disguised behavior?
- Will they be fooled by first impressions?
- Will they be trained to know what these predators are truly capable of doing?
- Will officers allow perpetrators to ride away into the night as occurred multiple times with serial killers Jeffrey Dahmer and Gary Ridgway, and numerous other violent predators?

From literary pages, we delve into fictional novels for two prime examples of predators who invade our collective nightmares. Nineteenth-, twentieth-, and twenty-first-century novels of fiction have shown a consistent commitment to the portrayal of literary misanthropes across a spectrum from psychopathic violent predators to nonviolent varieties who are scarred souls—tragically and emotionally damaged—but not violent. May they find redemption from the tenderness of others? Two examples—*The*

Strange Case of Dr. Jekyll and Mr. Hyde and *Le Fantôme de l'Opéra*—will show the nature of *spectrum disorders* such as the cold-blooded psychopath—Edward Hyde—to the psychologically scarred soul of Eric—the Phantom.

The Strange Case of Dr. Jekyll and Mr. Hyde

The Strange Case of Dr. Jekyll and Mr. Hyde, written by Scottish author Robert Louis Stevenson (1886/1995), is best known for its vivid portrayal of the *duality of human personality.* This duplicity represents respectability presented in the nurturing persona of Dr. Jekyll versus the impulsivity and conniving mind in the misanthropic Edward Hyde, deep into violent "dirty tricks"—and loving it!

The Strange Case of Dr. Jekyll and Mr. Hyde, **written by Robert Louis Stevenson (1886), is best known for its vivid portrayal of the duality of human personality. (Courtesy of the Library of Congress)**

As a mirror on moral character, the phrase "Jekyll and Hyde" has become accepted in popular culture to describe a person's hidden dark side, perhaps best described as a *misanthrope*—a person who hates other people or who has been consistently disappointed in relationships leading to palatable negativity and anger.

The novella *The Strange Case of Dr. Jekyll and Mr. Hyde* pierced the veil between the fundamental dichotomy of the 19th century's notion of outward respectability versus a hidden and fulminating inward lust, depicting moral and social hypocrisy, while providing yet another instance of a fulminating criminal mind. On the surface, Dr. Jekyll is portrayed as an honorable physician with many friends and acquaintances; he nurtures his patients and his reputation by virtue of an engaging personality. Transitioning to Mr. Hyde, Jekyll disappears and is replaced by a person who is small in stature, mysterious, criminal, secretive, sexual, and violent.

As time passes, Edward Hyde (personifying pathological psychopathy) grows in power within Jekyll. After taking the chemical potion that "released" Hyde in the first place, and henceforth repetitively, Jekyll requires it no longer as his demonic twin appears spontaneously—a prescient foreboding of the 21st century's neuroscience showing the relative balance or imbalance of the brain's potion (neurochemistry behind the personality and behavioral characteristics of psychopathy) and how it produces mental health, mental disorder, and violent criminality; it is how "order" becomes "disorder" (addressed in Chapter 10).

When Jekyll's chemical cocktail that originally triggered his transformation runs dry, he frantically scours the pharmacies of London seeking the same ingredients, but ultimately he realizes one of the original components had unique imperfections; therefore, the exact formula could never be duplicated. Realizing he soon will be Hyde forever, Jekyll leaves behind a testament before committing suicide by poison—pointing out that while in Jekyll he felt charlatanistic, in Hyde he felt genuine, years younger, energetic, and sexual. He stated in his final confession that although Hyde knew people recoiled from him, he reveled in their rejection; *he felt no remorse for his violence*—a cardinal trait of extreme gradations of pathological psychopathy.

Le Fantôme de l'Opéra

The Phantom of the Opera (*Le Fantôme de l'Opéra*), a novel by French writer Gaston Leroux, originally a Gothic horror novel, was published in the United States in 1911 some two years after it appeared in the original serialization in France. Andrew Lloyd Webber's musical version—the premier occurring in London (1986)—remains the most popular and longest running show in the history of musical theater.

In his original story, Leroux tells the story of a young girl, Christine, who is destined to be an opera singer and whose father, a musician, shared with her inspiring stories when she was a young and impressionable child about a mysterious "Angel of Music." Nearing death, her father tells Christine he will send the Angel of Music to hear her sing.

Soon after his death, Christine becomes a member of the chorus at the prestigious Paris Opera House where she begins to hear a voice singing "beautiful music of the night." She believes the voice to be the Angel of Music; however, it is the voice of Eric, a disfigured musical genius who was a worker during the opera house construction; he secretly built a room for himself in the catacombs beneath the opera house.

Thus enters Eric—the ghost or phantom—into the plot as a misanthropic misfit. For some time, he had extorted money from the opera house owners as a pledge not to interrupt performances and scare patrons away. The phantom, therefore, is a threatening, nonviolent misanthrope in contrast to Edward Hyde's violent and homicidal criminal. Had Eric been violent, he surely would have faced arrest at all costs, rather than simply have been viewed as an unwelcomed nuisance.

For a brief time, Christine is influenced by Eric to live with him in his underground lair—the catacombs—where she is never physically, emotionally, or sexually abused. Eric nurtures and tutors her voice. Shortly thereafter, a romantic triangle ensues between Christine, the phantom, and Raoul, a recently renewed acquaintance from childhood. With the mounting possibility of "protective" violence for any interloper (competitor) for his love of Christine, Eric feigns a threat to kill Raoul and destroy the opera house unless she agrees to marry him.

However, a tender kiss from Christine pierces the veil of the phantom's misanthropic rage for never feeling loved—the singular gesture of affection apparently overwhelms Eric to the extent that he releases Christine. With great ambiguity in her heart, she leaves Eric for Raoul.

The mask worn by Eric to cover his scarred face is yet another metaphor of deception—hiding the dark side of his grieving heart. As a misanthrope, Eric appears, at the end of the story, to have found redemption for his misanthropy by the simple gesture of Christine's tender affection. This provides a subtle hint of what may be possible for those feeling merely estranged from mainstream society. Eric may have developed a psychological conditions known as PTSD—post-traumatic stress disorder—from earlier abuses. The fact remains: there is hope for Eric's type of misanthropy. Did his natural brain condition provide him with an adaptive version of psychopathy—an adaptive neuropsychopathy—prophylactic against suicide until he perceives a way around his problems? In this literary license, is it a big stretch or small half-step?

The violent psychopath Edward Hyde versus psychologically tortured Eric personifies further differences *between spectrum psychopathy and DSM-inspired pure psychopathologies such as PTSD*. For example, the nurturing physician, Dr. Jekyll, became the violent psychopathic Edward Hyde through a "chemistry experiment"—a metaphor for the endogenous variety that cascades in sapient brains. Hyde grew to enjoy and ultimately prefer his alter ego; Hyde never suffered from a disorder. Eric, on the other hand, displayed a far different personality because of a lifetime of emotional scarring leading to rejection; he may have, through Christine, found redemption and a way out of his misery. Might Eric find another woman to love him? It seems entirely possible.

As literary misanthropes, Eric is miserable and sad in his psychopathology, while Edward Hyde is empowered and energized by violence and criminality in his pathological psychopathy. Big difference.

Edward Hyde, empowered, invincible (bulletproof), and callous to the feelings of others, flourished in his version of spectrum psychopathy, while Eric, miserable and sad, retained his hope for better treatment in his version of psychopathology. As we know in modern clinical forensic neuropsychology, *the only love a true psychopath feels is for his jagged self.*

INSIDE FORENSIC SCIENCE

The impact of modern neuroscience upon criminal mind analysis has, technologically, created new cutting-edge tools and improved products. New paradigmatic ground has been broken again with my 2010 Brainmarks Paradigm featuring the argument for adaptive psychopathy (or *neuropsychopathy*). Careers in forensic investigative science are becoming the most important applied science of the modern world—a world filled with violent criminality and terrorism in all its forms.

To those new to investigative science, the emphasis in this investigative field (as CSIs), in criminalistics (as laboratory scientists), and in criminal mind analysis (as profilers and *amicus curiae* advisors) is on behavioral science transitioning to forensic investigative science.

Homicide investigators, for example, have been trained traditionally in criminal justice as shrewd, clue-hungry detectives who leave no stone unturned; still, they have not been trained to *think as scientists*. That's changing in the age of neuroscience with scientific investigation on the front-burner. Forensic science is composed of various disciplines of study, principally criminal justice-inspired crime scene and homicide investigation, along with behavioral sciences of psychology and anthropology joined to the natural sciences of biology, chemistry, and physics to connect the *why* in criminal minds analysis.

Imagine CSIs, homicide detectives, medico-legal death investigators, laboratory criminalists, criminal profilers, and forensic psychologists not cooperating in investigations—not knowing or caring what other disciplines offer in forensic investigative science.

- Might cops on patrol benefit from insights embedded in tools of criminal and forensic psychology when they pull over cars on lonely country roads?
- Who might the officers have before them?

What if this? What if that? Criminal psychology and related disciplines offer additional information over and beyond the excellent criminal justice academy training to answer more completely "What if?" questions. Officers do not confront solitary persons as much as they confront his or her brain—a brain intent upon survival; a brain that is, by nature, deep into deceptive practices. Is it ready to hatch a criminal mind?

As a preview of things to come, the following prescient quote from Charles Darwin foreshadowed the fact that the future is now and right in our faces:

In the distant future I see open fields far more important than research. Psychology will be based on a new foundation that of the necessary acquirement of each mental power and capacity by gradation. Light will be thrown on the origin of man and his history. (Darwin, 1859/1882, p. 428)

Communicating with investigative colleagues across disciplines can speed up the process of apprehension and save countless lives. This kinship is best exemplified by learning the language and perspectives of related disciplines:

- How can criminal psychology expedite CSI's role at crime scenes?
- What can forensic psychology's study of criminal minds' *mens rea* (criminal intent) bring to criminal court?

- Can forensic neuropsychologists, equipped with high-resolution brain scanning technology, show *diagnostic evidence* of brain malfunction? Also, what is the role of brain fingerprinting?
- What happens when evidence ends up in forensic labs? What needs to be known by CSIs who gather evidence in the field?
- Must criminal justice–trained students become academically prepared to know as much as possible about *criminal mind*? Would they "read" crime scenes differently?
- Do antisocial criminals differ from cold-blooded psychopaths in personality, habits, and patterns? Should investigators know this?

THE NEW INVESTIGATIVE TOOL KIT

Forensic science academic training is most effective when it reflects *forensic investigative kinship.* An interdisciplinary "tool kit" linked to other disciplines is advisable in securing internships as departmental cooperation puts investigators on the same page. To that end, all bachelor's degrees in forensic sciences should include the study of interdisciplinary investigative sciences. Forensic psychology, criminal justice, anthropology, biology and chemistry, and other tangential disciplines, such as "cybercrimes" units investigating cyberbullying, must reflect interdisciplinary coursework. Mentioned earlier, we favor *double major degree programs,* or a collection of courses intermingled among various disciplines that offer corroborating advantages to students entering advanced degree programs. In this way, no one discipline is left out of the loop that might hamstring scientists in the process.

It all starts with evidence collected at crime scenes. Investigative "inputs" affect decisions models (logistics) far in advance of authoring criminal profiles.

The general public's obsession with reality-based television programming such as *CSI: Crime Scene Investigation* has contributed to a pop culture phenomenon known as "The CSI Effect" (Schweitzer & Saks, 2007). This syndrome evolved because of the general public watching a variety of CSI-related television programs. In this effect, jurors develop unreasonable expectations in real-life cases from evidence presented by forensic investigative scientists; jurors may wrongfully acquit guilty defendants when scientific evidence such as DNA evidence does not meet their television-inspired expectations, whether or not it is warranted in specific cases. In real life, evidence is often more sketchy and equivocal and seldom as "swift and certain" as presented in CSI-related programs. Jury selection has been affected by this effect by asking potential jurors if they are regular viewers of CSI shows.

In the pop culture phenomenon known as "The CSI Effect," jurors develop unreasonable expectations of evidence presented by forensic investigative scientists. Jury selection has been impacted by this effect. Now potential jurors are asked if they are regular viewers of CSI shows. (Photofest)

Criminology: Partnering with Criminal Psychology and Behavioral Psychology

Criminology is the scientific study of criminals, penal treatment, and *crime as a social phenomenon*. Over the past 20 years, the rise of modern criminal psychology has affected analysis of the individual criminal toward a standard for clinical assessment of his or her mental "state of mind" at the time of the offense. As an applied discipline, criminology *per se* has migrated toward a kinship with psychology (and neuropsychology) and away from criminal justice influences *per se* as in distancing itself from old-school "police psychology." Increasingly, criminal justice curricula is helping to drive the bandwagon of formal interdisciplinary education by requiring a collection of courses (multidisciplinary) with criminal and forensic psychology focus in preparation for CSI-oriented careers. For example, a CSI interprets crimes scenes differently with forensic psychology academic training.

Also relevant in the 21st century and inherent in special cases involving *severe* psychopathy evident in ultraviolent crime scenes "authored" by a violent psychopathic personality is the FBI-inspired investigative tool of *criminal profiling*. This technique is now *au courant* in criminal investigation worldwide because of its increased accuracy.

A persistent focus jointly shared by the expertise of criminal psychologists as professors in academia, clinical practice, and research versus forensic psychologists practicing in pretrial, trial, and post-trial jurisprudence courtside is this: Is the accused *psychotic* or in some way clinically disordered? If not psychotic, thereby not meeting the standard for an insanity plea, how severe is the mental defect or disorder? Is it severe enough to claim *diminished capacity*? Instead, might the accused be faking psychosis and is in reality a violent, cold-blooded psychopath?

Criminal Neurology: Forensic *Amicus Curiae*

For sure, the "smart practitioners in legal arenas" are *forensic neuropsychologists*—specialists who use brain-scanning technology. This technology is a cutting-edge relative to Computerized Axial Tomography (CAT) scans from the 1970s. Enter *criminal neurology* into jurisprudence suggested by this new breed of forensic neuropsychologists.

In the 21st century, *mens rea* (criminal minds' intent) is front and center in the gladiatorial venue of courtrooms in which a criminal's brain stands trial with the alleged perpetration by displaying his brain in high-resolution neuroscans. Judge and jury alike can view the colors—reds, yellows, and blues—from positron emission tomography (PET) scans that indicate quality of blood flow. Retained by prosecutors or defense attorneys as "hired guns" (expert witnesses with special knowledge), *criminal forensic neuropsychologists* dazzle legal arenas providing *evidence* of damaged brains pivotal in influencing verdicts. Lucrative careers as forensic *amicus curiae*—"friends of the court in matters of forensics" are becoming commonplace.

THE EVOLUTION OF HUMAN MOUSETRAPS

Early influences that shaped forensic investigative science—that is, *historical benchmarks* in the development of criminal psychology and criminal profiling will be addressed in society's quest to build a better mousetrap.

The late 19th century (1888) is a good place to start. Police surgeon Thomas Bond proffered a *psychological profile* of the White Chapel murderer, "Jack the Ripper." Bond, a physician, assisted in the autopsy of Mary Kelly, the Ripper's last known victim. In his notes (from November 10, 1888), he mentioned the *sexual nature of the murders* coupled with elements of *misogyny* (hatred of women) and *misanthropy* (rage against people). Bond continues:

> All five murders no doubt were committed by the same hand. In the first four the throats appear to have been cut from left to right, in the last case owing to the extensive mutilation it is impossible to say in what direction the fatal cut was made, but arterial blood was found on the wall in splashes close to where the woman's head must have been lying. All the circumstances surrounding the murders lead me to form the opinion that the women must have been lying down when murdered and in every case the throat was first cut.

Furthermore, Bond hypothesized the killer to be subjected to "periodic attacks of homicidal and erotic mania," with the mutilations possibly indicating *satyriasis* (male hypersexuality).

The early landscape of psychological profiles from police surgeons turned "criminal psychologists" continued decades later when psychiatrist Walter Langer (1972) presented a profile of Adolf Hitler. Langer viewed Hitler through the eyes of those who knew him, providing eye-witness accounts of his behavior, accounts of which produced a diagnosis *in abstentia* of a manic-depressive disorder (the 21st century's bipolar disorder) typified by bouts of mania followed by periods of depression and paranoia.

In 1956, Greenwich Village psychiatrist James A. Brussel (1968), New York State's commissioner of mental hygiene, studied photographs of crime scenes and personal notes sent to the press by the so-called Mad Bomber—a serial bomber who terrorized the city for 16 years (1940 to 1956). The UNSUB (*unknown subject* in FBI lingo) Brussel targeted was a former disgruntled employee of Con Edison, an obsessed and paranoid loner. The employee turned out to be George Metesky, who was charged with 47 separate crimes, including seven counts of attempted murder. In 1957, Metesky was adjudicated a "dangerously incapacitated person" and confined to a psychiatric center for the criminally insane.

Later, Brussel wrote a book about his *criminological approach*, which caught the attention of a veteran police officer, Howard Teten of California. Teten, an FBI agent since 1962, soon became part of the FBI's new Behavioral Science Unit at Quantico, Virginia. He and fellow BSU instructor Patrick Mullany added their expertise to Brussel's perspective by expanding methods of analyzing unknown offenders in unsolved (cold) cases. Soon, Teten, Mullany, and later Robert Ressler and John Douglas would foster insights into the criminal mind with *criminal investigative analysis*, characterized by inputs at crime scenes necessary for profiling, including logistics, decision models, and crime scene assessment—all of which contribute directly to authoring the profile itself, followed by investigation and apprehension. Criminal investigative analysis from the 1970s is the historical link to interdisciplinary forensic investigative science of the 21st century.

Early Influences Inspired by Fiction

Scottish author Sir Arthur Conan Doyle (1859–1930), in a series of fictional novels introducing his famous detective, Sherlock Holmes, demonstrated how early methods of police (detective) work eventually produced viable suspects. Indeed, Sherlock Holmes inspired the creation of the 20th-century discipline of *forensic science,* especially by his minute study of even the smallest clues beginning with *trace evidence* from shoe impressions, fingerprints, and handwriting analysis, now known as *questioned document analysis.*

Due to his slow-moving medical practice, Conan Doyle found time to write short stories, his favorite passion. His first crime story, *A Study in Scarlett* (1877), introduced the world to his famous detective 11 years before Jack the Ripper. Conan Doyle modeled Sherlock Holmes after Joseph Bell, his former medical school professor.

Webs of Deception

Perhaps Doyle's most popular crime novel ever, *The Hound of the Baskervilles* (1901), displays the importance of observation, reasoning, and *deductive reasoning* (also known as speculative logic). Astute criminal psychologists who are on the scent of violent criminals require an investigative mind.

Dartmoor, the physical setting of the story, is composed of moorland in Devonshire, England, featuring the Great Grimpen Mire, a foul-smelling swampland typified by thick and oozing quicksand. As the story unfolds, Holmes suspects that a *web of deception* is being woven by a clever criminal (perhaps a cunning *psychopath*?). Holmes correctly suspects this unknown suspect will attempt murder by resurrecting the legend of a demonic, spectral hound.

In any time frame reaching from classical philosophers to present-day investigators, *deception is always a central theme in criminal minds analysis.* This requires astute observation and deduction to unravel the mystery often spun by a brilliant psychopath—a cold-blooded killer.

Holmes decides to disguise himself as a hermit living upon the moor, a ruse to help further the investigation. The butler of Baskerville Hall,

Barrymore, is caught late one night signaling someone by candlelight across the moor leading to yet another mystery. (The butler is in fact signaling Seldon, a criminal and the brother of his wife. Along with Barrymore, she provides Seldon food and clothing.)

Ultimately, the most *deceptive ruse* of all belongs in the criminal mind (*mens rea*) of Jack Stapleton, a neighbor of the Baskervilles, who pretends to be the brother of a beautiful woman (to whom he is actually married and for a time is his co-conspirator).

Jack actually is the unknown son of Roger Baskerville, the brother of the recently deceased Sir Charles Baskerville, the wealthy owner of Baskerville Hall. The son, John Roger, becomes an embezzler of public funds, and later hatches a master plan by resurrecting the fable of the "killer hound" to dispose of the remaining Baskervilles and inherit his uncle's fortune as sole heir. Holmes correctly deduced this scheme by analyzing a large portrait of Sir Charles that showed a remarkable resemblance to Jack, *especially through the eyes*. Also, John Roger Baskerville displays the cold stare of a psychopath.

Holmes's correct deduction turns the criminal case around as an early example of the *powers of deduction and observation* in solving difficult cases, a parallel to the work of criminal psychologists and later to criminal profilers *who must imagine what most likely happened from evidence left behind at crime scenes*. Becoming astute observers to the smallest detail of CSI analysis comes with academic training, application in internships, and direct on-the-job experience. With training as CSIs, criminal psychologists make effective crime scene investigators, perhaps a trend in the making.

Throughout Conan Doyle's long literary career (as his medical, then later his ophthalmology careers failed), he became interested in miscarriages of justice by reversing two cold case files that led directly to the establishment of a Court of Criminal Appeals (1907) in Britain. But be forewarned: there was a *dangerous curve ahead*. The potential for a gigantic misstep in the evolution of criminal psychology loomed on the horizon in the theories of Freud.

Sigmund Freud: At the Paris Morgue

Almost no one thinks of Freud as an early contributor to forensic psychology. Yet, following a trail of evidence, there can be no question; he became an early contributor *due to his own deception*. In one grand gesture, Freud set a new standard for deceptive practices; he was one of the most famous contemporaries of Sir Arthur Conan Doyle. Freud was born in 1856, Doyle in 1853; Freud died nine years after Doyle (1930) in 1939.

Freud would become one of the most famous and controversial founders of an early school of psychology known as *psychoanalysis*—a theory that investigates *unconscious aspect of behavior*. Virtually unknown to students is Freud's direct observation of sexually abused children in the Paris morgue and the aftermath of the reversal of his Seduction Theory. Proposing that the mind held automatic repressions of unresolved conflicts in early childhood (especially of the oedipal complex variety—the supposed sensual or sexual attraction of young children to opposite-sexed parents), this theory provided developmental grist for those seeking answers to adolescent and young adulthood sexual misbehavior and, ultimately, *sexual criminality*. Would Freud's insight into the unconscious mind provide the long sought-after *mens rea* model for criminal psychology and in the courtroom with forensic psychology?

Freud's theoretical binge on unresolved sexuality in oedipal complex was nothing compared to his Seduction Theory purge—*the prime example of Freud's great deception*. Initially, his colleagues were outraged when they heard Freud's contention that parents may be sexually abusing their children. (Recall that Freud's sexual theories resonated in Victorian Europe where all discussion of sexual matters remained strictly taboo.)

In 1896, Freud theoretically professed that childhood seduction was the origin of *hysteria* and was due to early sexual traumas—"infantile sexual scenes" or "sexual intercourse in childhood"—in his words. It was his belief that these *early experiences were real, not fantasies*—long-lasting and damaging to children. Archivists contend that Freud believed the sexual acts were forced on the children, often by a parent (usually the father), and were not sought by the children.

Upon graduation from medical school, Freud traveled to Paris, France, to consult with the renowned neurologist of the day, Jean Martin Charcot. There, in the Paris morgue, Freud observed evidence of severe sexual abuse in some of the deceased children, thereby adding fuel to his theory of seduction. Immediately, Freud suspected childhood sexual abuse might be more rampant than imagined; if so, it could lead to death or permanent psychological *neurosis*—a condition referred to as *hysteria*. Upon hearing this news, colleagues begin to distance themselves from Freud. Sexual abuse by parents was just too outrageous.

What transpired in aftermath was this: Freud *reversed his Seduction Theory* by stating that sexual behavior between parent and their children was not real: just imagined. His clear act of deception changed the course of his life and transformed his theory into a worldwide movement. Although Freud observed the sexual abuse with his own eyes, many critics, including the former director of the Freudian archives, Jeffery Masson, believe that

Freud reversed his position and abandoned his Seduction Theory to save his reputation and his hallowed place in the Founder's Club of Psychology (Masson, 2003).

Modern archivists consider the Seduction Theory *reversal* to be the cornerstone of psychoanalysis. In other words, even though his reversal was contrary to what he observed, his theories became famous for showing the strength of *imagination.* Could imagination alone psychologically cripple a person, leading to severe emotional trauma? This became Freud's mantra of belief. Ironically, by admitting error in his original theory (what he observed with his own eyes) and attributing the experience to fantasies of sexual seduction, psychoanalysis became an international movement. This singular event occurred in 1908.

However indirectly, the reversal was tainted by deception and fraud. Freud accomplished a rare feat by showing the power of imagination and fantasy in driving violent, sexual crime. In this convoluted way, it can be proposed that Freud was an early contributor to what would become forensic psychology.

As a sidebar, obsessive and compulsive his entire life, when Freud neared death, he had prearranged with his physician to administer an overdose of morphine—an instance of *euthanasia* (easy death)—upon consultation with his beloved daughter, Anna. The deceptive stoic remained in control of his life until the bitter end. Upon death, Freud's body was cremated and his ashes were deposed in a Grecian urn, a present given him by Marie Bonaparte.

TAKING THE BEST FORK IN THE ROAD

Historically and paradigmatically, the correct fork in the road was taken in what would come to be called forensic investigative science. By following the Holmesian pathway of dogged investigation using gathered evidence, instead of the Freudian perspective of unconscious conflicts, early criminal psychologists connected criminal *mens rea* with crime scene evidence pointing to the identity of the offender (suggested in the fiction of Conan Doyle) and moved away from unconscious influences of behavior (suggested by Freud). Ironically, through deception, Freud contributed to the power of the imagination, fantasies, and deception as the fuse to sexually psychopathic crime.

Had early trailblazers taken the pathway suggested by Freud—and his theory of unconscious mind and its "complexes" erupting from past repressions, clearly *a nonscientific perspective*—imagine the confusion and misdirection of the new science of forensics, especially forensic psychology. In fact, FBI agents Teten and Mullany rejected aspects of James Brussel's focus on Freudian theory in *all* respects, while keeping *all* non-Freudian perspectives intact in teaching *applied criminology and abnormal psychology* at the FBI Academy. But another dangerous curve was ahead. And the next fork in the road was just as critical for the evolution of criminal psychology as a precursor to forensic psychology and onward to forensic investigative science. That necessary path would be *behavioral psychology*, better known to the world as behaviorism.

ALIGNING WITH NATURAL SCIENCE

One of the seven psychological pillars in the evolution of criminal psychology (Jacobs, 2008), suggested most recently in *Psychology of Deception: Analysis of Sexually Psychopathic Serial Crime* (Jacobs, 2009), was following the pathway of *behavioral psychology*, which became the focus of American psychology in the 1920s. This proved to be a theoretical departure from Freud and his reliance on the unconscious mind ascertainable through dream analysis.

Taking the behavioral pathway and analyzing *observable behavior* suggested by the *behaviorism* of John B. Watson and later by the *behavioral connectionism* of Edward Thorndike, and still later with instrumental and purposive learning of Edward Tolman and operant conditioning by B. F. Skinner, insistence on observation and objectivity in the analysis of behavior *aligned criminal psychology with natural science.* The continued evolution of modern criminal psychology and later to forensic neuropsychology was absolutely critical along this pathway, without which we have no empirical science of *sexually psychopathic serial homicide.*

A somewhat distant relative to classical and instrumental behaviorism, *cognitive-behavioral psychology* emerged in the 1950s as a bridge from learned behavioral habits and patterns to deviant thinking patterns (cognitive mapping) as the fuse to the "boiling and scheming" criminal mind. This fuse ultimately exploded into violent "acting out" behavior (in the commonly used expression "he just snapped"), which soon would be addressed and brilliantly analyzed in the 1970s by Samenow and Yochelson.

During the 1960s and 1970s, *dysfunctional parental upbringing* was connected to subsequent juvenile delinquency as *cognitive mapping* (powerful thinking maps of behavior) of the criminal mind was applied to criminal investigation.

SAMENOW AND CRIMINAL PERSONALITY

In the 1970s, Stanton Samenow, PhD, emerged as a clinical psychologist turned researcher investigating criminal behavior at St. Elizabeth's Hospital in Washington, D.C. Samenow, along with colleague Dr. Samuel Yochelson, MD, published research findings from a series of studies (Samenow, 1984; Samenow & Yochelson, 1976–1986). For decades following this research, many state correctional facilities and emerging clinical forensic psychologists involved in the criminal justice system adopted insights from Samenow and Yochelson.

Essentially, they uncovered *cognitive distortions in thinking* that necessitated gradual eradication to reverse criminal behavior, a position that remains embedded in modern criminology and 21st-century criminal psychology. As time has shown, some thinking patterns are more resistant to change than others, the prime example being *psychopathy,* which is viewed along a continuum (spectrum) with mild, moderate, or severe varieties. In Chapters 4–7, spectrum psychopathy is presented in light of 21st-century forensic investigative science's cutting-edge paradigm—the Brainmarks Paradigm.

COGNITIVE DISSONANCE

Psychologist Leon Festinger (1957) introduced a theory of *cognitive dissonance,* which suggests inconsistent beliefs—what others demand from adolescents—often result in psychological tension. This disequilibrium can lead individuals to change their beliefs to fit what they desire to do, rather than change for the sake of another's perspective as suggested by popular wisdom. By this theory, teenagers can become accomplished liars to hide evidence of doing the forbidden, just as spectrum psychopaths become deceptive to fool others. As a social cognitive theory, cognitive dissonance resonates throughout modern criminal psychology.

21ST-CENTURY FORENSIC PSYCHOLOGY

According to the *American Academy of Psychiatry and the Law (AAPL),* 21st-century forensic psychologists increasingly are becoming involved in the following:

- Criminal responsibility evaluation
- Civil or criminal competency evaluation
- Mental disability assessment
- Risk assessment
- Juvenile assessment
- Involuntary treatment or commitment
- Child custody issues

- Psychic injury cases
- Malpractice cases
- Correction cases

If students are contemplating a major in psychology, when they hear the word "forensics," they should think of legal and judicial venues, not the morgue. Morgues are under the direction of *forensic pathologists*, not forensic psychologists and forensic psychiatrists. Forensic mental health professionals use their expertise in human behavior, motivation, and pathology to provide psychological services in the courts, assist in criminal investigations, develop specialized knowledge of crimes and motives, provide counseling, and conduct forensic research (Ramsland, 2002).

The psychological specialty that seeks to understand violent offenders, their methods, and their motivations, and that seeks to deliver accurate criminal profiling in special crimes falls under modern criminal forensic psychology. *In forensics, the living learn lessons from the dead.*

REFERENCES

Brussel, James A. (1968). *Casebook of a crime psychiatrist*. New York: Bernard Geis Associates.

Conan Doyle, Arthur. (1901). *The hound of the Baskervilles*. London: George Newnes.

Cummings, Nicholas A., & O'Donohue, William T. (2008). *Eleven blunders that cripple psychopathy in America*. New York: Taylor & Francis.

Darwin, Charles. (1859/1882). *On the origin of species by means of natural selection*. London: John Murray.

Darwin, Charles. (1871). *The descent of man, and selection in relation to sex*. London: John Murray.

Festinger, Leon. (1957). *A theory of cognitive dissonance*. Stanford, CA: Stanford University Press.

Gerber, Samuel M., & Saferstein, Richard. (Eds.). (1997). *More chemistry and crime*. Washington, DC: American Chemical Society.

Girard, James E. (2008). *Criminalistics: Forensic science and crime*. Boston: Jones and Bartlett.

Good, I. J., Mayne, A. J., & Maynard Smith, J. (Eds.). (1963). *The scientist speculates*. New York: Basic Books.

Harris, Thomas. (1988). *The silence of the lambs*. New York: St. Martin's Press.

Hazelwood, Roy, & Michaud, Stephen G. (2001). *Dark dreams*. New York: St. Martin's True Crime.

Heilbronner, Robert L. (Ed.). (2005). *Forensic neuropsychology casebook*. New York: Guilford Press.

Holmes, R., & Holmes, S. (2002). *Profiling violent crimes: An investigative tool* (3rd ed.). Thousand Oaks, CA: Sage.

Jacobs, Don. (2003). *Sexual predators in the age of neuroscience.* Dubuque, IA: Kendall-Hunt.

Jacobs, Don. (2008). *Sexual predators and forensic psychology.* Plymouth, MI: Hayden-McNeil.

Jacobs, Don. (2009). *Psychology of deception: Analysis of sexually psychopathic serial crime.* Dubuque, IA: Kendall-Hunt.

Langer, Walter. (1972). *The mind of Adolf Hitler.* New York: Basic Books.

Larrabee, Glenn, J. (Ed.). (2005). *Forensic neuropsychology: A scientific approach.* New York: Oxford University Press.

Leroux, Gaston. (1911). *Le Fantôme de l'Opéra.*

Lytle, Michael, Director, Forensic Investigation Program, University of Texas at Brownsville/Texas Southmost College and Founding Faculty Member, Forensic Science Program, Marymount University. Interview, 2010.

Masson, Jeffrey Moussaieff. (2003). *The assault on the truth: Freud's suppression of the seduction theory.* New York: Ballantine Books.

McDonald, J. M. (1963). The threat to kill. *American Journal of Psychiatry, 120,* 125–130.

Ramsland, Katherine. (2002). *The criminal mind: A writer's guide to forensic psychology.* Cincinnati: Writer's Digest.

Samenow, Stanton. (1984). *Inside the criminal mind.* New York: Crown.

Samenow, S., & Yochelson, S. (1976–1986). *The criminal personality* (3 vols.). New York: J. Aronson.

Schweitzer, N. J., & Saks, M. J. (2007). The CSI effect: Popular fiction about forensic science affects public expectations about real forensic science. *Jurimetrics, 47,* 357.

Stevenson, Robert Lewis. (1995). *The strange case of Dr. Jekyll and Mr. Hyde.* New York: Barnes & Noble.

Stirling, John. (2002). *Introducing neuropsychology: Psychology focus.* New York: Taylor & Francis.

Chapter 2

New Tools from Neuroscience

Instead of looking at all of the evidence around the individual—footprints, fingerprints, DNA, and video cameras—if there is one central place where the crime is planned, executed, and recorded, it's in the brain of the individual. It's a whole different way of looking at how crime is investigated.

—Dr. Lawrence Farwell (ABC-TV Good Morning
America, 2004), originator of Brain Fingerprinting

Contrary to popular opinion . . . we don't see with our eyes, hear with our ears, smell with our nose, taste with our tongue, or touch with our skin. Technically, they are chemo-receptors attached to something grander. In fact, chemical conditions underlie all instances of normalcy, abnormality, genius, addiction, soaring achievement, and psychopathy. So, where's the headquarters for all this? The human hive for neurochemical activity is the brain. Quality of life depends upon chemistry and how it "marks" the brain.

—Don Jacobs (2009), *res ipsa* observation

GUILTY CAPTURED BY BRAIN FINGERPRINTING

Other than fMRI (functional Magnetic Resonance Imaging) scans, the most important new technological tool of *deception detection* (in guilty capture) is brain fingerprinting. Unlike what lies beneath old school lie detection—physiological monitors of heart rate, blood pressure, and Galvanic Skin Response (GSR)—proven by experience to be notoriously inaccurate and unacceptable in court—*brain fingerprinting*, registers changes in brain waves. Not a neuroscan, but rather a method of 21st-century analysis of deception, detection in criminal minds is based on a computer-generated method of *short-term memory detection from the hypothalamus* triggered by stimuli shown on a computer screen.

Dr. Larry Farwell, former faculty member of Harvard Medical School, pioneered computerized knowledge assessment (CKA) in the mid-1990s. Now known as brain fingerprinting, it has a proven record of application and utility—shown to be infallible in tests by the FBI and U.S. Navy. The technological capture of a guilty "brain fingerprint" has been ruled admissible in U.S. courts; it has been used both to exonerate and to convict.

The premise of this technology is that a brain spontaneously "erupts with memory traces" that cannot be faked or repressed; in fact, subjects have no conscious control whatsoever relative to recognition by the electrical outputs registered by electroencephalograph (EEG) in detecting brain wave patterns. This process utilizes *electroencephalography* technology, which records neuron activity as brain wave patterns relative to a baseline electron reading. Measurement quantifies the summation of electrical activity detectable at specific points on the scalp. A reading of P300 (or P3) is regarded as a *positive relative change* or a "recognition spike" of neural activity 300 milliseconds after recognition following stimuli from a question or visual cue. A negative change would record brain wave amplitude below the baseline reading, hence "unrecognizable," or a non-guilty response.

Memories Produce P3 Waves

Output readings occur in the *hippocampus region of the brain*—that is, the depository of short-term memory existing in a distinctive pattern (the P3 wave). The waves occur 300 milliseconds after recognition producing the "Aha!" moment—the nearly *instantaneous spark of recognition* scientists call the P3. This recognition presents the scientific earmark upon which the technology is based, uncovering "guilty knowledge" that determines whether or not a suspect's brain recognizes key crime scene evidence never before released to the press.

Event-related potential (ERP) is the index for examining how the brain processes information with the distinctive P3 paradigm expressed as a mathematical algorithm. It is the most promising index of deception detection because it is elicited by meaningful events—events withheld from news coverage and known only to perpetrators. Guilty knowledge is outside the conscious control of subjects. Because the brain *per se* recognizes the cue similar to a knee-jerk reaction, the subject's mind is powerless to control it.

THE SCIENCE OF MERMER

Electrical brain wave patterns are detected (noninvasively) through powerful headband sensors. A specific brainwave response called MERMER (memory- and encoding-related multifaceted EEG response) is elicited if—and only if—the brain recognizes noteworthy information objectified by the P3 wave.

Therefore, when details of a crime scene are presented to a subject that only he or she would recognize, a resulting MERMER is emitted in a P3 pattern. Words or images relative to crimes are flashed on a computer screen versus irrelevant images. Each stimulus appears for only a fraction of a second. Three types of stimuli are presented:

- Targets
- Irrelevants
- Probes

Targets are made relevant and noteworthy to *all* subjects; they are given a list of the targets before the *image montage* begins; they are instructed to press a particular button in response to the targets. Hence, *all* targets will elicit a MERMER.

Most of the nontarget stimuli—known as *irrelevants*—have no association at all to the criminal investigation; therefore, irrelevants do not elicit MERMERs. On the other hand, some of the irrelevants are relevant to the investigation and exist as *probes*—which are noteworthy to subjects with particular knowledge stored in the brain relative to the crime scene. Probes are things that only the individual who committed the crime could reasonably know; probes are selected from police reports. Hence, probes elicit a MERMER. For subjects lacking this knowledge, probes are indistinguishable from irrelevants with no MERBER elicited. In regard to terrorism, for example, affiliation to a group of secret conspirators would indicate insider (guilty) knowledge and would activate a MERMER, exposing a ring of terrorism.

No Place to Hide

The principal technology behind brain fingerprinting is that images of a crime cannot be concealed within cortices of a guilty brain; hence, guilty memories have no place to hide. Evidence stored in the brain will match evidence extracted at crime scenes by registering the P3 wave.

Brain fingerprinting utilizes a guilty knowledge test (GKT) by presenting relevant stimuli (such as the caliber of gun used in a crime) against irrelevant items included in the control group. As expected, relevant stimuli trigger P3 amplitudes—the subject recognizes relevant stimuli as meaningful, resulting in a positive score on the GKT. This paradigm proves whether or not certain relevant information is, in fact, stored in short-term memory in the brain of the subject, not whether the subject committed the crime.

Unlike old-school lie detectors, brain fingerprinting is entirely under computational control; thus, at no time does bias or subjectivity of the investigator affect the analysis of the EEG brain wave patterns. Brain fingerprinting already has altered the way we solve crimes and is destined to revolutionize the criminal justice system as the 21st-century tool of forensic investigative science.

FORENSIC INVESTIGATIVE NEUROSCIENCE

Twenty-first-century advances in medical technology have catapulted brain science into the orbit of neuropsychology. The science of the central nervous system defines neuroscience, whereas neuropsychology defines psychology at the tissue level within cortices of the brain. Before this century, biology alone was the best synonym for neuroscience. This chapter reflects major interdisciplinary tools available in forensic investigative neuroscience. Historically, it all began without fanfare in the 1970s with the FBI's KOC—known offender characteristics—obtained directly from the mouths of incarcerated predators. KOC, obtained by skilled investigators, captures shocking confessions, *modus operandi* (MO), and other indicators along with the backgrounds of violent predators who "author" horrific crime scenes.

Forensic neuropsychology is a new product for the 21st-century analysis of criminal minds; more accurately, it reflects underlying *neurological conditions of the brain*—the organ of behavior, cognition, and affect (feeling). This perspective utilizes neuroscans as noted previously to determine relative activity, or inactivity, of specific cerebral regions, including gradations of neurotransmitter pathway activation and hormone efficacy as they merge, interact, and drive behavior.

General neuropsychology is the interdisciplinary product of the scientific field of neuroscience, specifically, documenting the merging of neuropsychology with the following:

- Neurology
- Cognitive neuroscience
- Forensics

- Adolescent neurobiology
- Computer science models based on artificial neural networks

Neural networks are computational models of artificial neurons that duplicate biological networks—they reflect adaptive systems similar to brain wiring based on informational flow from internal and external information.

In forensic science, *clinical forensic neuropsychologists* become forensic *amicus curiae*—that is, "friends of the court in forensic matters"—as expert witnesses and trial strategists. They assess the accused for fitness to stand trial or present compelling neuroscans (brain scan images) showing evidence of a neurologically "broken" brain in arguments for *diminished capacity*. Additionally, they may be hired as consultants by pharmaceutical firms to contribute expertise in clinical trials for prescriptive drugs that affect central nervous system (CNS) functioning and efficacy required in the discipline of *psychopharmacology*.

In addition to academic research, contributions to theoretical advances in paradigmatic schemas for new perspectives (such as my upcoming Brainmarks Paradigm), and participation in criminal courtrooms as *amicus curiae*, the general practice of neuropsychology reflects *diagnostic assessment* of patients who are suspected of brain injury, lesions, or cognitive deficits. Practitioners are equipped with cutting-edge knowledge of the brain gained from interdisciplinary preparation in neuroanatomy, psychopharmacology, and neurology. Twenty-first-century tools include a battery of extensive neuropsychological tests to assess cognitive deficits and rehabilitation protocols for brain-impaired patients who experience the following:

- Traumatic brain injury (TBI)
- Cerebrovascular accidents ("strokes" or CVA)
- Aneurysm ruptures
- Brain tumors
- Encephalitis
- Dementia
- Mental illness
- Development disorders (attention deficit hyperactivity disorder [ADHD], autism, Tourette's syndrome)

Clinical neuropsychologists in hospital settings, laboratories, and courtrooms—also known as *clinical forensic neuropsychologists*—use functional neuroimaging from neuroscan technology that produces high-resolution images of a living brain in real time (the same brain that showed up at crime scenes). Neuroscans allow the accused to stand trial alongside his or her brain.

ADOLESCENT NEUROBIOLOGY

Because of imaging studies of the brain, the adolescent brain experiences increased capacities for handling cognitive complexity and accumulating experiences by way of *adaptive neuroplasticity*—the brain's ability to change its own connections and computational "wiring." An unprecedented window into the biology of the brain has opened in the last 10 years showing how cerebral tissues function and how particular mental or physical activities change blood flow.

Giedd (2009) documents the following three themes that have emerged from neuroimaging research into the biological underpinnings for cognitive and behavioral changes in the adolescent brain:

- Connections and receptors of neurons (brain cells) and neurotransmitter chemicals peak during childhood, then start a slow decline beginning in adolescence.
- Connectivity among discrete brain regions increase.
- The balance between frontal lobe regions and limbic system regions gradually modulate toward frontal lobe superiority toward maturity by the mid-20s.

Connections and Receptors

As adolescents interact in a variety of social milieus—especially in their "tribal" peer groups—neural connections form and reform giving rise to specific behaviors. This changeability (plasticity) forms the essence of adolescent neurobiology and underlies both learning potential and vulnerability to risky behaviors—merging together as "the adolescent brain paradox"—*a time of great opportunity and great danger.*

Gray matter volume (size and numbers of branching pathways), number of synapses (microspaces between brain cells), and densities of receptors decline in adolescence, level off during adulthood, and decline again in senescence. The pronounced overproduction, volume, and density increases observed in the childhood brain set the stage for *competitive elimination* in adolescence. Therefore, the activities adolescents choose during middle and late teenage years matter greatly as the brain is literally shaped and maintained by those activities.

Cognitive advances in abstract thinking revs up during adolescence as brain circuitry communication increases because of integration of the brain regions, such as the following:

- Physical links between brain regions that share common developmental trajectories.
- Relationships between different parts of the brain that activate together during tasks—reflecting "cells that fires together, wire together" (Hebb, 1940).
- Anatomically, white matter volumes (axons covered in Myelin sheath for 100 times faster responses) link various regions of the brain and increase in adolescence, thereby improving abilities in language, reading, memory, and response inhibiting (the slow rise of "second thoughts" of cognitive restraint).
- Brainwise, the focus of adolescence becomes pivotal in plasticity as myelin proliferation speeds up processing of experiences. Decreased plasticity contributes to drug addiction, poor study habits, and lack of motor activity seen in obesity as demonstrable downsides.
- The result is a more holistic brain advanced over the childhood brain preparing prefrontal regions to become the adult variety typified by integrating information from multiple sources allowing for greater complexity and depth of thought.

Changing of the Guards: From Limbic to Frontal

The relationship between earlier maturing limbic pathways—the seat of rewards systems tied to emotion, sexuality, and appetitive drives (eating), to late-maturing prefrontal regions within the frontal lobes (as "brakes" on inappropriateness and for regulating appropriate responses) is noteworthy. This pivotal refocusing from limbic to prefrontal defines the paradox of the adolescent brain. Frontal lobe circuitry is attempting to power-up as a regulatory agent in the prevention of inappropriate, certainly criminal, behavior. Successes in mitigating limbic superiority include the following:

- Increases and specificity of attention span
- Response inhibition (Learning to say "No!")
- Regulation of emotion, organization, and long-range planning

Structural MRI studies show that high-level integration of the brain characterized by robust regulatory control does not reach adult levels until the mid-20s to early 30s. A study reported by Giedd speaks volumes in this regard,

> Among 37 study participants (aged 7–29) the response to rewards in the nucleus accumbens (a region rich in dopaminergic neurons related to pleasure-seeking) of adolescents was equivalent to that observed in adults, but activity in the adolescent orbitofrontal cortex (involved in motivation and second thoughts) was similar to that in children. (2009)

There is no question that the late maturation of the prefrontal cortex (PFC)—essential to judgment, decision making, and impulse control—has affected social, legislative, judicial, educational, and parental orbits circulating around adolescent issues. Countless numbers of adolescents are saved daily from unintentional self-destruction by this insightful decision made by the legal profession.

From the standpoint of Evo-Devo and adaptation, it is not surprising that the brain is particularly changeable during adolescence—a time when our species must learn how to thrive, survive, and connive in multiple environments. This changeability is far and away the most distinctive feature of our species, making adolescence a necessary paradox—*a time of great risk versus a time of great opportunity*. Those who successfully navigate this critical stage survive to become thrivers and connivers—plowing deeply into deceptive practices and, perhaps, nonviolent but potentially toxic dirty tricks.

Finally, it is no longer a mystery why so many adolescents enter the criminal justice system at such tender ages. With all the changes in the landscape of the brain, it is no wonder that this developmental stage is so wrought with vulnerability as adolescents continue to cling to tribal-inspired dangers. With brains still baking in the oven of living tissue, it is no wonder it takes a village to raise one child into adulthood.

NEUROSCANS: SHOWCASING THE BRAIN'S THEATRICS OF MIND

Through the evolution of brain neuroimaging—high-resolution neuroscans made possible by gradual advances in medical technology—a wide pathway has been paved for the analysis of a living brain viewed in real time. What can now be analyzed and documented is how the brain "works" or not due to functionality observed in blood flow. This "theater of mind" is the technological tool forensic investigative scientists had been waiting for since the days of Wilhelm Wundt, an early founder of psychology, who postulated that brain regions (structures) must lie behind behavior. Later, this perspective became an early school of psychology known as Structuralism thanks to Wundt's pupil Edward Titchener. But where were these brain regions? How did these regions power-up? Unfortunately, the only brain visible in Wundt's day was dark gray and lifeless lying on the autopsy table. It would take almost a century before neuroscans disclosed ways our sapient brain functions.

We now know the brain lies behind all thinking, feeling, affect states, and behavior with localization of function configured in a *modular format*. This holistic compartmentalization is powered-up by discrete neurotransmitter chemistry (as well as hormonal boosts) giving sapient brains personalities in psychological animation geared toward life's wondrous experiences, including the sexualized violence in the brain's "dirty tricks"—that is, the sexually psychopathic serial crime and criminal minds behind it all. The established importance of the modularity of the brain to discrete localization of function is restated by Kenneth M. Heilman, MD, in his book *Creativity and the Brain* (2005). This "discrete localization" is due entirely to pathway interconnectivity and powerful neurochemistry activated in these regions following the well-established cortical principle of *"what wires together fires together."*

I might add that his remarks explain, in the carefully chosen words of a scientist, the central importance of the Brainmarks Paradigm— how modularity and localization "mark" the brain in discrete chemical pathways.

LITERAL HEADQUARTERS FOR THINGS THAT GO BUMP IN THE NIGHT

It is our contention within the Brainmarks Paradigm that an adaptive gradation of psychopathy (neuropsychopathy) is a beneficial and natural brain condition. In this gradation of spectrum psychopathy, no dysfunction exists; it represents the natural ordering of the brain for survival value. However, further across the dial from spectrum psychopathy is *pathological psychopathy*, also because of a brain condition—a disordered and dysfunctional brain condition. Is it possible for "ordered versions" to become "disordered versions?" Currently it is unknown whether this condition occurs. The often-hypothesized external causes of the criminal variety of psychopath are presented in Part III. Until we know more, where do we go for answers to this brain condition? Bolstered by evidence of dysfunction from neuroscan diagnostic interpretation, it appears the headquarters (literally) for the pathological version of psychopathy is contained within a *ring of cerebral tissue* deep in sapient brains. What causes this region to be, theoretically, disordered is not known.

The Ring of Fire: The Paralimbic System

Some evidence is accumulating that the midbrain limbic system (MLS) when connected (minimally, partially, or when damaged by trauma) may become the breeding ground for pathological psychopathy evident in sexually psychopathic serial crime. This 21st-century insight is bolstered by fMRI scans of these regions showing diminished blood flow. Does this describe its mere appearance alone in the scan, or does it *diagnose dysfunction*? A for-sure answer remains elusive as forensic neuropsychologists acting as *amicus curiae* can be persuasive on either side of this critical issue.

If an internal brain compass existed, the readings on the dial of the compass when placed in the exact center of the limbic system would show parameters in four directions of the paralimbic system—our hypothesized neurological site of both neuroadaptive psychopathy and, in disorder, of pathological psychopathy. The northernmost segment reaches the entire top of the corpus callosum—the "hard-body bundle" of tissue connecting the right hemisphere to the left hemisphere deep in the brain. The eastern segment (toward posterior cortices of the brain) borders the occipital lobe, known to activate sight. The western segment (toward anterior regions of the frontal lobes) borders on the prefrontal cortex (PFC). Finally, the southernmost segment extends into the temporal lobes and most especially encapsulates the amygdala. The facts most encouraging about this "ring of psychopathy" suspected in the etiology of pathological psychopathy (the "disordered version") is what each structure is known to initiate but fails, producing instead "disorder." For example, in *anterior* sapient brain cortices,

- The anterior cingulate is the cortical site for decision making, empathy, and affect (emotion); when disordered, all of these very human characteristics are dampened, especially empathy and affect.
- The orbitofrontal PFC produces the "last tollbooth" of rational decision making, impulse control, behavioral flexibility, and consequences from learning; in disorder, impulsivity and never learning from mistakes takes the place of cognitive control.
- The ventromedial PFC merges feelings with cognitive "brainstorming"; in disorder, affect becomes blunt or inappropriate, marked by a lack of appropriateness to the situation reported.

In *posterior* sapient brain cortices, for example,

- The posterior cingulate produces emotional processing connected to emotional memory; in disorder, affect becomes more blunted and actions become disconnected from memory.
- The insula alerts the mind to pain perception; in disorder, it produces a high tolerance to pain.
- The temporal lobe integrates emotion, perception, and social inter-actional cues; in disorder, it disintegrates empathy and acts as a disconnect to social cues.
- The amygdala is the "alarm system" of the brain in the evaluation of sensation such as feeling "creepy" and emotional selectivity; in disorder, driven further by self-absorbed narcissism, grandiose enti-tlement is produced.

PATHOLOGICAL PSYCHOPATHY: TWO MINDS SUPERIOR TO ONE

The regional interconnectivity of the paralimbic system therefore prompts sensations, feelings, decision making, and impulse control (or not) for emotional and cognitive processing. The most promising argument for this region existing as prime headquarters for diminished capacity in pathological versions of psychopathy is their output (or more correctly, lack of it) *produces psychopathic traits* saturated by sexual "dirty tricks"—violence laced with perverted sexuality.

Neuroscans are showing impairment in these cortical regions (Kiehl & Buckholtz, 2010) that ultimately produce *blunted emotion* (also observed as blunt affect or inappropriate affect) and particularly damning traits of *never learning from experiences and infusion of on-the-fly impulsivity.* Yet, psychopaths at first blush seem bathed in bright affect; they seldom succumb to depression and seldom commit suicide. It's as though they feel psychologically empowered as the misanthropic Edward Hyde living within a respectable and camera-friendly persona of Dr. Jekyll. Two minds proving to be better than one: Hyde being the real McCoy, while Jekyll performs as the "front man"—all smiles and full of playful mischief. Yet, as poor decisions and impulsivity pile up around Jekyll, Hyde all the while continues to feel bulletproof to others commenting on Jekyll's mistakes. "So what?" Jekyll confesses, "I'm only human," as Hyde slithers around inside his cortical nest.

Brainwise, pathological psychopaths are amazing in their cortical differences. Recognizing shallowness of affect (reflecting an almost child-like quality of emotion) gives rise to an interesting, but not particularly scientific, experiment. When encountering a new acquaintance, try engaging that person in conversation for as long as possible, preferably for about three hours. Here's what you might notice, eventually. Moderate to severe psychopaths eventually show emotional fatigue from forced insistence on taking them off their cognitive course. They may show irritation, roll their eyes, become fidgety, and seem frustrated with your imposition. *You may have just observed Hyde emerging.* Run, don't walk away! Yet, here's a seeming contradiction. Once considered incapable of sustained focus, it is now believed pathological psychopaths can have a laser focus *but only on things that jazz their violent fantasies.* They can remain engaged in their pathological perversions even at great risk to themselves. Loitering for hours at the scene of their crimes, revisiting "dump sites" or constantly moving corpses, even when surveillance video running nearby are possible activities.

HISTORICAL ROOTS OF BRAIN IMAGING

As we marvel at metabolic functioning in bright reds and yellows captured in positron emission tomography (PET) scans, or cortical clarity in high-resolution fMRIs, we can literally study and observe the "colors of the mind." We have come a long way since the research-inspired "Decade of the Brain," which ended in 2000, yet in practice continues unabated today.

In 1918, neurologist Walter Dandy injected filtered air directly into the lateral ventricles of the brain by trephination—holes he had drilled into the skull for that purpose. He performed what was known as ventriculography under local anesthesia. This dangerous procedure carried significant risk to patients *prima facie*, but stood as the forerunner to the modern varieties of noninvasive imaging.

In 1927, professor of neurology and Nobel laureate Egas Moniz of Lisbon introduced cerebral angiography as a way to visualize both normal and abnormal blood vessels, a practice with modern refinements still used in the 21st century. (Interestingly, this is the same Egas Moniz who received the 1949 Nobel Prize in Medicine for his work on the controversial prefrontal leucotomy—a procedure known as lobotomy in the United States.)

Still more advanced technology was soon to arrive. In 1961, Oldendorf, followed by Hounsfield and Cormack (1973) revolutionized earlier attempts with noninvasive imaging known as CAT scans.

Computed Axial Tomography Scans

Introduced in 1973, CAT scans remain one of the more common imaging technologies used by physicians to analyze internal structures of various parts of the body, including the brain. Approximately 52 million CAT scan images are performed each year, making CATs one of the more common imaging technologies in the medical field. By the use of numerous X-ray beams and a rotating X-ray detector, beams are passed through the cranium and brain at different angles. Sensors detect the amount of radiation absorbed by tissues and possible lesions. A computer program uses the differences in X-ray absorption to show cross-sectional images of the brain; these images (or slices) are known as tomograms. With higher resolution than a traditional X-ray, CATs can spot irregularities in cortical tissue and ruptures in vessels. An iodine compound may be injected into the bloodstream to increase the contrast, allowing visualization of vascular health or damage. In initial stages of forensic investigation, CAT scans may be of interest to clinical forensic investigative scientists.

The cost of a single CAT scan can range between $270 and $4,800; the tremendous cost difference is broken down into two fees: technical and professional. The procedure itself—the technical fee—occurs with the patient receiving the CAT scan; this procedure has the most potential for saving a considerable amount of money, due to such contingencies as the age of the scanner and facility that houses it. The professional fee associated with having the radiologist interpret the result is far more straightforward and less negotiable.

Magnetic Resonance Imaging Scans

Based on nuclear magnetic resonance imaging from chemistry, the NMRI, soon shortened because of negative connotations surrounding the word "nuclear" thus becoming the MRI, became commonplace during the 1980s. The scan works by hydrogen nuclei acting as magnets that absorb radiation at different frequencies, therefore, detecting hydrogen in organic compounds, such as tissues and organs, which can be reflected in stunningly clear images. Brain dysfunction in soft tissue—aneurysms, stroke, tumors, and brain trauma—can be detected at a glance.

It has been estimated that more than 26 million MRI scans are done every year at a cost of $18 billon. Although insurance covers most of the cost, with the growth of high deductible plans, higher co-pays, and catastrophe-only coverage, U.S. patients increasingly are paying more out of pocket for scanning diagnostics. Forty-seven million uninsured people are faced with the full cost of an MRI if they need one. Major hospitals can charge between $1,750 to $2,200 per visit with outpatient centers charging more bargain-basement prices between $700 and $1,000.

Functional Magnetic Resonance Imaging Scans

Brain-functioning scans are among the most powerful diagnostic tools available to medical specialists in neurology, among neuropsychologists, and among forensic investigative scientists. In 1992, traditional magnetic resonance imaging became "functional"—with an upscale MRI with the ability to map the functions of various brain regions satisfying the modular model of the brain.

Similar to PETs and SPECTs (soon to be addressed), fMRI scans measure *blood flow in parts of the brain that become active;* the scans do not require the use of a radioactive tracer. Understanding blood and oxygen levels in the brain and body help in conceptualizing how fMRIs work. Erythrocytes (red blood cells) "pick up" oxygen that it supplies to tissues. For example, as blood moves through the lungs, red blood cells pick up oxygen—it binds to hemoglobin in red blood cells allowing oxygen to transform hemoglobin into oxyhemoglobin, which releases oxygen into tissues whereby oxyhemoglobin becomes deoxyhemoglobin—a paramagnetic molecule—behaving like a tiny magnet able to be attracted to a magnetic field. This is the basis of the fMRI that traces blood flow without the use of a radioactive tracer.

fMRI Deception Detection

Of particular interest to the forensic investigative scientist is the use of the fMRI scans in deception detection. In 2005, researchers at the Medical University of South Carolina (MUSC), in collaboration with Cephos Corporation and the Department of Defense Polygraph Institute, generated a 90 percent accuracy rate in the largest ever (at the time) fMRI-based deception detection study. Following publication of the study, Mark George, MD, one of the authors of the study remarked,

> I have been thinking about imaging and lie detection for more than 15 years now, and it is gratifying to see this important advance. We have known for years that certain brain regions are involved in attending to a complex problem, with others involved in stopping over-learned responses. Finally, we know all about the brain regions involved when you are anxious. These different brain events (attending, not telling the truth, worrying about the lie) *are all part of telling a lie.* We were able to break through an important barrier and use this to predict individual responses through continual refinements in technology (higher field strengths of scanners) as well as developing sophisticated methods of imaging data analysis that allow us to pick out brain patterns during responses.

Cephos founder and CEO Steven Laken, PhD, noted that for the first time, deception detection is moving away from stress responses (polygraphs) to the actual involuntary brain activity required for communicating and disseminating lies,

> The positive peer reviews coupled with the outstanding feedback from our board of legal, forensic and scientific advisors afford us every confidence that fMRI-based deception detection will soon begin to transform the judicial system much in the same way scientifically sound DNA analysis has.

According to nationally known criminal defense attorney, Robert Shapiro,

> There is enormous potential for Cephos' deception detection services to change the world of litigation; I'd use it tomorrow in virtually every criminal and civil case on my desk. This technology will revolutionize how cases are handled by allowing the truth to prevail undeniably.

Positron Emission Tomography Scans

The PET scan measures changes in blood flow associated with glucose metabolism in brain functioning. Positively charged particles—positrons—are detected due to radioactively labeled substances injected into the body that "piggyback" on glucose. PETs work due to the fact the brain utilizes glucose for energy; by labeling glucose with a radioactive "tag," the injected "tracer" substance can be followed to areas of the brain where it is metabolized or used. Also, underutilized cortical regions can be charted and analyzed.

When evaluating PET scans, areas of highest metabolic activity appear red colored, followed by lower intensities in yellow, next by green, and lastly by blue reflecting lowest intensity. (I consistently have referred to the blue category of low intensity as "cool-coded" in several publications.) PET scans are beneficial due to the radioactive tracer being relatively weak and short acting, therefore, radiation exposure is low.

Single Photon Emission Computed Tomography Scans

The SPECT scan is based on the decay of a radioactive tracer, technetium-99m, which emits a single gamma-ray photon. Technetium-99m is an isotope widely used for studying internal organs. SPECTs look specifically at blood flow and indirectly at metabolic activity like PETs. A radioactive isotope is first bound to a substance injected into the patient that is readily absorbed by brain cells. The SPECT gamma camera slowly rotates around the head recording data, while a computer reconstructs crystal clear three-dimensional images of brain activity. Data for brain trauma, mood disorders, anxiety disorders, addictions, attention deficit disorders (ADD), and psychotic disorders have been obtained as research criteria. Normal SPECT scans reveal homogenous and uniform tracer accumulation throughout the cerebral cortex with the cerebellum being the area with the most activity.

Three-dimensional surface images and active brain images are common types of SPECT scans. Blood flow is evaluated on the cortical surface by surface images, which often are caused by brain trauma and substance abuse. Symmetrical activity across the cortex indicates a normal brain. By contrast, the active brain image compares average brain activity to the hottest 15 percent of activity appearing in the cerebellum or occipital lobes. In a normal three-dimensional active brain image, increased activity is observed at the back of the brain and average activity everywhere else.

In the 21st century, all major pharmaceutical drug manufacturers—Big Pharma—use three-dimensional brain images showing drug efficacy when applying for Food and Drug Administration (FDA) approval of a new drug application; PET and SPECTs show how a proposed drug affects the metabolism and function of the brain. SPECT scans cost on the average about $1,000 per session, usually less than PETs and fMRIs.

REFERENCES

Brodsky, Ira S. (2010). *The history and future of medical technology*. St. Louis, MO: Telescope Books.
Buxton, Richard B. (2002). *An introduction to functional magnetic resonance imaging: Principles and techniques*. Cambridge: Cambridge University Press.
Ewing, C. P., & McCann, J. T. (2006). *Minds on trial: Great cases in law and psychology* New York: Oxford University Press.
Farwell, L. A., & Donchin, E. (1991). The truth will out: interrogative polygraphy ("lie detection") with event-related brain potentials. *Psychophysiology, 28,* 531–547.
Farwell, L. A., & Makeig, T. (2005). Farwell brain fingerprinting in the case of *Harrington v. State*. Open Court X 3-7, Indiana State Bar Association.
Farwell, L. A., & Smith, S. S. (2001). Using brain MERMER testing to detect concealed knowledge despite efforts to conceal. *Journal of Forensic Sciences, 46* (1), 135–143.

Farwell, Lawrence. (2004). Mind-reading technology tests subject's guilt: Brain reading technology becomes new tool in courts. Interview on *Good Morning America*, March 9.

Giedd, Jay. N. (2009). *The teen brain: Primed to learn, primed to take risks.* New York: Dana Foundation.

Heilbronner, Robert L. (Ed.). (2005). *Forensic neuropsychology casebook.* New York: Guilford Press.

Heilman, Kenneth M. (2005). *Creativity and the brain.* New York: Psychology Press.

Herman, Gabor T. (2009). *Fundamentals of computerized tomography: Image reconstruction from projection* (2nd ed.). New York: Springer.

Jacobs, Don. (2008). *Sexual predators and forensic psychology.* Plymouth, MI: Hayden-McNeil.

Jacobs, Don. (2009). *Brainmarks: Headquarters for things that go bump in the night.* Dubuque, IA: Kendall Hunt.

Keppel, Robert D. (1997). *Signature killers.* New York: Simon and Schuster.

Kiehl, Kent A., & Buckholtz, Joshua W. (2010). Inside the mind of a psychopath. *Scientific American Mind*, September–October.

Michaud, Stephen J., & Hazelwood, Roy. (1999). *The evil that men do.* New York: St. Martin's True Crime.

Purcell, Catherine E., & Arrigo, Bruce A. (2006). *The psychology of lust murder: Paraphilia, sexual killing, and serial homicide.* New York: Academic Press.

Chapter 3

Criminal Minds Capture

There are grounds for cautious optimism that we may now be near the end of the search for the ultimate laws of nature.
—Stephen Hawking (1988, p. 157)

KNOWN OFFENDER CHARACTERISTICS:
RES IPSA EVIDENCE

Before neuroscience entered into the technological sweepstakes of criminal minds capture and before abnormal psychology, criminal psychology, and criminal investigation combined forces to become forensic investigative science, testimonies from incarcerated violent predators spoke volumes in what has come to be called Known Offender Characteristics (KOC), reflecting *behavior that can now be directly connected to conditions in the brain*.

Collection of KOC provided the first *systematic endeavor* from FBI special agents and other investigators to interpret criminal minds directly from the mouths of incarcerated killers. "They spilled their guts and enjoyed that attention," according to agents who at first were convinced they would not participate in the program. In fact, KOC documented in a systematic way *res ipsa evidence* of criminal characteristics, habits, patterns, family histories, incarceration histories, mental health issues, addictions, and other pertinent information never before archived. (The utility of *res ipsa evidence* is addressed in detail in Chapter 6.) For now, it is sufficient to know that such evidence "speaks for itself" and continues to show up in the pretzel of psychopathic characteristic of criminal minds evident in violent, *cold-blooded sexualized varieties*. Indeed, what early investigators learned from KOC is observed repeatedly in violent offenders who continue to commit similar crimes and whose brains are "marked" in particular ways along known chemical pathways in specific regions of sapient brains.

FBI INVESTIGATION OF THE ATLANTA CHILD MURDERS

In the summer of 1981, an infamous string of murders in Atlanta, Georgia, put the new tool of *criminal profiling* into the crosshairs of media scrutiny. Was this a viable investigative tool, or simply crystal ball-gazing? Criminal profiling first came under the harsh glare of media and public scrutiny when it claimed center stage in the high-profile murders of many black youths in Atlanta, Georgia. Due to pleas from victims' parents and appeals from local law enforcement, the FBI Academy at Quantico, Virginia, sent FBI profilers John Douglas and Roy Hazelwood to test the brash and controversial new tool.

Aces Up the Sleeves

Unknown to the general public and those closest to the investigation of the Atlanta child murders, the FBI had an ace up their sleeve—a KOC database created directly from the mouths of convicted serial killers. Compilation of KOC was the result of the pioneering work of FBI special agents John Douglas and Robert Ressler who interviewed all of the known serial murderers across the country. "Creature features" from this study showed predators to be like trapdoor spiders who preferred comfort zones, such as geographical places where they felt the most comfort trolling for prey, or favored places for disposing of the bodies. Predators shared the deceptive ruses they used to lure victims into their comfort zone, and most important, how they could never stop serial rampages; their fantasies of control, manipulation, and lust for killing were too overwhelming. As previously stated, KOC was instrumental in shaping early investigative protocols that now have become the principles of forensic investigative science.

In a matter of hours upon arrival in Atlanta, the profilers never wavered from their initial belief that the UNSUB must be an African American man, a person who would feel comfortable moving within the milieu of an all-black community; a light-skinned Caucasian simply would have stood out like a red flag. Still, a considerable dose of investigative skepticism troubled police officers working the case, as well as agents within the FBI. How could "a profile" be worth the paper it was written on? How could knowledge of psychology, victimology, and crime scenes target one offender? The ace up the sleeve of FBI profilers John Douglas and Roy Hazelwood was KOCs that indicated habits and patterns of personality, possible ruses, such as impersonating police officers, as lures, and ways the UNSUB captured his prey—victims who never saw it coming.

Douglas and Hazelwood created a criminal profile that surprised and shocked everyone. However, it fit the accused, Wayne B. Williams, with uncanny accuracy. The document suggested the offender was a young black male, a police buff who routinely impersonated police officers. This ruse allowed the predator ready access to young, unsuspecting victims. He also "recruited" local youths as a "talent scout." In the end, it was the profile's great accuracy that caused observers to comment, "It was as though the agents were watching the killer's every move even when he committed the murders and dumped the bodies" (remarks of commentator: *Inside the Mind of Criminal Profilers*, 2001, Films for the Humanities and Sciences).

A profiler (or forensic investigative scientist) does more than proffer written documents intent on apprehension; they also help plan trial strategies. For example, during the trial, Douglas predicted Williams would fake a heart attack in court as the tide of evidence turned against him. He did. Also, Douglas suggested a cross-examination strategy in interrogating Williams, who chose to enter the witness stand—a dangerous decision wrought with arrogant miscalculation. Douglas's strategy was calculated to cue the rage Williams hid under his cool-crafted persona. During questioning, the FBI agent instructed the prosecuting attorney to invade Williams's personal space, by grasping his hands and in a low, barely audible voice, inches from William's face ask: "What was it like to wrap your fingers around your victims' throats? Were you frightened, Wayne?" Shocked and caught off guard, Williams replied, "No."

Realizing he had implicated himself in a murder, Williams angrily jumped from his seat blasting the attorney with the following: "You're not going to implicate me with your profile!" When jurors actually experienced the outburst of rage in the middle of the proceedings (along with forensic evidence of hair and fiber samples gathered at the crime scene matching samples found in his home), they were convinced. They convicted Wayne B. Williams of the Atlanta child murders and sent him to prison for life.

Criminal profiling utilizes data from the *crime scene* evidence and *victimology*—why this specific victim and not another? Besides the document, agents are encouraged to use good common sense, and their own unique investigative experiences. It all begins in the mind of the profiler with "what likely happened."

Could there be accurate profiling without addressing underlying psychological principles? The answer clearly is "no." Admittedly, borrowing training protocol from criminologists and criminal justice academy training may offer sketches of perpetrators based solely on crime trends, statistics, and criminal typologies. But this overview would lack significant and important pieces of the psychological pretzel of violence, such as the following:

- Personality proclivities
- Emotional and sexual motivations
- Behavioral habits and patterns characteristic of violent offenders

Our first example of the application of KOC to criminal minds is the psychology of sexual sadism and compliant victimology.

Example 1: Sexual Sadism and Compliant Victimology

The pioneering work into KOCs by former FBI agent Roy Hazelwood provided unprecedented insight into the behavior of sexual sadists and compliant victims, our first example of documenting characteristics of criminal minds from the mouths of monsters. The definition of *sexual sadism* is a sexual perversion in which gratification is obtained by the infliction of pain of a physical and sexual nature with accompanying mental anguish and fear. In many cases of sexual sadism, the sadist keeps victims alive as long as possible to prolong perverse sexual appetites. The *fait accompli* of serial sexual sadism is rape or murder. (The word "sadist" comes from the exploits of the Marquis de Sade in the 19th century, who delighted in inflicting sexual cruelties on his entrapped "lovers.")

What would drive the behavior of compliant victims such as female co-offenders who help recruit victims of sadistic love? By what psychological power does he control, manipulate, and dominate her? According to Hazelwood, the sadist follows five steps in creating his perverse companion, the compliant co-offender. (No better example of this condition exists than in the book *Lethal Marriage* documenting the crimes of Canadian serial killers Paul Bernardo and Karla Homolka). The steps are as follows:

1. Through astute observation of body language, the sadist identifies a vulnerable co-offender—a naïve, dependent, immature, and highly controllable female. Often, such a compliant person has a diagnosable *dependent personality disorder*— a well-researched pathological personality disorder. She displays behavior consistent with codependency, that is, being a "doormat" for others. She may have had abusive parents or an abusive relationship with a boyfriend or ex-husband. In any event, the sadist appears as the "rescuer."
2. The sadist charms her with his "smooth talk" and seemingly gentle nature. He may lavish her with gifts, offer physical protection, financial

support, or whatever he perceives as the "legitimate" answer to her problems. The victim perceives him as a loving and caring "nurturer," worthy of her love. Dependent women often are swept away by his demeanor and persona—deceptive behavior inherent to psychopathic personality.

3. Soon, she is totally dependent on him and under his emotional "spell." He encourages her to engage in perverse sexual practices that she most likely considers deviant, or at the very least "kinky." The "small steps" he so craftily uses to lure her into his perverse world eventually leads to the shaping of full-blown perversities that evolve into habitual sexual practices. This shaping of sexual perversity accomplishes two control mandates: First, it demolishes her fragile will and "esteem," along with any sense of normalcy regarding sexuality. And, second, she becomes isolated from others—the *fait accompli* of sexual sadism. After a relatively short time, the co-offender becomes a sexual "slave."

4. The sadist uses domination, manipulation, control, and physical punishment for lapses. The compliant co-offender feels hopeless and depersonalized, which eventually will play a central role in victimization. Sadly, she is worse off in the sadist's hands than in any prior dysfunctional relationship.

5. Through his use of mind control and physical punishment, she complies with his every demand, partly to avoid his wrath. He has succeeded in a "makeover" of her cognitive maps of thinking. The sadist has changed her fragile, or nonexistent self-esteem, into the persona of a "bad," "stupid," "inferior," or "inadequate" depersonalized slave. She is now a pure example of pathological codependency.

Example 2: Signature Sexual Offenders

Criminologist, homicide detective, and true crime author Robert Keppel presents his own paradigm to explain sadistic homicide offenders that contributed to a "sexual signature" KOC. His term for KOC is *signature killer* because of the unmistakable presence in all crime scenes of the killer's sadistic "calling card"—a *signature* or in FBI lingo, "personation."

According to Ressler and others, signature relates to motive, emotionality, and, ultimately, the reason violent predators continue to kill. *Addictionologists* know why serial predators feel compelled to continue criminal behavior—they operate out of a full-blown addiction in which every aspect of the crime is sexualized and obsessively compulsively repeated.

According to Keppel, the basis for understanding even the most minor sexual offenses (in his words "Sex Crimes 101") is the realization that anger expressed through control drives serial killers. To analyze serial crimes, Keppel uses the following categories to describe the perpetrator's psychological dynamics manifested at the crime scene *from their own accounts.*

1. *The Anger-Retaliation Signature.* This signature often displays overkill against the victim as an anger-retaliation symbol. The killer chooses to retaliate against the real source of his anger by using a symbolic victim. Examples of serial killers who follow this typology include Arthur Shawcross and John Wayne Gacy. According to Shawcross, he murdered women because his mother rejected him, while Gacy murdered "lost boys" who sought consolation from him as retaliation against his alcoholic father who never expressed genuine emotion and love. (Serial killers are so dangerous because they are not what they appear to be. They may pose as roofers or service technicians while canvassing victims door to door. They may return several months later in what appears to be a random, chance occurrence, or they may dress as a clown, as Gacy did, to entertain children.) The anger-retaliation killer seldom kills his own mother; he chooses someone like her. He chooses victims who represent domineering women in his life, whom he believes are responsible for his troubles—unless the killer is homosexual and seeks to destroy young males. According to Keppel, examples include mothers who were overly controlling, promiscuous, physically or sexually abusive, or who inspired fear and terror in their children, or fathers who rejected their sons.

2. *The Picquerism Signature.* The serial killer who is a picquerist is a sexual deviant who becomes sexually aroused by biting the victim or by penetration of the skin through cutting, slicing, or stabbing with a long-bladed knife. In rare cases, picquerism may involve sniper activity. Victims are not victims of chance. The killer may stalk his victim for weeks or months, choosing those who fit his preferred type. Picquerist crimes are particularly gruesome because of deep and violent stab wounds. Knife penetration and the control of every aspect of bringing his victims death drive this type of signature homicide. After six picquerist murders near San Diego, California, a 25-year-old black male, Cleophus Price, became identified as the serial killer.

3. *Sexual Sadism Signature.* According to Dr. Richard Walter, a forensic psychologist at Michigan State Penitentiary, the three Ds of sexual

sadism are dread, dependency, and degradation. Prolonging the sexual "high" in each stage by inflicting as much pain and misery as possible provides the killer with *modus vivendi*—sexualized feelings related to sadism, such as breaking his victim's will to resist. Delaying the victim's death prolongs the sadist's desire for psychological terrorism. If death comes too fast, the serial sexual sadist feels cheated.

Example 3: Sexual Addiction and Pathological Psychopathy

According to Jacobs (2008), a signature often provides evidence of the *addiction factor* that highlights the violent criminal mind in serial rapes and serial homicides. Because of many factors relative to learning and neurochemistry, offenders often have various chemical addictions (such as alcohol or methamphetamine) in addition to addiction to sexual burglary—the "thrilling high of sexual control"—generated in the brain's pleasure pathways. The same pathways explain addiction to any drug, such as alcohol, marijuana, cocaine, or MDMA (ecstasy). It is now known that serial killers dread killing the victim because the act of restraining the victim and controlling the victim produces the high, not the murder *per se* in a variety of cases.

Again, violent offenders seem to enjoy talking to investigators about their habits and patterns. The relentless addiction factor ironically from their own brain chemistry compels serial killers to obsessively and compulsively go from one kill to another; serial killer Ted Bundy called it the "brutal urge." It only recedes when the killer feels "spent" in the aftermath of the murder. The same frenzy that describes this addiction may describe two lovers tearing off each other's clothes and having consensual sex in a wild display of shared passion; parallels to wild displays of sexuality are striking to the organized serial offender albeit from his perspective. This factor is startling news to so-called experts who inject *decision* into the motivation of serial psychopaths while missing the significance of the psychological ramifications of addiction and neurochemistry that lie behind emotion. Erotic fantasy—that is, anticipation of sexual control—not cognitive decision-making—drives serial crime.

The most important ingredients that now can be teased apart by forensic investigative scientists are the documentation of the following:

- How sources behind the killer's driving force in erotic fantasy relative to the crystallization of his sexual fantasies drive his crimes
- How he is savagely driven toward *mens rea*

- How his all-encompassing fantasies drive the physical perpetration of full-blown *actus reus (the criminal act)* exemplified in MO and signature
- How the brain becomes "spent" from endorphin release in the aftermath of the crime

To the neuroscientist, every step from imagery to debauchery to aftermath is due to neurochemistry and neurohormones driven by fantasies and deviant cognitive "mapping," with a goal of reaching sexual climax indicated by his MO and in signature, by his emotional fixation to the crime. This view explains why some serial killers experience revulsion at the memory of the crime the next morning when alcohol (or other drugs) wears off. But, as Bundy explained in his last interview before lethal injection—"the brutal urge always comes back stronger than ever" (*The Last Interview of Ted Bundy* by Dr. James Dobson, Films for the Humanities and Sciences).

Example 4: Paraphilias

The essential feature of KOCs related to *paraphilias* comes from field observation and direct word-of-mouth experiences from violent offenders. Paraphilias are recurrent, intense sexually arousing fantasies, sexual urges, or behaviors by name that involve the following:

- Voyeurism: clandestinely observing others as a "Peeping Tom" in various stages of undress or engaging in sexual activity
- Frotteurism: touching or rubbing against a nonconsenting person
- Sadism: causing the emotional suffering of another
- Masochism: receiving emotional humiliation or suffering
- Pedophilia: sexualizing children

Voyeurism

A budding sexual offender shows signs of sexual deviance early in developmental stages. The act of observing unsuspecting individuals, usually strangers, who are naked, who are in the process of becoming naked, or who are engaging in sexual behavior is known as voyeurism. The act of looking or "peeping" (i.e., a "Peeping Tom") is to achieve sexual excitement, and generally the killer seeks no sexual activity with the observed person. Convicted killer Richard Ramirez began his serial killer "career" by observing hotel guests in various stages of nudity.

Clinically, voyeurism constitutes clinically significant distress or social or occupational impairment in the voyeur, unless psychopathy is a factor, in which case entitlement takes the place of distress. For psychiatric hospital admission and insurance purposes, voyeurism is designated 302.82 in the DSM.

Frotteurism

Frotteurism involves touching or rubbing against a nonconsenting person. The behavior usually occurs in crowded places where the individual can escape more easily. He rubs his genitals against the victim's thighs or buttocks or attempts to fondle her genitalia or breasts with his hands. While doing so, he usually fantasizes an exclusive, caring relationship with the victim. Most acts of frottage occur when the person is 15 to 25 years old, after which frequency generally declines.

As a teenager, Jeffrey Dahmer often fantasized lying next to a nude male and listening to his heart beat, a fantasy that fueled his murderous rampage against homosexual males. After strangling his victims, Dahmer often laid next to their corpses to fondle them. Later, he often cannibalized them.

Such fantasies, sexual urges, or behaviors cause clinically significant distress or impairment in social, occupational, or other important areas of functioning, again if psychopathy does not mitigate distress. DSM designates this condition as 302.89.

Sexual Sadism and Sexual Masochism

While inflicting psychological or physical suffering upon a victim, the sadist is the "giver" of that pain, suffering, and terror, which is seen on the victim's face and in her response. In psychopathology, the fantasies, sexual urges, or behaviors cause clinically significant distress or social or occupational impairment in the perpetrators. In violent sexual psychopathic crime, no distress or social impairment is observed, *as the criminal is remorseless and empowered*—the victims had it coming.

Conversely, the masochist is the "receiver" of pain and humiliation from beating, binding, or suffering. These fantasies, sexual urges, or behaviors cause clinically significant distress or social or occupational impairment (but not in psychopathy). The DSM designates sexual sadism as 302.84 and sexual masochism as 302.83. Sadomasochism combines characteristics of the two paraphilias.

PSYCHOLOGICAL PERSPECTIVES IN CRIMINAL MINDS CAPTURE

The following psychological perspectives provide theoretical foundations in criminal minds capture. Along with KOC, they constitute the rationale for the design of the mousetrap—the *criminal profile*—so effective in identifying and apprehending society's most elusive predators.

Behavioral Psychology

Behavioral psychology (behaviorism) focuses on learned behavioral *patterns and habits.* In various social milieus (social contexts of learning) *formative influences* are known to "shape and maintain" behavior, including normalcy, psychopathology (defined exclusively by the DSM), and pathological psychopathy, mixing violence with perverted sexuality. Said another way, a person does what he sees, or what he thinks about, or fantasizes about every day. FBI profilers trained in behavioral and abnormal psychology contend that *behavior lies behind personality*; therefore, a knowledge of *behavioral psychology* is essential in connecting the behavioral dots—habits and patterns—ascertainable as KOC, specifically in the cold-blooded violence of psychopathic personality disorder.

As will be addressed in Chapter 9, predatory "toxic" parenting appears to reinforce features of *antisocial behavior* promulgated by severe physical or sexual abuse that emotionally and physically disfigures children and adolescents. In literary misanthropes, Edward Hyde was "born" of chemistry that produced his pathological psychopathy, whereas Eric, the phantom, displayed gradations of psychopathology from his past experiences of never feeling loved. Behavioral psychology perspective maintains that what occurs in childhood may be significant and should be addressed. Behavioral psychology seeks some measure of empirical verification from rigorous laboratory evidence that most often is gathered in *comparative studies* of animal behavior.

Forensic Psychology

Forensic psychology has deep roots in both criminology and behavioral psychology, especially with regard to the analysis of criminal minds from expert witness testimony from forensic psychologists, psychiatrists, and neuropsychologists—professionals who specialize in criminal behavior. In the 21st century, startling new evidence from high-resolution neuroscans that show blood flow profiles of cortical tissue are revolutionizing evidence in criminal courts. Highly paid professionals provide expert insight extracted from crime scene evidence and victimology. Forensic psychologists suggest the state of mind of perpetrators, trial strategies to follow, and protocols for or against insanity pleas. Forensic neuropsychology has deep roots in biology, neurology, and in interpretation of neuroscans in diminished capacity cases.

Cognitive-Behavioral Psychology

Historically, the cognitive-behavioral perspective of psychology focused on the relationship between aberrant thinking, focus, and motivation produced by powerful *neurocognitive maps* of behavior as a consequence of learning and quality of thinking. Twenty-first-century *cognitive forensic neuroscience* has evolved out of this perspective connecting the central nervous system's connectivity with neurocognitive mapping with conniving and calculating criminal minds. This perspective, more than any other, explains why *addiction to hardcore violent pornography* on a neurologically wired brain of sexual perversion is a contributing factor in sexualized violence. Connecting two perspectives—cognition (thinking) and behavior (acting-out inappropriately)—creates the *mens rea* intent of criminal minds.

Abnormal Psychology (Psychopathology)

Pure psychopathologies target dysfunctional family relationships, and chemical imbalances, such as chronic depression, anxiety, and all affect (emotional) dysfunctions as well as major (chronic) mood disorders, such as bipolar disorder and schizophrenia. In diagnosing the violent perpetrators of serial crime, abnormal psychology most often documents severe personality disorders often connected to criteria for antisocial personality disorder. As we will contend, pathological psychopathy is a *qualitatively different personality disorder* than antisocial personality disorder because of the central feature of deviant sexual psychopathy and other differences outlined in an upcoming chapter. Our view rests on the Neuro School research into psychopathy presented in Part II. Discussed at length in Chapters 4–7, features of Cluster B DSM personality disorders—narcissism (narcissistic personality disorder), histrionicism (histrionic personality disorder), and borderline personality disorder can be more correctly viewed as variations of spectrum psychopathy in the Brainmarks Paradigm.

Developmental Psychology

Developmental psychology targets unsatisfied emotional "crises" brought about by incompetent parenting (with strong elements of emotional detachment or ambivalence). This appears especially true in the tradition of Erik Erikson's classic psychosocial stages of life span development. More severe dysfunction in self-image and in relationships may occur due to predatory "toxic" parenting effects on development (see Chapter 9). It has been a long tradition in developmental psychology to view stages and phases of development as influential in anchoring personality.

Primate studies show that insufficient tactile stimulation (i.e., Harry and Margaret Harlow and John Bowlby) and concomitant effects of emotional scarcity, lack of attachment, and lack of bonding is known to *retard* brain development, thus producing low oxytocin and vasopressin— the chemistry known to lie behind social bonding and pair bonding. Stunted emotional behavior and severe neurological deficits in the development of the cerebellum—the brain region most affected by lack of tactile stimulation and motor stimulation before age two—rewires neurological systems. How can a person be rehabilitated to normalcy if he or she were never habilitated in the first place?

NEUROPSYCHOLOGY AND ADDICTIONOLOGY: "COMPELLED" BEHAVIOR VERSUS "CHOICE" BEHAVIOR

The combined disciplines of *neuropsychology* and *addictionology* identify powerful neurotransmitters and neurohormones underlying thinking (cognition), emotions (affective states), and behavior. The two disciplines also indicate how normal gradations of endogenous chemistry can become imbalanced through cortical rewiring from a myriad of causes, not the least of which is obsessive-compulsive behavior tied to addiction.

Neuropsychology is the study of behavior at the tissue (cortical) level of the central nervous system and brain relative to neurotransmitters— chemical messengers of the brain—and neurohormones—blood messengers in the body that target remote cells. Understanding addiction and its effect on neurological systems provides insight into *compelled behavior* versus so-called *choice behavior*. The brain is, of course, the organ of addiction primarily because of the prevalence of DA that cascades from the substantia nigra of the midbrain *per se* and is transported via pathways into the MLS (collectively, midbrain *per se* and the limbic system *per se*), which is further connected to DA-rich pathways of the medial forebrain bundle (MFB) and the nucleus accumbens (NAcc) of this region, as well as the ventral tegmental area (VTA) of the midbrain *per se*. As a major pathway, the mesolimbic dopamine system (MLDAS) of the MLS is connected to another major chemical pathway, the mesocortical dopamine system (MCDAS) of the frontal lobes involving the entire brain in intoxication and addiction. It is well known that many violent killers often have multiple addictions.

Severe neurological abnormalities can transpire in neurocognitive *mapping* when exacerbated with addiction to sexually explicit images, including hardcore violent pornography, which some forensic investigators document as the single most devastating influence in the development of serial killers.

Evolutionary Neuroanatomy and Development (Evo-Devo)

The evolutionary neuroanatomy of brain development can no longer be ignored; my argument of psychopathy being both neuroadaptive as well as pathological makes res ipsa sense based upon psychopathy being a spectrum brain condition. My Brainmarks Paradigm of Neuropsychopathy addressed in Chapter 4, with ramifications discussed over the next three chapters of Part II, connects adaptive neuropsychopathy to brain evolution. Is *res ipsa* evidence compelling enough to suggest an *adaptive gradation of psychopathy* as a "gift" of nature as the brain most likely to survive and thrive?

Neurologist Paul McLean's Triune Brain presents the brain as two-thirds predatory because of the *reptilian brain* (brainstem) connections to the primitive MLS, which exert neurochemical influences associated with violence.

Criminal Profiling Capture

In the early 1990s, the key ingredients of profiling—psychological, emotional, and behavioral—made up the profile's first media moniker, known as the psycho-behavioral profile. *The Silence of the Lambs*, the Academy Award Best Picture of 1992, mentioned it by the same moniker. Psychological principles enable an in-depth analysis of the mind of a violent criminal capable of rapacious behavior—preying on others in sexualized ways. According to the ex-FBI special agents and modern founders of criminal profiling, Robert Ressler, John Douglas, Roy Hazelwood, and others, it takes years of training, expertise, research, maturity, and experience—especially experience—to author effective profiles.

In 1978, FBI special agents Robert Ressler and John Douglas modified the Teten-Mullany Applied Criminology Model of serial killers into the

Organized/Disorganized Model. This model remains influential into the 21st century. From 1979 to 1983, FBI agents hatched the Criminal Personality Research Project, the dream and literary child of FBI special agent Robert Ressler. The undertaking was truly a landmark for the FBI, which at the time showed limited interest in what motivated murderers, rapists, and child molesters. The study took dead aim at the psychological and behavioral characteristics of violent criminals related to familial backgrounds, incarceration history, mental health issues, specific crimes, crime scenes, and victimology. Ressler and Douglas essentially created the first axes-like tool of criminal differential diagnosis similar to the model of the DSM.

FBI special agents obtained this information firsthand by entering correctional facilities in conjunction with road school engagements, where agents taught FBI techniques to local law enforcement agencies. The agents spoke with offenders individually, augmenting personal interviews with homework and poring through stacks of forensic evidence, such as court transcripts, psychiatric assessments, and police reports. The exhaustive study resulted in the creation of the following list of crime scene protocols. The current dichotomized *organized versus disorganized model* follows the presentation of the six steps of Crime Scene Analysis (CSA) capture, which are:

1. *Profiling Inputs.* CSA's initial stage is evidence gathering. This includes all crime scene materials gathered at the crime scene, such as photographs of the crime scene or of the victim. Evidence includes comprehensive background information on the victim, autopsy reports, and forensic information relative to the "psychological autopsy" of the crime scene, such as postulating what occurred before, during, and after the crime. Profiling inputs are the CSA's foundation. Any errors or miscalculations in this evidence-gathering stage can lead investigators in wrong directions.
2. *Decision Process Models.* Logistics is the best word to describe CSA's second stage. A logical and coherent pattern must emerge from this stage, an emerging picture of the perpetrator suggested by the crime scene. Was a serial perpetrator responsible? Or, does the evidence point to a single instance of a crime (the offender's one and only crime)?
3. *Crime Assessment.* Reconstruction best describes the third stage. What are the sequence of events and the behavioral characteristics of victim and offender? What "role" did the victim play? What "role" did the offender play? Analyzing this stage allows investigators to piece together the emerging criminal profile gradually.

4. *Criminal Profile*. The actual profile begins with the fourth protocol, which includes background data, behavioral characteristics, and the perpetrator's physical description. This stage provides suggestions based on personality type for the most effective ways to interview the offender, if apprehended. The goal at this stage is identification and apprehension.

5. *Investigation*. This is the application phase during which law enforcement agencies receive the actual profile to aid in the perpetrator's apprehension. New information continually modifies the original profile, sometimes on a day-to-day basis.

6. *Apprehension*. The last stage of CSA is crosschecking the profile with the apprehended offender. This stage has built-in difficulties in the event the offender never is caught, police arrest him on another charge, or he ceases criminal activity.

TYPOLOGY CAPTURE: ORGANIZED VERSUS DISORGANIZED

Organized versus Disorganized Offender Dichotomy

The following taxonomy represents behavioral characteristics of violent sexual psychopathic serial killers relative to the Organized Offender characteristics.

The Organized Offender

The organized serial killer appears to have the following behavioral characteristics:

1. Average to above average intelligence
2. Socially competent
3. Skilled work preferred
4. Sexually competent
5. High birth order status
6. Father's work stable
7. Inconsistent childhood discipline
8. Controlled mood during crime
9. Use of alcohol during crime
10. Precipitating situational stress
11. Living with partner
12. Mobility with car in good condition
13. Follows crime in news media
14. May change jobs or leave town (Ressler, 1992)

The Disorganized Offender

The disorganized offender appears to have the following behavioral characteristics:

1. Below average intelligence
2. Socially inadequate
3. Unskilled worker
4. Sexually incompetent
5. Low birth order status
6. Father's work unstable
7. Harsh discipline as a child
8. Anxious mood during crime
9. Minimal use of alcohol
10. Minimal situational stress
11. Lives alone
12. Lives or works near the crime scene
13. Minimal interest in news media
14. Significant behavior change (e.g., drug/alcohol abuse) (Ressler, 1992)

Organized Offender Application: Ted Bundy

The poster-boy predator for the organized offender is the serial killer Theodore "Ted" Bundy. Applying his personal vitae to the following delineation of organized versus disorganized offenders is instructive. In terms of IQ (Intelligence Quotient), the organized offender is almost always average to above average in intelligence. Bundy was in law school at the time of his offenses and possessed a "gift of gab" along with above average academic skills. In contrast, the disorganized offender is usually below average in intelligence and may not have a high school diploma or a GED (General Educational Development test). The organized offender is socially competent and sophisticated, meaning that he has a grasp on the way society works and possesses the requisite interpersonal skills to maintain at least a persona of "normal" social relationships. Bundy made friends easily and possessed strong manipulative skills that made him appear "engaging".

The judge who presided over his murder trial berated Bundy for his offenses (paraphrased): "I would have liked to hear you argue in court someday . . . you would have been a good lawyer . . . but you chose the wrong path." The organized offender is proficient at acquiring and keeping skilled jobs, as was the case with the offender's father. Bundy was adopted into a home with a stepfather who had a stable work record.

The disorganized offender is socially incompetent; displays socially inadequate behavior, such as disturbed or nonexistent social relationships; and is a "job-hopper," an unskilled laborer following in the footsteps of his father's spotty work history.

The organized offender often has success in sexual relationships with girlfriends, wives, or ex-wives. Bundy had girlfriends and even married one of his admirers who witnessed his trial. While in prison, conjugal visits by his wife produced a daughter.

The disorganized offender is sexually incompetent. When interviewed on death row, disorganized offenders report never having experienced a mutually satisfying sexual relationship with the opposite sex. The disorganized offender bases sex on control, domination, degradation, or abuse.

A history of inconsistent discipline characterizes the organized offender's childhood. Researchers documented this fact in Bundy's parent-child relationship. On the other hand, harsh discipline characterizes the disorganized offender's history of discipline.

During the crime's commission, the organized offender's mood is somewhat stable, enhanced with the abuse of alcohol. Bundy was in a state of intoxication during the commission of his crimes. The disorganized offender's mood is anxious with minimal use of alcohol during the commission of the crime.

A precipitating stressor or "trigger" for the crime exists for organized offenders, whereas minimal situational stressors exist for disorganized offenders. (In Bundy's case, having to leave law school due to finances was the "trigger.")

Organized offenders live with a partner (a wife or girlfriend), whereas disorganized offenders live alone. Because of a lack of transportation or a fear of mechanical breakdown, the disorganized offender lives close to the crime scene, while the organized offender displays a wider range of mobility with dependable transportation. Bundy drove a Volkswagen Beetle in good repair.

The disorganized offender displays minimal interest in the media coverage. The organized offender follows news coverage avidly (true in Bundy's case). After the crime, the organized offender may leave town or change jobs. Bundy left town and eventually moved from state to state. In contrast, although the disorganized offender never strays from home, his behavior changes radically, as observed in increased drug or alcohol abuse.

Individuals with full-blown psychopathic personalities marked by lack of empathy have many sexual relationships with people they depersonalize "as things to be used." The difference between the garden-variety nonviolent psychopath and the violent sexual psychopath is telling. The sexual psychopath, a sexual pervert for life, kills and becomes known to the world as a serial killer.

PERSONALITY CAPTURE: HARE'S *PSYCHOPATHY CHECKLIST–REVISED*

Robert Hare's PCL-R (2003) is a diagnostic tool used worldwide to assess psychopathic characteristics. Peer-reviewed research and clinical application have confirmed the test's utility as a valid and reliable tool for more than 30 years. Hare urges the test can be considered accurate only if administered by licensed and experienced clinicians. The most current edition, the PCL-R, lists four factors that summarize 20 assessed characteristics known to typify the clinical condition of psychopathy. Factor 1 is labeled *selfish, callous, and remorseless use of others*. PCL-R Factors 1a and 1b are correlated to *narcissistic personality disorder* and *histrionic personality disorder* characterized by extraversion and positive personality affects—beneficial traits in the psychopath's many splendored social deceptions documenting the "con artistry" of his social lures making him so dangerous. Factor 2 is labeled *chronically unstable, antisocial socially deviant lifestyle*. PCL-R Factors 2a and 2b are strongly correlated to criminality, especially antisocial personality disorder that is associated further with anger, criminality, and impulsivity leading to violence punctuated by lack of remorse.

Answers to the questions are scored on a three-point scale: zero points are given if a question does not apply; one if it somewhat applies, and two if it fully applies. The score of "1" is what the Brainmarks Paradigm would argue exists as a general indicator of adaptive neuropsychopathy. Also, the checklist is what can be referred to as a *QAI psychometric*, meaning following a question (Q) an answer is provided (A), scored by subjective interpretation (I) that is based on antecedent information from the responder's file, or from the examiner's expertise. (This is not unlike my 25-year-old instrument measuring adolescent behavior collected in autobiographical essays in which the question (Q) "Who am I and why?" is followed by answers (A) in essay form, followed by interpretation (I) based on antecedent information from prior responses.)

After lifestyle and criminal behavior assessment, the instrument assesses traditional "markers" of psychopathy, such as glibness (a "slippery" persona) associated with superficial charm. Grandiosity is noted in pathological lying, typified by lack of remorse, callousness, and a cunning and manipulative personality. Poor behavioral control observed in impulsivity and failure to accept responsibility for behavior is likewise noted.

Quantifying the responses with rating points across the continuum of zero to two creates scores on the PCL-R from the following factors:

Factor 1: Personality expressed in aggressive narcissism

- Glibness and superficial charm
- Grandiose sense of self-worth
- Pathological lying
- Cunning and manipulative
- Lack of remorse or guilt
- Shallowness of affect
- Lack of empathy
- Failure to accept responsibility for one's own behavior

Factor 2: Socially deviant lifestyle

- Need for stimulation and proneness to boredom
- Parasitic lifestyle
- Poor behavioral control
- Promiscuous sexual behavior
- Lack of realistic long-term goals
- Impulsivity
- Irresponsibility
- Juvenile delinquency
- Early behavior problems
- Revocation of conditional release

Traits not correlated with Factor 1 or Factor 2

- Many short-term marital relationships
- Criminal versatility

Interestingly, studies examining the relationship between antisocial behavior and suicide found that suicide was strongly correlated to Factor 2, reflecting antisocial deviance but not correlated to Factor 1 reflecting affect (emotional) states. As the DSM's antisocial personality disorder relates to Factor 2 and psychopathy relates to both factors, this fact would confirm Hervey Cleckley's assertion that psychopaths are relatively immune from suicide. Conversely, individuals with a clinical diagnosis of antisocial personality disorder have relatively high suicides rates.

NEUROLAW: THE BRAIN STANDING TRIAL WITH THE ACCUSED

Neurolaw is an emerging interdisciplinary field christened by the impact of brain-scanning technology from neuroscience, especially forensic neuropsychology. *The brain can now stand trial along with the accused.* Also, high-tech brain scans have paved the way for a meaningful dialogue between medico-legal experts and neuroscientists regarding legal standards for criminal culpability. Consider the following:

- How will new insights from brain imaging studies affect motive and sentencing? Is there a new standard for intent? Does a person with a damaged brain receive a lighter sentence than a person showing no damage?
- Will increasingly accurate deception detection in the brain lead to more accurate criminal verdicts?
- Does neuroscience hold the key to final determination of guilt or innocence?
- The *American Heritage Dictionary* definition of "diminished capacity" is the demonstrated lack of ability to comprehend the nature of a crime or to restrain oneself from committing a crime.

The definition of diminished capacity is not ambiguous; however, the way individuals come to suffer from it raises questions and is reviewed over the next several paragraphs.

According to modern neurological-based research, some violent criminals may suffer from this syndrome—diminished capacity—to one extent or another. The next question is whether or not society should recalibrate the scales of normalcy versus "mental defects" as scientific "excuses" for violent behavior. Should we mitigate the sentence from death to a long prison sentence without the possibility of parole?

Most of what we know chemically and functionally regarding criminal minds has been available for a relatively short period of time or has just emerged over the horizon. Forensic investigative practices call for the acceptance of fact-based evidence to convict criminals. What we know in 10 more years will eclipse what it has taken centuries to catalog.

- How can we ascertain what is in the mind of a dangerous or violent person?
- How can we use this information to limit that person's access to society?

As law and forensic neuropsychology struggle to develop technologically advanced methods, principally the neuroscan (high resolution brain scans), to analyze the criminal mind via brain conditions, society is being forced to acknowledge that the brain is the foundation of behavior. Theoretically, "brain conditions" show up in the neuroscan thanks to advances in this groundbreaking technology. Look what technology has accomplished in DNA analysis from a decade ago. Yet, why are some sapient brains in society cast to the farthest end of a measurable continuum of violent behavior, whereas others land somewhere in a range most of us consider normal to somewhat normal?

Neurolaw involves new and evolving technology, pointing to the condition of the brain for answers to legal questions, most notably: "what was the condition of the mind (literally the brain) at the time of the commission of the violent crime?" Does the image of the brain from the neuroscan show function or dysfunction? When the scan is applied to legal questions of culpability, is it diagnostic evidence or merely descriptive of how a given individual brain works? What do scans really tell us? Do low blood flow and other "imperfections" evident in scans *cause* violent behavior? The determination of the argument of "diagnostic" versus "descriptive" will be up to the jury to decide. Absent good, hard science from case law, neurolaw is an evolving neuroscience that leaves many questions to be determined as a matter of fact, not law.

John's Brain

A representative problem faced by neurolaw is equivalent to the condition of brain development depending on many varied circumstances in modern society. If we consider "John" as the subject of scientific scrutiny, we can discover many important things about "John" and his brain (suggested by the essay *Neurolaw,* by Barry Grubbs).

- Did John (and his brain) have what we consider a normal healthy upbringing?
- Did John suffer any physical abuse or abuse of any other kind that might contribute to his inability to adjust to the world in the same way we are all expected to due to an impaired brain?
- Does John suffer from a personality disorder? Is he depressed or anxious? Does John's brain have chemical imbalances?
- Are John and his brain addicted to drugs, alcohol, or pornography?

In sum, does John have a damaged brain sufficient enough for diminished capacity?

These queries make up an initial round of questions followed by others that are even more focused and concentrated on the finest detail of the personal social experience of "being John and being his brain." It is, after all, what individuals live through in formative years that tends to determine, maybe not exactly, what our lives will be like as adults, or so contend traditional developmental psychologists. It is not difficult to predict that by the time John (or anyone else) acts out violently, he surely knows "right from wrong," which raises the following questions:

- What if he is psychotic and is incapable discerning right from wrong?
- Might the perpetrator show in his handiwork a cold-blooded quality? He knew it was wrong, but so what?
- What circumstances might suggest "diminished capacity," mitigating the normal decision-making process, and if so proven, affect sentencing guidelines?

This is just a small sampling of what neurolaw must determine. Forensic neuropsychologists are sure to prepare their presentations based on academic studies, such as the one that follows, in attempts to bolster their cases.

Careful clinical studies by brain specialist and neuroscientist Adrian Raine has led to consistent results that can be used to predict what types of mental characteristics reflective of brain health or dysfunction might contribute to violent tendencies. Brain damage from a childhood head injury is only one example of the kind of trauma that can lead to a decrease in the brain function necessary to effectively "blend" into normal society. What if the alleged trauma was not due to a physical injury, but rather to an emotional trauma? Does emotional trauma show up in neuroscans? Negligent or abusive treatment or what is commonly known as "toxic parenting" may be presented in court to establish diminished capacity. Is it really to blame? What does the scan show? What effect does alleged child abuse have on criminal culpability?

Child abuse is defined in many ways in modern culture. Physical violence against children or adolescents is only one of the ways parents and other influential adults can alter the development of the mentally and physically fragile brains of young people. What is becoming more certain with each study is that in nonviolent adults, parental nurturing often produces emotional competency in young adults. Children of addicted parents, and those raised in abusive environments, are more likely to emerge with "toxic brains."

NEUROLAW AND NEUROSCANS

Brain imaging scans (neuroscans) tell a story that cannot be ignored. SPECT scans and fMRI results may reveal visible damage to the tissue of the brains of those who are affected by physical and mental abuse. Reduced blood flow to certain regions of the brain can be linked to a decrease in the ability to function and normally can be observed in PET scans. Did the traumatized regions cause the accused to act out violently?

Adrian Raine reports that results from neuroscans conducted on serial killers reveal a staggering trend and consistently point to some forms of permanent brain damage. Whether or not the idea is appealing, evidence suggests that the production of violence may be identified in a neuroscan. Violent behavior has not been determined to be caused by viral infections but rather caused by a complex combination of physical, genetic, emotional, and social ingredients that work together to trigger violent behavior.

In the final analysis, we have to be prepared to accept that the delicate organ we have long taken for granted as a dependable and predictable source for our mental and emotional capacity is likewise highly susceptible to certain destructive inputs that may result in permanent damage. A damaged brain can often inflict more than its share of damage on those who are subject to its influence. The modern analysis of the criminal mind using forensic investigative science benefits greatly from the halls of academia and research labs with scientific discoveries that provide courtroom-strength answers to one of the most haunting questions asked about violent criminal behavior: "Why did they do it?" If knowing what kinds of physical and emotional conditions lead those with evidence of a damaged brain to an unnatural propensity for violent behavior, it is crucial that such knowledge be shared. This new view of the violent criminal could be effective in the courtroom when the sentencing of the most dangerous offenders takes into account the criminal's *diminished capacity for rational behavior*, for example the following:

- Should we release a murderer after only 20 years of incarceration?
- Should we ever release that same murderer if we know that what is wrong cannot be made right?

Raining Down on Neurolaw

Perhaps the precursor to neurolaw and questions of diminished capacity was the 1992 study by neuroscientist Adrian Raine, who discovered damage to the prefrontal regions of the brain—regions responsible for regulatory control over inappropriate behavior. Raine found frontal lobe damage in 41 out of 41 murderers in his study. Raine used PET scans, which measure glucose uptake in regions of the brain when stimulated by tasks, to measure whether they received sufficient blood flow (or inefficient flow). Blood flow was shown in splotches of blue indicating low activity that resulted in a lack of inhibitory control of aggressive impulses. Raine also found that murderers are not all the same; he had images to prove it. When murderers were divided into (1) those who committed cold-blooded, premeditated killing versus (2) those who killed impulsively, the impulse killers' prefrontal regulatory control showed to be the poorest functioning.

Raine's study supports previous work by researchers at the University of Iowa showing that healthy people who suffer damage to the PFC can become impulsive and antisocial. Interestingly, the model for this result occurred in the mid-1800s when a railroad worker—Phineas Gage—received massive damage to his PFC and led to transforming the like-able Gage into an impulsive and vulgar man. The Gage Study became the model study suggesting that damage to specific regions of the brain affected personality and behavior and often did so in violent ways.

Raine's finding were consistent with years of research by Dr. Dorothy Lewis, a professor of psychiatry at New York University School of Medicine as well as Dr. Jonathan Pincus, chief of neurology at the Veterans Affairs Medical Center. Based on standard neuropsychological tests alone and enhanced by brain scans on serial killer Joel Rifkin, the most prolific serial killer in New York's history, Pincus showed Rifkin's brain was vulnerable to violent behavior.

Clinical forensic neuropsychologists who testify for the defense may have the inside track in the courtroom when powerful and highly con-vincing brain images are used to show alleged dysfunction causing diminished capacity. When scans reveal "dinged up" PFCs as "cool-coded" spots indicating low glucose activity, for example, the implication of diminished prefrontal regulatory control may mitigate the profundity of the crime in the sentencing phase, or it might not.

A poorly functioning amygdala, for example, has been advanced as a major factor in explaining cold-blooded psychopathic crime. This pivotal brain region lies behind normal individuals' ability to feel fear when fear-inducing stimuli are presented. When damaged, underdeveloped, or not well connected, we are not fazed by fear stimuli in the least. The same is true for sexual predators who brazenly steal children in broad daylight from the front yards of their homes.

Regardless, advances in and the application of neuroimaging has set the stage for the collision of medical technology in legal proceedings with the all-important interpretative or diagnostic aspect of brain scans. *What do they mean?*

Interpretation is sure to take center stage among forensic neuropsychologists, as they tangle with legal experts. Brain scans show what they show, but the question remains: Will neuroscans be perceived as diagnostic or merely descriptive? Legal scholars seem to support the diagnostic view rather than the descriptive one, but which one reflects true conditions in the brain? Time will tell.

TRUTHFULLY, HONESTLY, DECEPTIVELY: AUTOBIOGRAPHICAL ESSAYS

It is well known in 21st-century neuroscience that final prefrontal connectivity, augmented by psychological maturity gained from life's hard knocks, "marks" the adult version of the sapient brain. Finally in the driver's seat, we have three rearview mirrors—age, experience, and cognitive "second thought"—giving us a mature, self-reflective *looking before leaping* mentality. Sapient brains thus marked by a functional PFC characterize what is mandated by the evolution of the sapient brain *away* from adolescent deceptive practices and dangerous dirty tricks from the chemical dominance of the MLS and *toward* making cool, calm, collected, and self-reflective judgments. Truly, the adult version of the brain turns a new leaf toward *shades of honesty and truthfulness.* Not that the adult-version sapient brain is ever purged of adaptive neuropsychopathy, which would defeat the purpose of the cascading chemistry of the DANE brain and serotonin, boosted by testosterone, which is the principal montage of mood-brightening neurochemistry providing "psychological armor" with mood and affect-sustaining chemistry.

In cortical and chemical metamorphosis, the sapient brain is capable of "wiring" and "rewiring" itself from a variety of social cues such as "looking before leaping." Is it evolutionarily mandated that the more mature we get, the better we are at making really good decisions? What better time in life to face the prospect of truthfulness over deceptive practices and to wrestle anew with morals and ethics than the arrival of a couple's progeny? Parents need truth and honesty to set the standard—the line in the sand—for their children who they know soon will be committed to deceptive practices and dirty tricks, just as they once were.

As part of my 2010 collection of autobiographical essays from college students, one essay will close out each part's final chapter. Students were asked: "Who Am I and Why?" Identities remain anonymous, but the essays, for the most part, are only lightly edited and presented as written. For further reflection and analysis, each autobiography is followed by a few comments that shed further light on how their brains were marked by the chemistry behind adaptive neuropsychopathy.

REFERENCES

Babiak, P. (2007). From darkness into the light: Psychopathy in industrial and orga-nizational psychology. In Herve, H. & Yuille, J. C. (Eds.), *The psychopath: Theory, research, and practice*. Mahwah, NJ: Lawrence Erlbaum Associates.

Changeux, Jean-Pierre. (1985). *Neuronal man: The biology of mind*. New York: Oxford University Press.

Cooke, D. J., Forth, A. E., & Hare, R. D. (Eds.). (1998). *Psychopathy: Theory, research, and implications for society*. Dordrecht: Kluwer.

De Becker, Gavin. (1997). *The gift of fear*. New York: Dell Books.

Douglas, J. (with Olshaker, Mark). (1995). *Mindhunter: Inside the FBI's elite serial crime unit*. New York: Pocket Books.

Douglas, J. (with Olshaker, Mark). (1998). *Obsession*. New York: Pocket Books.

Douglas, J. (with Olshaker, Mark). (1999). *The anatomy of motive*. New York: Pocket Books.

Esherick, Joan. (2006). *Criminal psychology and personality profiling*. Philadelphia: Mason Crest.

Farwell, L. A., & Smith, S. S. (2001). Using brain MERMER testing to detect concealed knowledge despite efforts to conceal. *Journal of Forensic Sciences, 46* (1): 135–143.

Forth, A. E., Newman, J. P., & Hare, R. D. (Eds.). (1996). Issues in criminological and legal psychology: No. 24, *International perspective on psychopathy* (pp. 12–17). Leicester, UK: British Psychological Society.

Hare, R. D. (2003). *Psychopathy checklist–revised technical manual* (2nd ed.). Toronto: Multihealth Systems.

Hawking, Stephen W. (1988). *A brief history of time: From the big bang to black holes*. New York: Bantam.

Holmes, R. M., & Holmes, S. T. (2002). *Profiling violent crimes: An investigative tool* (3rd ed.). Thousand Oaks, CA: Sage.

Jacobs, Don. (2008). *The psychology of deception: Sexual predators and forensic psychol-ogy*. Plymouth, MI: Hayden-McNeil.

Jeeves, Malcom. (1994). *Mind fields: Reflections on the science of mind and brain*. Grand Rapids, MI: Baker Books.

Mattson, James, & Simon, Merrill. (1996). *The pioneers of NMR and magnetic resonance in medicine*. Jericho, NY: Dean Books.

Owen, David. (2004). *Criminal minds: The science and psychology of profiling*. New York: Barnes and Noble Books.

Ressler, Robert. (1992). *Whoever fights monsters*. New York: St. Martin's Press.

Ressler, Robert. (1998). *I have lived in the monster*. New York: St. Martin's Press.

Reynolds, Cecil, & Fletcher-Janzen, Elaine. (Eds.). (2006). Brain SPECT imaging. In *Encyclopedia of Special Education*. Hoboken, NJ: John Wiley & Sons.

Rosen, Jeffrey. (2007). The brain on the stand. *New York Times Magazine*. Available at: http://www.nytimes.com/2007/03/11/magazine/11Neurolaw.t.html?_r=1.

Simon, R. I. (1996). Psychopaths, the predators among us. In R. I. Simon (Ed.), *Bad men do what good men dream* (pp. 21–46). Washington, DC: American Psychiatric Publishing.

Verona, Patrick E., & Joiner C. J. (2001). Psychopathy, antisocial personality, and suicide risk. *Journal of Abnormal Psychology, 110* (3), 462–470.

Autobiography of Rachel's Life: Determination—Life in Desperation

December 18, 1984: The day I was born, the day determination was born. What is in a person's mind that determines whether they succeed or fail? Could it simply be determination? Or, are we destined to become a product of our environment?

Corpus Christi, Texas, was the impoverished city I eventually bloomed from. All around me was illegal drugs, sex, alcoholism, but more importantly, neglect. I come from a family of four siblings, two sisters, one brother, and myself. My mother married "my sperm donor" when she was just a mere 14 years old. He was 15. My mother would soon give birth to her first born, a son, and my father-figure. In the remaining years she birthed my two sisters and me. By the time I was three years old, much too young to remember, my parents were separated; from then on, *my siblings and I would be forgotten.*

All of my childhood memories seldom include my mother being present, but they always include my sisters and brother. My mother started abusing narcotics and alcohol—they became her world, her "liquid" children. Subsequently, we became the last thing on her mind. One of my earliest childhood memories consists of her telling us to go outside and play. When we returned, in her eyes, was the look—a "glazed over" look in her eyes—that I can vividly recall seeing and there was the smell, the sweet smell of marijuana. We weren't naïve; we knew even then, that something was not right. Something was wrong with our lives.

We grew up in deplorable conditions. Conditions no kid should ever be exposed to. I recollect wanting new shoes all the time. Mine were worn down, so used. I never had any new clothes to wear to school like all the other children. By the time I was 10 years old, in the fifth grade, we must have transferred schools at least 20 times, but this time was different; this time I would actually come across a friend that would show me love.

We lived in a run-down, mouse- and cockroach-infested apartment. Right next door was a cantina, "Los Amigos"; my mother bartended there to all the drunks, the perverts—the nasty repugnant men and women. Of course, the music was always blaring from all the live bands that played there on a nightly basis. The music that stuck in my head was *Tejano* and *Cumbia*. Soon, though, the music no longer perturbed me, I could fall asleep as though it was just a lullaby.

The men—repugnant, vile, and drunken—never stopped bothering me. I recall going into the cantina to tell my mom I was hungry, or maybe just to bother her, and those perverts would stare at me. They would whistle at me, a 10-year-old little girl. Seriously?! One time I walked out our back door of the apartment just to realize that I had barely missed stepping on feces, not dog feces, but the human variety. Who could have the audacity to defecate on some one's doorstep? Those repugnant, drunken men, that's who.

However, there is a good memory that comes from the blue, rundown apartment on Highland Street, in the guise of my best friend. I remember her like it was yesterday. The sparkle in her eyes when she looked at me, the look of love in her eyes. The way she glistened in the hot sun, is still so fresh in my memory. I don't remember where she came from or how she got there, but she was there with me. She was there when I needed someone to show me love; there when I tried to scare her away; there when I needed someone to talk to; there when I needed someone to play with. Her name was Brownsie and, yes, she was a dog; not to me though, to me she was a constant companion in my short, sad, lonely little life. She was the inspiration to what I ultimately hope to become, a veterinarian. She showed me what it meant to be loyal, determined, and ultimately a great friend.

I remember one time I tried to get her to leave. With tears in my eyes I kicked her. It was awful, but nothing compared to what I thought the owner of the apartments would do to her; he hated dogs and zoned in on mine. To my surprise though, she stayed. She didn't care that I had hurt her. She still loved me. She was still loyal to me. It was like she comprehended that I needed her as much as she needed me. Eventually, she disappeared; nowhere to be found. I looked everywhere for her but to no avail. Maybe she thought she had served her purpose and moved on. Maybe the owner of the apartments had done away with her. Maybe she got picked up by animal control. I don't know, and will never know what happened to her, but I will never forget the brown, loyal friend with the sparkling green eyes; she had always been there for me when no one else was. By losing her, why didn't I "cave in"? Honestly, I don't know.

Ten years old was the first time I would smoke a joint (marijuana cigarette), and I would continue abusing this "awesome" drug for six years. This drug that calmed my mind; the drug that I knew my mother had smoked all those years; the drug that gave my mother that "look" in her eyes. Was I destined to follow in her footsteps? Was I destined to become everything that I despised in her? I didn't care, I didn't know any better. Marijuana got me through my depressing young life. But, it started to throw me off course of what Brownsie had inspired in me—how to love another. None of that mattered though; even an education was so far out of my reach. After all, who cared if I went to college and became a veterinarian? Nobody even cared if I attended primary school. No one in my family had an education, let alone a decent job. Kids are just products of their environments. Isn't that how society works? Some educated people think so.

By the time I was 13 I was pregnant, impregnated by a pedophile, Kojak. He was a sick, demented man, 13 years my senior. He was a tall, blonde, blue-eyed, handsome man. I never looked my age so when we met I told him I was 15, he told me he was 20. We were both accomplished liars. He was too old to be gallivanting around with a 15-year-old girl. In reality, I was only 11 years old and he was 24 years old. He soon found out my real age, but he insisted on staying with me. I found out his real age a year after we began dating, but by then it was too late to let go; we were "in love" after all.

The first year of our relationship was great. He gave me attention until my heart was content. He loved me, so I thought. De facto, he was just using me, getting his fix—sexual thrills—off being with a little girl. I realize that now, but I didn't know any better then, although I thought I did. When I found out I was pregnant, I hid it from everyone, everyone but him. I trusted him. I thought he would take care of me and we would live happily ever after—every neglected child's dream. I was dead wrong. Kids and their fantasies, they are sadly so miscalculated; now I know.

He soon started becoming domineering, jealous, and psychopathic. I guess he was already a psychopath; he just hid it very well. My sisters lived just a block away, but I wasn't allowed to go over there—his way of controlling me, making sure no one "knocked sense into my head." How could my mother not care that her 13-year-old daughter was living with a pedophile, with a grown man? Truth was I wasn't her problem anymore. Soon, my already distressing life would begin to unravel. Kojak would come in late at night, alcohol fresh on his breath, with a pure evil look in his eyes—a cold, dark, and empty look in his red-rimmed eyes. Then he would start beating me. At first, he would just hit me where no one else could see the bruises. One day though, my sister did see a bruise on my arm. I thought I would die if she found out the truth. After all, I was the smart one. I shrugged it off nonchalantly, telling her I had bumped into the door. Truth was I needed help; I needed someone to see beyond my careless, happy persona. I couldn't ask for help; how embarrassing would that be!

I recall Kojak coming into the house one night after being at another girl's house, ostensibly sleeping with her. Anyhow, he came in and used me as his own personal punching bag. I did nothing to provoke him; I simply greeted him with a smile. I was curled up in a fetal position begging him to stop. He continued punching, kicking, and slapping me until he became exhausted. I was pregnant when the abuse started and I couldn't believe that he could hit me with the knowledge of his unborn child inside me. The beatings were getting worse. I needed to get away from him. I was terrified and traumatized.

As was so often the situation, he was not home late one night; that's when I finally built up the courage to leave. I started down the street. I didn't know where I was going. I couldn't go to my sister's house. I was ashamed I had let myself become a victim of this man. Not 100 yards from the house, he appeared from nowhere, like a demon waiting to drag me back to Hell. He directed me to return to the house. I didn't listen to him this time. I had reached the limits of sanity. I was tired of being his punching bag, tired of being a victim. So, naturally he dragged me by my hair, back into the house. I was no match for him, a 200-pound man. He began doing what he did best, beat me. The next day came, as usual, and he left me alone at home while he was out using his charming skills on some other unfortunate poor girl.

There was no doubt in my mind this would be my time to leave. I was going to get away regardless of what happened. I ran as fast as I could to my sister's home. Not long after I arrived, he appeared at the door, pounding on it, trying to kick it in. I called my brother and they got into a fistfight while everyone watched; my brother was no match for him. I felt horrible that I had gotten my family involved in my problem. My brother was beat to a pulp.

Believe it or not that sick, psychopathic pedophile came around the next day, begging for forgiveness. He promised me he would never lay another hand on me. Of course, like most victims of domestic abuse, I believed him. I went back to the house with him! He resumed where he had left off. One day, not long after I returned, he became upset with me because his beer had become watered down in the hot summer sun. He punched me in my stomach. I gasped for air as he poured his drink on my head, all the while laughing hysterically like it was a big joke to him. I miscarried that night in the bathroom of our rundown apartment. He sat there the whole time, watching me, laughing while I was in excruciating pain during miscarriage. It didn't matter to him. He never tried to get me any medical attention. I never went to the hospital.

Life went on as usual. One night he was on the phone with a girl—talking to her right in front of me—courting her right in front of me. Before he hung up the phone, he told her he loved her. Finally, hearing this, I had enough; he had betrayed me for the last time. I proceeded to walk out the door barefoot and he grabbed me, pulled me inside and pinned me up against the wall. I was so angry. I was ready to fight back and I did just that. I punched him in his face as many times as I could and as hard as I could. His nose began to bleed. He became enraged at the fact I dared fight back. I didn't care if this was going to be my last day on Earth. He gave me a good beating all right, like he was fighting another man. No part of my body was off limits to him this time. He hit me in my face. I remember blacking out several times, but I wasn't going to let him beat me to death without a fight. Before I knew it, he had corned me in a bedroom and ordered me to lie on the bed. By this time I was exhausted. So, I just laid there waiting for my fate. He was holding a razor to my neck at this point and with one last punch to my eye he became satisfied and fell asleep.

The next day would be the beginning of my freedom from this monster.

As we walked to the store, I with an eye patch over my swollen, black eye, we crossed paths with one of my sisters. There was no explaining my abused face this time. She went home and called the cops. However, secretly, I met up with Kojak later on that night. I agreed to meet him at a restaurant down the street, after he begged me for forgiveness yet again. Yep, he promised he would not hit me anymore. *Why do victims of abuse believe their abusers when they tell them this lie?* Thankfully though, I didn't have a chance to meet him the next day. The police had reported my mother to child protective services and the next morning they were banging on the door. At the time I thought they were there to ruin my life. Realistically, they were my saviors. They were there to knock some much-needed sense in my head—to force us to believe that *children are not supposed to live without parental supervision.*

For the next three years, my sister and I were transferred from foster home to foster home. History has a way of repeating itself and I became pregnant yet again when I was sixteen. But, I had changed. I quit smoking pot, careful not to cause any harm to my baby. The state soon found out that I was pregnant and kicked me out of foster care. Was I really that bad? Everywhere I turned, someone rejected me all over again. Child protective services sent me to live with my brother who had now lived in Granbury, Texas. Where was this foreign place?

On my 17th birthday, I was grateful for my move; I had my beautiful son four months later. I graduated high school one year later, the first of my siblings to do so. I was proud of myself. Against all odds I had done what everyone told me I'd never achieve. *It happened because I was determined it would happen.* Better yet, I began to attend college two years later, after giving birth to my second child, a little girl.

It's been a long, hard road to get to this point. I'm now on my way to achieving my dreams; at the bottom of all this, I wanted to make my long-lost friend Brownsie proud. Wherever she is, I know she still loves me. Now, I'm twenty-five years old; I own my own house, car, and a parcel of land. I don't know what determines who will fail or succeed in life, but could it just be determination and the will to survive? I like to say that anything is possible with a little determination. Kids don't have to be a product of their environments. Everyone has a choice.

RACHEL'S BRAINMARKS

How could a young girl at the tender age of 11 possibly survive at the hands of an abusive pedophile? And, with only siblings to lean on without the love, guidance, and protection of her mom—a mom who had opted out of her life with alcohol and drugs—how could she somehow find the strength to finally say "enough is enough"? A synonym used earlier for the functioning of adaptive neuropsychopathy is *determinism.* Indeed, considering her parental rejection and her pedophilic "lover's" violent abuse, why not give up and "cave in?" Brainmarks suggests that Rachel displayed the "will to survive" alone without parents, without nurturing, without love, and without a belief in divine intervention because her powerful brain churned out enough "psychological armor" to deliver her life later into the calmer waters of the PFC. Now, Rachel is thriving and surviving as a single parent who is a great mom. I see her on campus making her dreams come true; I am willing to wager she has found a new "Brownsie" along with a new lease on life.

Part II

The Brainmarks Paradigm
of Adaptive Neuropsychopathy

par-*uh*-dahym	concepts in academic disciplines that produce systematic insights and knowledge; in spectrum varieties, strength of symptoms are presented in gradation across a continuum
uh-**dap**-tiv	able to change by ongoing adaptation
neuro-sik-op-*uh*-thee	an evolutionarily mandated natural brain condition featuring a life-affirming mild version of psychopathy
dih-**sep**-tiv **prak**-tisz	intentionally, systematically, and deceptively misleading others for personal gains

Introduction to Part II: Headquarters for Calculating Minds and Deceptive Practices

Man will occasionally stumble over the truth, but usually manages to pick himself up, walk over or around it, and carry on.
—Winston Churchill (Klotz, 1996, p. 412)

Nature has nurtured selected species with three "gifts" of adaptability for thriving and surviving amid slings and arrows of fierce competition: camouflage, regeneration, and metamorphosis. Camouflage allows potential prey to hide in plain sight from a stalking predator. Color and marking allow them to blend in so well to the surrounding environment—rocks, trees, or vegetation—they appear to be what they are standing around, or part of what they are perched upon. As long as the potential prey can remain frozen in place and get lucky, by having the wind blow in a favorable direction, for example, they likely will survive another day. It works both ways, however. Predators are likewise permitted to stalk, sneak around, and blindside unsuspecting prey when not protected by deception. *Nature is full of curve balls as the original pattern for species deception.*

Does camouflage ability suggest self-awareness? Do animals know they are virtually hidden? Considering what we know in the 21st century about animal intelligence, it most likely is true they are self-aware. The splendid white polar bear hides his black nose with its great paw with its black, razor-sharp claws clutching beneath. Unsuspecting prey see nothing but pure white until, of course, they feel searing pain and see red—their own blood.

A species of butterfly looks like a green leaf as it sits on leafy twigs. Due to color and markings, a big predatory cat—the lynx—blends in with surrounding tree bark—prey have no idea what is happening until fang and claw tear them to shreds. Or, by the same principle, the lynx survives by being hidden in plain sight thanks to background coloring and markings.

In an instance of *regeneration,* a bird dives into the path of a crustacean— a crab, lobster, or crayfish. It grabs one of the creature's 10 legs in its strong beak and takes to the sky, only to lose its grasp seconds later, left "holding the leg," so to speak. The crab frees itself as the trapped leg literally falls off, only to grow back in about two weeks. Fish, salamander, and some mammals show regenerative abilities. Humans have regenerated fingertips, ribs, and entire livers with as little as 25 percent of the original organ left to sprout another.

The most spectacular example of nature's changing room is biological metamorphosis in which species conspicuously and abruptly morph— changing their entire physical form to something else. What once was a repulsive worm becomes a beautiful butterfly. Species *Homo sapiens,* however, takes the grand prize for being the most deceptive of all creatures great and small. From normal minds to criminal minds, the staggering presence of deception is as necessary as taking the next breath. Psychologically, from charmers to pathological liars, we become what we need to be.

All species old and new owe a debt of gratitude to nature for being the original designer of deception. This leaves us with an important question: Do we ever really know what stands before us?

Chapter 4

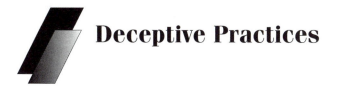 **Deceptive Practices**

I state my belief and present my evidence that a syndrome of psycho-pathy of everyday life [Jacobs: if I may—adaptive *neuropsychopathy*] actually exists.

—Martin Kantor (2006, p. 4)

There's no shortage of psychopaths who con people into doing things for them, usually to obtain money, prestige, power, or, when incarcerated, freedom. In a sense, it is difficult to see how they could do otherwise *given a personality* [Jacobs: If I may—a sapient brain] *that makes them "naturals."*

—Robert Hare (1993, p. 110)

It should come as no surprise that behavior characterized as "decep-tive practices" comes from sapient brains deep into "calculating minds." This is a commonly made observation by anyone who cares to notice. Now, thanks to the improved products and new technological tools in deception detection presented in Part I, we have evidence of neurological regions that give animation to deceptive behaviors buried deep in cortices of the brain. As evidence of this very human condition, if you are safely past late adolescence, revisit your own childhood and early adolescence for proof:

- Did you ever lie to your parents?
- Did you participate in very dangerous or impulsive things with your friends that your parents would have objected to, had they known?
- Did you keep secrets and clandestinely "plot" to gain advantage over a rival by spreading rumors?

- Did you join others in ignoring or bullying a targeted classmate?
- On occasion, did you then (and now) intentionally mislead others or offer partial explanations intent upon leaving out pertinent facts to your advantage?
- Even now do you intentionally and seamlessly manipulate conversation away from topics that could expose you to others in a negative light?

In sapient brains, deceptive practices have a long history; they are not generic to violent criminal minds. In a spectrum of gradation, strength-wise, do they account for original sin in the Garden of Eden? It can be argued forcefully that entire world religions evolved and continue to exist as "guiding lights" *away* from the sins of the Father of Lies—that is, the original source of deceit in "deceptive practices" and in extreme varieties of violent and sexualized "dirty tricks" of Chapter 7. National headlines and popular television shows blaze nightly with the violent criminal varieties. Ecclesiastical canons provide an array of metaphorical rituals—juice and wafer and holy water—as evidence of our petition to purge our wicked and deceiving hearts. The prophet Jeremiah tells us, "The heart is deceitful above all things, and desperately wicked" (Jeremiah 17:9). Throughout history, human behavior has been portrayed as *tragically flawed;* temptation appears too much for our 2.5 pounds of cortical tissue to resist. As further proof, it is a common practice to say, "All's fair in love and war!" But, although history is bloated with tradition, neuroscience is lightly muscled with research.

A primary focus of 21st-century *forensic neuroscience* is what is going on inside the brains that produce criminal minds, especially the nightmarishly violent and sexually psychopathic version. New tools are convincing forensic investigative scientists that it is not so much what is outside of our craniums that matter, but rather, *what is inside that really counts.* What else could account for normalcy, abnormality, violent, and sexually perverse criminality? Many incorrect assumptions leading to cause and effect of human flaws remain persistent even when proven inadequate by standards of neuroscience. Misguided answers continue to loiter in the minds of sapient brains, especially those with brains "marked" for deceptions supporting hidden agendas.

Deceit and lying cut though the fragile fabric of trust that binds families and communities together. Exemplary in this regard are extramarital affairs marked by deception and devastating dirty tricks that shatter hearts and send children into the orbit of single parenting. Deceptive practices have toppled and disgraced the powerful across millennia accounting for

Conspiracy to Commit Wire Fraud; Wire Fraud

JOSEPH WAYNE McCOOL

Aliases:
Joe McCool, Joe Wayne McCool

DESCRIPTION

Date(s) of Birth Used:	October 3, 1947	**Hair:**	Gray
Place of Birth:	Myrtle Point, Oregon	**Eyes:**	Blue
Height:	6'2"	**Sex:**	Male
Weight:	230 pounds	**Race:**	White
NCIC:	W253072313	**Nationality:**	American
Occupation:	Unknown		

Scars and Marks: McCool has a scar on his right knee and right wrist.
Remarks: None

CAUTION

Joseph Wayne McCool is being sought for his alleged involvement in a ponzi scheme that was based out of Mesa, Arizona. Sometime before February, 2004, McCool allegedly conspired with two other individuals, who have since been arrested, to operate The Brixon Group, Ltd., which fraudulently solicited millions of dollars from the public. McCool solicited and induced members of the public to invest approximately $10 million in Brixon by making fraudulent and misleading representations concerning how the money would be used, the rates of return, the security of the investments, and their own qualifications to conduct such investments.

Reportedly, McCool promised investors that their money would be invested in European investment programs and used as reserves for high-yield insurance company portfolio investments. Investors were told that Brixon would generate returns of 10 percent per month. Investors were also falsely promised that they could not lose their principal investment because the principal was insured by the State Bar of California. Furthermore, McCool was represented to investors as a banking expert who successfully managed a large private trust in Europe before operating Brixon.

Additionally, McCool reportedly failed to disclose to investors that he did not invest money for the benefit of the investors; instead, he allegedly converted a substantial portion of the invested money for personal use and used new funds received by Brixon to make payments to earlier investors. Additionally, investors' money was never insured against loss. When Brixon failed to make promised payments to investors, McCool responded by telling investors that the money was tied up in Europe due to the United States Patriot Act and various international banking problems.

On May 11, 2006, a federal arrest warrant was issued by the United States District Court for the Southern District of California after McCool was charged with conspiracy to commit wire fraud and wire fraud. Additionally, McCool may be in the Philippines.

If you have any information concerning this person, please contact your local FBI office or the nearest American Embassy or Consulate.

FBI wanted poster for Joseph Wayne McCool. (From http://www.fbi.gov/wanted)

financial greed that has practically bankrupted entire world economies. In the 21st century, we stand on the brink of a meltdown of traditional values because of financial deception and investor dirty tricks. The list of every-day criminal offenders is long, but three in recent memory will suffice: "wealth managers" Bernard Madoff (2009), Allen Stanford (2009), and

Wire Fraud; Mail Fraud; Telemarketing Fraud Against the Elderly; Aiding and Abetting

OMID TAHVILI

Photograph taken in 2005   Photograph taken in 2005

Aliases:
Omid Roshan, Omid Roushan, "Nino"

DESCRIPTION

Date(s) of Birth Used:	October 31, 1970	**Hair:**		Black
Place of Birth:	Tehran, Iran	**Eyes:**		Brown
Height:	5'9"	**Sex:**		Male
Weight:	165 pounds	**Race:**		White (Persian)
NCIC:	W683726392	**Nationality:**		Iranian
Occupation:	Unknown			

Scars and Marks: Tahvili has tattoos on his right and left arms of the face of a small child, a tattoo of a large cross on his back that connects to a circular flame design over his right shoulder (see photos below), and a tattoo of a pointed flame design over his right arm just above his chest. He also has a scar above his right eye.

Remarks: Tahvili may be in Germany; Tehran, Iran; Toronto, Canada; or Spain. He may have a moustache and goatee. Tahvili is considered extremely dangerous.

CAUTION

Omid Tahvili is wanted for his alleged role as the owner and operator of a fraudulent telemarketing business in Vancouver, British Columbia, through which he obtained approximately $3 million from hundreds of primarily elderly victims in the United States. The business operated from 1999 to May of 2002. Tahvili and his co-conspirators allegedly informed the victims that they had either won or had a very good chance of winning a lottery, but that they would have to pay an advance fee in order to obtain the winnings. None of the victims received any of the promised winnings.

A federal arrest warrant was issued for Tahvili on January 30, 2003, by the United States District Court, Central District of California, after he was charged with mail fraud, wire fraud, telemarketing fraud, and aiding and abetting.

On November 15, 2007, Tahvili escaped from a correctional institution in British Columbia, Canada, where he had been in custody since July of 2005 on an unrelated kidnap and assault charge. There is currently a Canada-wide arrest warrant related to the escape from custody.

SHOULD BE CONSIDERED ARMED AND DANGEROUS AND AN ESCAPE RISK

If you have any information concerning this person, please contact your local FBI office or the nearest American Embassy or Consulate.

FBI wanted poster for Omid Tahvili. (From http://www.fbi.gov/wanted)

Shalom Weiss (2000). Violence against a person's life savings and investments is yet another way to destroy a life from remorseless psychopaths deep into deceptive practices fueled by self-absorbed narcissism.

Lying, stealing, cheating, and cover-ups have an even more sinister side with violent and *psychopathic sexual burglary*—portrayed as the extreme dirty tricks of pathological psychopathy. In violent criminal minds, it appears that society's most elusive predators—sexually psychopathic

Failure to Appear (Mortgage Fraud)

JULIEANNE BALDUEZA DIMITRION

Alias:
Julie Anne Baldueza Dimitrion

DESCRIPTION

Date(s) of Birth Used:	March 22, 1972	**Hair:**	Black
Place of Birth:	Hawaii	**Eyes:**	Brown
Height:	4'11"	**Sex:**	Female
Weight:	120 to 140 pounds	**Race:**	Asian
NCIC:	W440768252	**Nationality:**	American
Occupation:	Unknown		

Scars and Marks: None known

Remarks: The Dimitrions were last known to be in the Mililani area of Oahu, Hawaii. Julieanne Dimitrion has expensive tastes in clothing, specifically high-end lingerie, designer purses, and shoes.

CAUTION

Julieanne Dimitrion and her husband, John , were indicted in February of 2009 for mortgage fraud. In April of 2009, they pled guilty to operating a fraud scheme in which they used their companies to convince distressed homeowners to relinquish their homes with the premise of improving the victims' financial position. They promised to invest the proceeds of the home sales, but instead the Dimitrions used the victims' money to fund their own lavish lifestyles. As a result, multiple families in Oahu, Hawaii, lost their homes. The Dimitrions were scheduled to be sentenced in the United States District Court in Honolulu, Hawaii, on July 6, 2010, but failed to appear at the sentencing. A federal arrest warrant for failure to appear was then issued for each of them.

REWARD

The FBI is offering a reward of up to $1,000 for information leading to the arrest of Julieanne and John Dimitrion.

If you have any information concerning this person, please contact your local FBI office or the nearest American Embassy or Consulate.

FBI wanted poster for Julieanne Baldueza Dimitrion. (From http://www.fbi. gov/wanted)

serial rapists and murderers—are increasing in numbers and incidents. Around the world, this is cause for alarm and for reasons "why."

Without question, these facts account for our pressing need to understand the foundation of criminal minds. In the search for reasons behind calculated deception and violent dirty tricks, we must analyze sources of *pathological psychopathy*—the syndrome behind many instances of violent criminal minds, the focus of this book. Psychopaths account for estimates of 20 percent to 35 percent of the population of incarcerated inmates, but their crimes are laced with violence and perverted sexuality committed in serial time frames. It is most troubling that incarceration or rehabilitation fails as they display *the highest recidivism rates of all criminals.* It is true that they never learn from their mistakes. But, what do we really know about psychopathic versions of deception? Why does it appear so prevalent in sapient brains?

As a psychology professor and department chair of behavioral science, the results from my 25-year study of adolescent sapient brains come from autobiographical essays—from the "horses' mouths." This became the focus of what has become my life's work: Why is the adolescent sapient brain so prone to deceptive practices and adolescent versions of dirty tricks? Why does their behavior seem so whimsical and careless at times as though entitled to do whatever they please without regard for other's feelings? Could this be a "red flag" indicating some gradation of criminal minds to come, or is it just human nature?

ADOLESCENTS RAISE PARENTS AS MUCH AS PARENTS RAISE ADOLESCENTS

The bios (autobiographical essays) spoke volumes—they taught me how to listen to adolescent sapient brains and not be so quick to judge; as if they "were raising me" with experiences documented in their essays. I did become a cobbler of sorts to the workings of their "mental workshops" within their all-encompassing experiences in peer tribes. With such energy and creativity buzzing inside their young sapient brains, why would some come so close to danger, to death, to criminality, and to hatching criminal minds? In the 21st century, is participation in social networking sites a way to self-medicate by diversion? Through tweets, Facebook, and so-called compatibility sites, does daily networking increase their sense of empowerment in peer tribes?

From my academic training and early years as a college professor, I followed without question the paradigms suggested by my chosen discipline of psychology. Over the years, I observed the behavior of my students, my children, and friends, and the behavior of colleagues while conducting a 25-year study of our sapient brain's output articulated into everyday behavior. In a sense, don't we all do that to some extent? One event would shift my perspective away from conventional wisdom in an unanticipated direction toward the creation of my new adaptive or beneficial version of psychopathy, long overdue and absolutely required.

From legal theory, I borrowed a well-known common law principle still used today—*"res ipsa loquitur"*—common evidence allowing behavior to "speak for itself." In the evolution of forensic investigative science, scientists cannot ignore what all of us observe every day. Eventually, *cause and effect* connects the dots of everyday raw materials of observation, which the

Federal Bureau of Investigation (FBI) documented in the 1970s with KOC—
known offender characteristics. This vital information came from studying
personality characteristics of violent offenders "in their own words," similar to the bios of my students. Of similar importance, not every instance of
behavior or human interaction is subject to rigorous laboratory study; it is
not practical and would likely produce misleading results. However, the
first step in documenting habits and patterns in sapient brains is the *res ipsa*
step—attempting to quantify what we see every day. (Chapter 6 addresses
the significance of astute observation of behavior, particularly violent
behavior as it "speaks for itself" in spectrum analyses.) As an evolving
neuroscience, *forensic investigative neuroscience* has provided compelling
answers presented over the course of the book (introduced in Chapter 2).

STUDENT BIOGRAPHIES: WHO ARE YOU AND WHY?

The seminal event that prompted my paradigmatic shift was an
ongoing assignment that lasted 25 years and counting. I asked students
in introductory psychology to write end-of-semester autobiographical
essays addressing factors they believed to be important in their own
development. On the surface, the assignment was simple: "Who Am I
and Why?"

During the 1970s and fresh out of a master's degree program, I was
only a few years older than most of my students. Apparently, I was close
enough to their age to be counted somewhat worthy of being embraced
by their tribe milieu. Over the ensuring years as I grew older, my luck continued as the brutally honest and insightful responses continued to match
patterns from earlier essays.

Subsequently, over another two decades, I read nearly 20,000 essays.
What I gathered from the autobiographies of typical college-age students
(mostly 18 to 21 years of age) did not mesh with the *zeitgeist* of my boomer
generation's lukewarm analysis of adolescent development as years of
"storm and stress." No explanation was given for exactly what was meant
by this expression other than an explosion of hormones that produced
chaotic behavior at times. But, what *were the specific conditions in the brain*
that produced such powerful changes in mind, body, and behavior? What
could it be, but the workings of sapient brains?

ADOLESCENT BRAIN'S FASCINATION AND STIMULATION
WITH DANGEROUS SHENANIGANS

What appeared in the autobiographies from the beginning and continuing into my 2010 crop of bios was adolescent fascination with "dangerous

shenanigans"—at-risk behavior covered up by deception that placed the adolescent peer tribe below the radar of the nurturing bond of family trust—as though teenagers were living apart from traditional emotional shelters afforded by family. Interspersed into this "tribe-apart" entitlement was a considerable amount of psychological deception covering up what often turned out to be *really bad choices*—choices that produced teen pregnancies, drug addiction, family upheavals, school problems, runaways, suicide ideation, and serious clashes with the law. Sure, some teenagers seem like "old souls," who seldom strayed far from parental bridles (did they really?); but they appear clearly in the minority viewed as "do-gooders" by the majority.

Evidence from the bios spoke and continue to speak volumes: if parents knew then and now even 10 percent of what their teenagers are really doing when absent from supervision, they are geniuses. Year after year, page after page, students consistently convinced me that parents do not know what they think they know about their own kids. What is up with the adolescent sapient brain?

Therefore, directly from the bios, parent-teenager relationships were uniformly, on the surface, typified by trust or more akin to "wishful thinking"—from parental perspectives—whereas within peer tribes, teenagers painted a picture of deceptive practices and dirty tricks—often engaging in dangerous activities—almost whimsically as though *entitled to do so.* Is adolescent-strength entitlement when joined to the hip of narcissism a precursor to criminal minds? Do entitlement and narcissism so evident in young sapient brains fill some other need of living? Could they be beneficial and adaptive to survival? So, after decades of reading bios, I finally got the significance of the autobiographies through *my thick skull.* What developmental dynamic could possibly account for this seemingly universal theme that appeared over and over in adolescent essays from the 1970s continuing to the present? The answer is presented in the next paragraphs; and while it is not surprising, it is compelling. A subtle hint is fair: it is all about the continuum of the brain condition of psychopathy; in spectrum analysis, if a far right-side describes pathology (disorder), by definition there must exist a more normally "ordered" far left-side. *It is as plain as the nose on our faces.* In fact, Robert Hare's *Psychopathy Checklist–Revised* (PCL-R) has proven for more than 30 years what my Brainmarks Paradigm contends: *psychopathy is both a normal brain condition in mild gradation and a severe and irreversible personality disorder in severe gradation.* Point-wise, it is the difference between assigning a score of one versus a score of two on his remarkable checklist. It is what is best described as a simple discovery by Nobel Laurent

Szent-Grogyi: *"seeing what everyone else has seen and thinking what nobody else has thought."*

In adolescent sapient brains what *developmental dynamic* could possibly account for the seemingly universal theme of fascination with danger, deceptive practices, and adolescent varieties of dirty tricks? Said another way, in the face of participating in risky behavior, why do adolescents appear so casual, unconcerned, and bulletproof? They act as though they are inoculated against any dangerous adventure. *As it turns out, they are.* What else could the answer be but a brain condition? Not just any brain condition, mind you, but a *demonstrative brain condition.* On such a grand scale as that of living another day, might this condition be due to brain evolution, whereby the focus on helpful traits is deposited into cortices of the brain? Based on the same principles that assist survivability, what genetic "gift" could so empower sapient brains?

Since 2000, while researching how criminal minds analysis had changed from Stanton Samenow's *Inside the Criminal Mind* (1984), I rediscovered the brilliantly advancing insights into *pathological psychopathy* evolving as it has over time from Hervey Cleckley's *The Mask of Sanity* (1941), Robert Hare's *Without Conscience* (1993), Adrian Raine and Jose Sanmartin's *Violence and Psychopathy* (2001), and Martin Kantor's *The Psychopathy of Everyday Life* (2006). These works all address the well-researched and peer-accepted construct of spectrum psychopathy—that is, gradations of psychopathy across a continuum—typified by mild to moderate, and moderate to severe gradations—these gradations are the same criteria used by psychiatrists and clinicians in the language of the American Psychiatric Association's (APA, 2000) *Diagnostic and Statistical Manual of Mental Disorders* (DSM).

To understand cold-blooded criminal violence mixed with perverted sexuality and to gain a foothold on the violence capable from psychopathic criminal minds, we must enter into the domain of a well-researched psychological paradigm of *psychopathy.* As each chapter will contribute portions of our modern understanding of this brain condition, still misread in many quarters as only a personality disorder, it is imperative that we embrace its origins. *As far as we know, there is no psychopathy gene.* What can no longer be denied as a condition of spectrum psychopathy, however, is the fountainhead source of psychopathy from the specific neurotransmitter and hormone chemistry we can name as well as others perhaps still unknown. An adaptive neuropsychopathy has been in sapient brains for a long time. It is present at birth; in fact, brain chemistry is with us before birth.

In cascades that can be mapped in rapid-transit pathways of the brain, our endogenous chemistry "marks" the brain in ways we are just now beginning to understand. Might we be born with a Teflon coating—prophylactic against sapient brains "caving in" or losing the "will to live"? Additionally, from our life experiences might we learn very early (created by chemical cascades) that deceptive practices give us distinct advantages? In first meeting another sapient brain, for example, we may encounter nonthreatening and engaging behavior characterized by a natural magnetism and openness that subsequently is shown over a short time to disguise self-absorbed narcissism, augmented by an arrogant bulletproof entitlement of doing whatever he chooses; so that, in the end, arrogance is misread as confidence. Will we see him for who he truly is? Or, will we be summarily duped by his magnetic charms? This natural charmer will be observed to effortlessly adapt on the fly to any contingency. In the time it takes to bat an eye, this glib, superficial charmer becomes whatever he needs to be. And, as it turns out, the female brain is often vulnerable to his charms. Here's why. Even casual observations preliminary to mating behavior suggests that females possess a distinct vulnerability of being blindsided by a handsome and charming male. The male charmer spins his cocoon of silky promises interspersed with lies around her, cemented by his engaging smile and handsome features; she becomes transfixed. She may soon become "putty in his hands." This drama initiated by charm is due in large part to a brain condition fueled by the DANE brain, soon to be addressed, and the bonding chemical oxytocin; like an enchanting mist of cascading brain chemistry, a romantic halo effect is produced to consume her, stimulated of course, by his charming smile and engaging humor, perhaps punctuated by gentle caresses and tender kisses. The results are universally observed as "falling head over heels." Behind the scenes, and in dramatic fashion, brain scans show her brain saturated with infatuation in MLS regions plus the bonding "glue" (oxytocin) making her increasingly vulnerable to being controlled and manipulated by her *indescribably delicious charmer*. Darwin would agree with the substance of Prince Charming.

> The most vigorous individuals, or those who have most successfully struggled with their conditions of life, will generally leave most progeny. But success will often depend on having special *weapons or means of defense, or on the charms of males*; and the slightest advantage will lead to victory [in the preservation of species and in mate selection]. (*Origin of Species*, p. 261)

Ultimately, the steep downside of a moderate to severe psychopathic charmer is devastating for those who trust and try to love him: he is incapable of love; he is without conscience and free of guilt for all the damage he brings to those *who never see it coming*. Inside Jekyll, fulminating with anger and sexual shenanigans, resides the violently empowered Hyde.

From behavioral psychology, we know that by age three or four children learn subtle deceptive practices that connect to rewards (due to operant conditioning principles of reinforcement). Also, these early deceptive practices contribute directly to the development of *cognitive mapping*—the powerful thinking maps of "manipulative behavior"—that produces staggering examples of calculating minds.

When children get away with "murder," why wouldn't they continue with their own brand of deceptive practices? Effortlessly, they learn early in life which parental buttons they can push to get their way. It is indeed alarming that any criminal justice system that does not hold adolescents accountable on first offenses, enhanced by additional consequences for compounding offenses, *clearly fails our youth*.

BRAINMARKS: A PARADIGM OF ADAPTIVE NEUROPSYCHOPATHY

To me, following on the heels of psychiatrist Martin Kantor's right-on account of *Psychopathy of Everyday Life* (2006), evidence for an ultramild to mild gradation of an adaptive, beneficial, and restorative psychopathy is compelling, startling, and observable everywhere. We address this contention in Chapter 6 that evidence for spectrum psychopathy "speaks for itself"; therefore, I refer to the legal doctrine of *res ipsa* liberally throughout the book as applied evidence of its existence as an argument for the *adaptive version of psychopathy* (henceforth, "neuropsychopathy").

What sapient species have had a hard time getting through our thick skulls is the prospect that in mild gradation, psychopathy includes a neuroadaptive brain condition, and this condition is beneficial to the continuing evolution of sapient brains. This condition accounts for behavior that is *determined* and *resilient* in the face of unimaginable pain and devastation such as finally recognizing one has been duped by the lies of a psychopath. What else could rescue us repeatedly from the brink of suicidal despair? A person becomes paralyzed out of the blue and spends his life in wheelchair. How did he tolerate this condition? Parents lose all three of their young children in a devastating rear-end collision. They escape unharmed. How do they regroup and go on? This condition is especially true for children and adolescents who, due to their young ages, have no life experiences to fall back on in times of major life upheavals, humiliations, and failures.

By all means, for those who insist on adding additional layers of insulation on top of this adaptive condition are not only welcomed to do so, but encouraged to do so. This would include, but is in no way exclusive to, spirituality, the power of prayer, religious beliefs, philosophical views such as Stoicism, and positive ethics. Whatever works to enrich one's life and promote longevity is entirely relevant in the human hive of sapient brain development.

What a preponderance of behavioral scientists and researchers have agreed upon from at least the 19th century onward is that, in extreme gradation, spectrum psychopathy represents a severe, violent, and irreversible personality disorder. This fact is addressed in my spectrum paradigm as *pathological psychopathy*, and in more common clinical semantics, as *Psychopathic Personality Disorder* (PPD). Pathological psychopathy is what Hare's PCL-R (2003) has measured empirically since 1980. Herein is a point of procedure that has long been ignored: in spectrum analyses, there cannot be an extreme right-side (featuring "disordered" behaviors) without having an extreme left-side (featuring normal or "ordered" behaviors) separated by a middle continuum of robust symptoms. This will be addressed at length in Chapter 10: Order Becoming Disorder as the long-overdue paradigmatic shift in spectrum psychopathy. Of particular interest is the robust moderate zone of florid psychopathic characteristics that suggests the potential for greater or for lesser influences upon behavior as the person ages and matures.

As a natural brain condition, ultramild to mild gradations of psychopathy foster an impeccable self-interest accompanied by bulletproof entitlement. The scientific community has had proof of this condition for 30 years by way of the most universally accepted measure of psychopathy: Hare's PCL-R (2003). This instrument, used worldwide, requires a score of at least 30 of possible 40 points for a clinical diagnosis of psychopathy.

What about the traits measured in lower scores? What do these scores indicate?

Lower scores resonate as ultramild to mild conditions proof of mild gradations of psychopathy. What else could they mean?

Connecting this quantitative measurement to modern perspectives in the biological evolution of sapient brains is known collectively as evolutionary development (Evo-Devo) and is addressed in Chapter 5. The brain's powerful neurochemistry cascading in specific cortical regions of interconnected pathways produces nature's psychological armor, powerful chemical inoculations to survive amid fierce competition from rivals who seek to crush resolve. In a sense, every day would be a struggle to survive if not for nature's "gift" of adaptive neuropsychopathy. Thus, we seldom reach the point of hopelessness as hope embellishes an already resilient brain saturated in adaptive neuropsychopathy. As religious scholars contend, faith "moves mountains," so apparently does adaptive psychopathy.

Now, it appears as obvious that interdisciplinary forensic neuropsychologists can take clues from spectrum psychopathy, evolutionary psychology, and biological Evo-Devo to produce a compelling argument that the brain that lies behind behavior at all ages is indeed a conniving brain—that is, a brain that is really good at producing "survivors and thrivers" through self-absorbed narcissism, behavioral entitlement, and on-the-fly adaptability to almost any contingency. Replacing the seriously outdated brain of "storm and stress," I purpose that sapient mammals are accomplished "dreamers and schemers" who are deep into the use of deceptive practices as *adaptive dynamics* geared toward species survival.

The major focus of the four chapters of Part II, what would become my Brainmarks Paradigm of Adaptive Neuropsychopathy, hit me like a ton of bricks in the early months of 2010. The telling bios emerged as a documentary on evolutionarily mandated brain neuroanatomy. Our brains truly must be marked by chemistry and cortices powerfully geared to survival amid dangerous and contentious competition. Nationally known researchers—especially Robert Hare and Martin Kantor—came within a hair's width of saying the same thing in insightful and courageous publications—respectively, *Without Conscience* (1993) and *The Psychopathy of Everyday Life* (2006).

As scholars, we no longer need to split hairs, but rather unapologetically admit that what we see every day as outputs of sapient brains is an *adaptive* gradation of *psychopathy* as a natural brain condition. In severe gradation, it is a severe personality disorder separated by a moderate zone of robust psychopathic characteristics that present a bundle of challenges for parents and society in general. Twenty-first-century researchers indeed may shake their collective heads and ask: "How could what all of us see every day and research every day not represent a universal brain condition?" Forensic investigative scientists and attorneys in the midst of forensic cases can verify such evidence from deceptive practices and dirty tricks. The entire judicial system—as caretakers of truth and justice in all societies—exists as deception detectors determining at trial which side, plaintiff or defendant, is lying the most.

Over the next four chapters, personality traits and behavioral characteristics of what we have come to call psychopathy are laid bare for the analyses of all interested parties to pick apart, weigh, and decide. The powerful endogenous neurochemistry covered in Chapter 9 is pivotal in this regard. The powerful chemical neurotransmitters discussed in this chapter always have been in sapient brains, boosted by *hormones* of the body, that light up specific pathways of the brain. Lying behind affect (emotion) and cognition (thinking), dopamine (DA), norepinephrine (NE), phenylethylamine (PEA), testosterone, and perhaps unknown others afford sapient mammals highly effective and resilient psychological armor of survival dynamics. All of the aforementioned endogenous chemicals will be addressed in Chapter 9: The DANE Brain. Without chemical cocktails that produce determination, resilience, entitlement, and narcissism that border on arrogance, child, adolescent, and young adult sapient brains simply would wilt, sadden, or cave in from the influences of others who are more than ready to impale fellow humans upon spears of conniving and deceptive practices as well as to an assortment of dirty tricks. *Gaining advantages over others is the point.* Every individual develops his or her own version of advantages with strategic skills; by adolescence, life becomes a dramatic chess match. Look no further than the halls of Hormone High School for proof. In our view, without adequate gradations of an adaptive and beneficial version of psychopathy our hope that things will get better is weakened. By this reasoning is "hope for a better tomorrow" nothing more than a gradation of mild psychopathy? Overwhelming and unrelenting stress, sadness, and despair are equivalent to taking a pickax to dwindling self-esteem.

The trouble for me, really for all of us, is that adaptive neuropsychopathy masqueraded for centuries as only a personality disorder. There can be no question after reading Chapters 4–7 that *psychopathy is both a natural brain condition* and *a severe and irreversible personality disorder producing cold-blooded violence mixed with perverted sexuality in extreme cases.*

Indeed, a little psychopathy goes a long way.

Currently it is unknown how ultramild to mild gradations or moderate gradations might be transformed into pathological gradations as observed in Psychopathic Personality Disorder. Additionally, the middle ground of moderate psychopathic traits presents special problems for parents faced with "parenting-out" considerable strength of gradation in anticipation of the arrival of the brain's regulatory control of the prefrontal cortex (PFC). The arrival of the PFC of the frontal lobes signals the cortices that "reflective thought and judgments" have entered the cranium.

What better way for owners of brains to survive and thrive amid everyday competition, problems, and ambiguities of living than with a brain powered by powerful chemistry promoting bulletproof narcissism and permissive entitlement—that is, permission to do whatever one desires and without guilt—leading ultimately to the power of deceptive practices and perhaps crossing the line into the violent and sexually laced crimes ("dirty tricks")? Learning to leave facts and events out of explanations to hide information from competitors that might throw unfavorable light on us is engaging in deceptive practices—that is, the traditional sins of omission. Obvious examples include outright lying or misrepresentation of a rival's behavior intended to cast doubt or suspicion in their direction. By engaging non-violent deceptive practices in everyday behavior, sapient brains may feel entitled to the following:

- Attack others behind their backs, yet smile in their faces
- Appear as a model citizen on the surface, yet author cowardly "poison pen" anonymous letters seeking to bring down a rival
- Tell hurtful lies and spread vicious rumors
- Seek to make others miserable through calculating minds, by dominating and controlling behavior that on the surface may appear supportive

Might "prey" get defocused in the process of being attacked, bothered, or bullied? Might they lose concentration and become defocused; maybe they will have a serious accident. *Maybe they will die.*

Perpetrators of deceptive practices hatched by calculating minds gloat in the limelight of self-importance; they have known all along they are far smarter, perhaps "blessed," and far more brilliant than everyone around them, especially the "bottom feeders" they feel entitled to prey upon. *Anyway, the weak and the stupid had it coming.*

UNDERSTANDING BRAINMARKS

Principles of the Brainmarks Paradigm, first purposed in *Brainmarks: Headquarters for Things That Go Bump in the Night* (Jacobs, 2009a), addresses how cortices of the brain are marked by chemical connections, transitions, and modulations that operate on discrete, but connected, neurological regions. By this cortical circuitry, affect (emotion and mood) are fired up by powerful endogenous chemical pathways that trigger emotion and contribute to behavioral actions, including behavior associated with violet criminal minds, and dramatically in perpetrators who display a cold-blooded affect with a chilling lack of remorse.

In principle, chemical cascades can be viewed as marking the brain in ways that keep helpful traits that produce the chances of living another day; traits promoting survivability—a condition we have identified as *adaptive neuropsychopathy.*

This condition allows sapient brains by way of behavior to thrive and survive the many gut-wrenching disappointments, toxic parenting fiascos, relationship disasters, and general malaise, negativity, and despair encountered in living regardless of millennia time frames. As a result, a thriving and surviving brain is sure to be a conniving brain deeply entrenched in human drama characterized by dreaming and scheming, lying and conniving, and achieving by deceiving. Getting away with deceptive practices has survival benefits. Magnifying the disordered side, 180 degree across the continuum (spectrum), *pathological psychopathy* exists in a violent, sexually predatory, and irreversible brain condition known as Psychopathic Personality Disorder (PPD).

In paradigmatic sciences, a *typical, or ordered* left-side of the continuum reflects more normalized attitudes as helpful traits opposed by an *atypical or disordered* right-side. Separating the two poles creates a moderate zone of gradation. This is exactly the diagnostic configuration presented in the DSM with a continuum of "severity specifiers" indexed as mild, moderate, and severe. Again, in spectrum paradigms, there can be no disordered side without reference to a somewhat ordered side approximating normal behavior. Hence, the Brainmarks Paradigm recognizes in ultramild to mild gradations (1) a distinct left-side or ordered side, as the sapient brain best suited to thrive and survive; (2) in contrast, the right-side or disordered side, which defines pathological psychopathy as the brain of violence and ultimately cold-blooded murder; and (3) the moderate or middle zone of the spectrum, which is characterized by robust characteristics of psychopathy. These gradations pose special challenges for both the owner of the brain and those who attempt to parent-out aspects of it.

Determination and resilience appear to be bred into cortices of brains rich in neuroadaptive psychopathy. Just as a brain is marked for sex, language acquisition, and the appetitive drive, thereby marking sapient brains to be accomplished in sexuality, speaking, and finding a meal, likewise, a brain marked for survival, more than likely survives. Accumulated failures do not pack the punch they seem destined to accomplish. As Truman Capote once remarked, "Failure is the condiment that gives success its flavor."

Front and center within the Brainmarks Paradigm is the brain's powerful neurochemistry, especially fresh and robust in youth, marking sapient brains with chemistry and hormones that support survivability as helpful traits. Deceptive practices—the subject of this pivotal chapter—historically have not been addressed in sapient brains as strategies for survival. The destructive right-side of the continuum of psychopathy has been addressed since the 18th century and in modern times has been quantified by Hare's PCL-R (2003), which measured perhaps unintentionally adaptive neuropsychopathy—residing on the far left-side of spectrum psychopathy—since 1980.

THE WILD BOY

Although powerful and defining, nature and genetics have limitations. A good example of this is genetic "windows of opportunity" known to close, thus shutting out the development of helpful traits that could have been realized from learning in social milieus. No better example exists than the development of the feral child, *Victor, the Wild Boy of Aveyron*. Jean Marc Gaspard Itard, a young medical student, adopted Victor (as he came to be called) into his home to educate him in the human skills of language and empathy. However, Itard soon became disillusioned with Victor's lack of emotional and social progress, leaving a historical note that the brain is indeed highly influenced by developmental windows that when closed shut out vital learning opportunities. In Brainmarks phraseology, Victor's brain had been marked by characteristics and traits from neurochemical cascades that produced behavioral traits, patterns, and clusters. With his genetic pedigree, surrounded by no human interaction whatsoever, his *behavioral survival agendas* worked for approximately 12 years (Victor's suspected age at capture in 1791). At that time, he was discovered roaming naked and alone in the woods near Saint-Sernin-sur-Rance, France. Victor's brain had been marked by his unique environmental circumstances just as 21st-century experiences are known to modify brain wiring. Apparently, developmental windows of opportunity had closed permanently and could not be reopened, evidenced by his inability to acquire empathy, social connection, or language.

BRAINMARKS IN THE HANDS OF HIGHER EDUCATION AND PEDAGOGY

Brainmarks has proven to be an excellent teaching tool in the classroom. Demonstrating conceptual examples of "how the brain works" always has been and continues to be a challenge for professors. For example, we know how cortices and chemistry interact, suggesting that individual brains come marked not only for the sake of survival but also for the many splendored things the brain is capable of producing. Yet, we do not know exactly how these functional properties produce power and light, such as consciousness and individual perception, and we never may know.

Without the brain's amazing *capacity to adapt to practically any adverse condition*, such as genocides, plagues, natural disasters, ravages of war, atomic bombs, horrific and emotionally draining divorces, and deaths, the species would have become extinct millennia ago. The dinosaurs had their chance. Apparently, dinosaur brains were missing a vital ingredient of adaptive chemistry.

In Brainmarks, ultramild to mild gradations of psychopathy are theorized to include a congenital brain condition geared toward sustaining life regardless of practically any and all adverse conditions. This is accomplished, neuroadaptively, through powerful neurotransmitters and hormones, enhancing a chemistry of determination, resilience, entitlement, and narcissism, which ultimately produce a proneness to survive. This view represents a paradigmatic shift in understanding spectrum psychopathy. In this view, psychopathy is:

- Neuroadaptive for survival at one end of the spectrum (ultramild to mild gradation), colloquially, the "ordered" end
- Violence-oriented and predatory at the opposite end of the spectrum with an irreversible personality disorder, colloquially, the "disordered" end
- Robust and characterized by a middle zone of gradation between the two poles of order versus disorder, which is typified by traits and characteristics that mean potential trouble or toward lesser gradations making way for the development of the regulatory power of the PFC as arbitrator of adult behavior

In Brainmarks, the arrival of the PFC is theorized to mitigate moderate psychopathy within adult sapient brains. Thus, parents become hard-headed realists who tend to overthink every situation. This is not the case in adolescence, where impulsivity and narcissism gravitate toward brashness in deceptive practices.

Ironically, as it now stands, parental attempts to parent-out the very conditions that assist survivability in adolescent mild versions of psychopathy may require rethinking. Until more is known, might parents start by having frank discussion about the perils they fear in their offspring's powerful, but not yet mature, brains? While some deception in their peer tribes appears unavoidable, might parents share with their children some of their own experiences in this regard? What apparently is mandatory is the parenting-out of more moderate versions of psychopathy that produce exaggerated narcissism and self-entitlement. If this moderate zone of gradation is not modulated, behavior certainly can be expected to be problematic with potentially devastating consequences.

Regardless, we now know that a little psychopathy goes a long way.

In practicality, when parents are sufficiently engaged in their adolescents' lives, they should not be shocked to see deceptive practices. Reminding their kids to "make good choices" and "be careful" are ample testimonies to parents who secretly may fear that deceptive practices are in fact clandestinely occurring. As Judge Judith Sheindlin is fond of saying on her popular reality television show, *Judge Judy*, "you can always tell when teenagers are lying, their mouths are moving." It seems that learning to be honest—"just putting the truth out there"—is never quite mastered by the adolescent brain. But, parents, for sure, must make the effort to do so early. *This condition to be honest becomes the line drawn in the sand.* Within adolescent peer tribes, in which competition is fierce to fit in and be accepted, parents should not expect perfection but rather many shortcomings and failures. Still, the line in the sand must be evident with clear consequences in place for accountability. With no consequences for missing the mark, parents can lose their children before they realize it may be too late to save them.

VARIATIONS ON A THEME

According to Dr. Susan Wallace, associate professor (retired), Baylor University, Texas, and adjunct professor, Weatherford College Behavioral Science,

"Adaptive neuropsychopathy" explores a concept that has existed for many years in the field of anthropology that maintains the Homo sapient brain became adapted for life 100,000 years ago. An adaptive gradation of psychopathy alerts us to the fact that this 100,000-year-old brain evolved *mechanisms for adaptation and survival* for almost any contingency. If our non-human primate cousins with which we share 98 percent of our DNA can use *deception that provides others with false information* (Cheney & Seyfarth, 1990), kill members of their own species for no reason except war (Goodall, 1986), and hide physiological manifestations of anxiety from a rival (de Waal, 1982), why should *Homo sapiens* not process the same qualities in spades. Well, of course they do. What Professor Jacobs has done in his book is bring forth the astounding theoretical evidence of *psychopathy as a neuroadaptive brain mechanism.*

JOHN NASH EDITS A FAMOUS ECONOMIST

While a student at Stanford University, math genius John Nash solved a common social problem encountered by males when competing for female attention. In revising legendary economist Adam Smith, Nash proved to his friends seated at a local bar that Smith was "only half right." The father of modern economics, Adam Smith, contended that "social outcomes are best served by every man acting on his own initiatives," one of his most famous quotes (Nasar, 1998). At a local college hangout, a tall, attractive, and flirtatious blonde enters surrounded by her less attractive dark-haired friends. Nash, who is surrounded by his math peers, ponders strategies by quoting Smith and suggests an editorial revision:

Adam Smith needs revision. If we all go for the blonde, not a single one of us is going to win her as she loves the attention from all of us; being summarily rejected, we then go for her friends, but they will all give us the cold shoulder because nobody likes being second choice. . . . So, what if nobody goes for the blonde? We don't get in each other's way. *We ALL win. It's the only way we all get laid.* So Adam Smith was only half right; now, *we do what's best for ourselves AND what's best for the group.* (Nasar, 1998 [emphasis added])

This is exactly the situation with the modern understanding of spectrum psychopathy—it is only half right; it needs revision based on the relentless march of neuroscience and forensic investigative science augmented by the timely insights of Hare and Kantor, and bolstered by everyday (*res ipsa*) applied evidence. If Adam Smith can be revised, by extension, so can Pinel, Cleckley, Hare, Kantor, and others. Truly, psychopathy in severe gradation is a violent personality disorder, but also it is a normal and necessary brain condition.

In 2004, as I began to conceptualize how best to teach college students elements of clinical *forensic neuropsychology*—neurological and neurochemical conditions that make up criminal minds—a paradigmatic shift began to materialize in my mind; a paradigm that was inlaid with neuroscience, especially neuropsychology. This paradigm depicts how the brain must be marked by its own endogenous chemistry within discrete cortical regions responsible for firing up emotions and thinking as *precursors to behavior*—behavior that is normal (ordered), robust but not criminal (disordered), and violent and pathological. Also, why is the brain such an adaptive and resilient organ for survival regardless of what is thrown at it?

Then, like a bolt from the blue, might the brain come marked at birth with gradations of what we have come to call psychopathy because of modularity in the functioning of the brainstem and midbrain limbic system (MLS) agendas jazzed by powerful neurochemistry, such as dopamine (DA) and norepinephrine (NE), and later in puberty, by copious amounts of testosterone, PEA, and perhaps beta-endorphin? If this is so, the sapient brain comes marked by feelings of narcissism (bloated self-importance), emotional entitlement (self-centered right to do whatever one wants without consequence), and bulletproof resolve—behavior "shrink-wrapped" in psychological armor as a shield to sadness and despair.

BRAINMARKS OF THE HIGH-GAIN DANE BRAIN

Here is a short list of endogenous chemistry that requires no leap in logic to purpose chemical underpinnings of habits, traits, and patterns producing adaptive psychopathy. Located in the midbrain *per se* is the major source of DA, the *substantia nigra* (literally, "dark substance") region of the basal ganglia. It activates two related regions, the *nucleus accumbens* (NAcc) and ventral tegmental area (VTA), comprising dopaminergic neurons projecting into twin superhighways of powerful excitatory connectivity—the *mesolimbic dopamine pathway* (MLDAP) connecting to the *mesocortical dopamine pathway* (MCDAP)—terminating in the PFC. In this way, delivery of energizing DA is guaranteed to be brain-wide. For most, DA is robust in adolescent brains.

Likewise, the production of NE with its excitatory effects on adrenergic neurons mediating *arousal* and priming receptors to be activated and jazzed by an array of orienting stimuli (including DA) is due entirely to the tiny *locus coeruleus* (literally, "blue spot") located in the brainstem. Adrenergic receptivity (receptors with NE effects) produces orienting, focusing, motivated, and passionate behavior with contributions from dopaminergic activation ("ergic" means activating receptors "working as DA or any other chemical"). By the combined chemical cascades of DA and NE—the DANE brain—we find chemically induced narcissism and laser-focused entitlement—a chemical prescription for neuropsychopathy punctuated by liberated DA and NE (the subject of Chapter 9).

PEA released by the hypothalamus of the limbic system *per se* is chemically similar to amphetamine (speed), acting as a releasing agent for both DA and NE. Hence, it is another chemical engineer of jazzed sensibilities from the DANE brain—a speeding locomotive producing feelings of euphoria and invincibility (soon to be turbo-charged by liberated testosterone at puberty). The DANE brain usually gets what it wants.

Testosterone, known as the hormone of aggression and sexuality due to its powerful and energizing effects on the brain at puberty, is a steroid hormone secreted by testes, ovaries, and adrenal glands. This androgenic hormone lies behind aspects of mating behavior and sexuality across the spectrum from normal (ordered) to the most aberrant (disordered) varieties.

We have yet to mention oxytocin, known as the "cuddle chemical" and theorized to lie behind *mate bonding and social bonding, a critical chemical apparently missing in violent sexual predators.*

In light of this quick scan of energizing and entitling chemicals available 24 hours a day, can there be any doubt that they engineer our most powerful emotions—*hedonism, sexuality, focus, motivation, passion, euphoria, and bulletproof entitlement*—that, in the end, define what we seek to capture in our lives? In mild gradation, the forces of chemical cascades inoculate us against sadness and despair, and ultimately, we propose they exist as a strong tonic against suicide.

True, we all have been young, we all have felt bulletproof and entitled, and we all have been self-absorbed narcissists. We have been deceptive, too, and to some extent continue to be. As a species, we share a remarkable survival history of thriving and surviving by conniving; as we continue to dream and scheme. We be*lieve* we can do anything—even if it takes a lie. The prevalence of liberated chemistry that lies behind our successes in deceptive practices and dirty tricks will be discussed over the next three chapters. Bolstered by decades of empirical research from Robert Hare, PhD, Adrian Raine, PhD, and Martin Kantor, MD, and others, the Brainmarks Paradigm is simply the next step in the evolution of an adaptive neuro-psychopathy brought forward into 21st-century neuroscience.

The Brainmarks Paradigm delineates how the brain must be marked for both order and disorder and can be summarized as follows:

- As a neuroadaptive condition (neuropsychopathy), ultramild to mild psychopathy is theorized to exist as a normal brain condition.
- As pathological psychopathy (not psychopathology from the DSM diagnoses), extreme gradation of psychopathy is a well-researched condition indicating the reality of PPD and producing violent, cold-blooded sexual predators.
- Psychopathy in moderate severity appears as cluster disorders now existing within the DSM Cluster B personality disorders: Narcissistic Personality Disorder (NPD), Histrionic Personality Disorder (HPD), and Borderline Personality Disorder (BPD). In a magnanimous error,

Antisocial Personality Disorder (APD) cannot be equated to PPD, not by a long shot. We repeat, APD is not in the same orbit with PPD, the variation of which is presented in an upcoming chapter.

SEVEN PRINCIPLES OF ADAPTIVE NEUROPSYCHOPATHY

The following principles of neuroadaptive psychopathy (neuropsychopathy) form the basis of the Brainmarks Paradigm and provide rationale for the paradigmatic shift in understanding psychopathy *as a natural brain condition present at birth.*

1. The paradigm is committed, first and foremost, by a dedication to *brain functionality*—the place to look for answers as the organ of sapient behavior. The brain's cerebral architecture is vastly populated with neurons in regional interconnectivity launching chemical pathways that produce powerful chemistry such as DA, NE, PEA, and testosterone. These chemicals make up *the chemicals of neuropsychopathy*—producing feelings of superhuman, bulletproof entitlement—prophylactic to dangerous and impulsive conditions of living. Enhancing the aforementioned chemical cascades, brainstem and MLS regions of cerebral interconnectivity wire together to inoculate sapient brains against insult and abuse, such as the extreme negativity of toxic parenting and the unsavory influences of social milieus that would crush fragile self-esteem in young sapient brains.

2. The role of powerful neurotransmitter chemistry is enhanced by hormones of the body, as well as other unknown peptides and enzymes, traverse interconnected pathways in the brain, such as the mesolimbic and mesocortical chemical pathways, that connect to the more ancient regions of the brain geared to survivability—the brainstem and midbrain limbic system MLS—thereby producing nature's bulletproof psychological inoculation against losing the will to live.

3. Once the chemical and cortical conditions above are understood in light of modern neuroscience, especially neuropsychology, a critical question is asked and answered in light of this new paradigm: to what purpose is the brain so modularly, cortically, and chemically aligned?

4. The answer for the necessity of powerful cascading chemistry comes from excellent documentation: the overriding fact of our species's remarkable abilities of surviving and thriving objectified in ways that display traits and conditions—"helpful traits"—geared

to survival of the fittest. By surviving adolescence and by ongoing adult experiences, a regulatory PFC comes onboard to dampen neuropsychopathy or the more troublesome moderate versions to produce the adult version of sapient brains.

5. Next, what cluster of traits, characteristics, or conditions would best guarantee success in survival scenarios, especially in young sapient brains? There exists no better conditions or characteristics leading to species' thriving and surviving than feeling practically superhuman, due to the array of chemically induced psychopathic traits, not the least of which is self-absorbed narcissism leading to emotional entitlement (or "a truly astounding egocentricity that justifies life be lived according to one's own rules" [Hare, 1993]). How many exhausted parents of adolescents have been witness to this "astounding egocentricity and arrogance" in their own children?

6. Ironically, this condition at birth and subsequent development is a guard to life spontaneously caving in on those with less gradations of neuropsychopathy, thereby producing overwhelming feelings of despair, depression, grief, and perhaps ultimately, suicidal ideation. In this sense, *suicide is the failure of adaptive neuropsychopathy.*

7. Ultimately, neuroadaptive psychopathy is a *helpful trait encouraging survival* even in the face of impulsivity producing dangerous activities creating bad choices, which, again ironically, leads to *precocious development of the* PFC (as in, learning lessons from doing really stupid and dangerous things). Those who survive adolescence do so by learning *how to live amid danger*. In the process, connections from the MLS "wire together and fire together" into mature prefrontal regions, especially the orbitofrontal prefrontal cortex (OFPFC)—ultimately defining the dynamics of reasoned judgment so crucial to survival. In our view, adaptive neuropsychopathy makes sapient brains the most fit to survive.

FIRST-DEGREE PSYCHOPATHY

Representing evolutionary mandated behavior geared toward survival of the fittest with chemical neuropsychopathy as the glue—what we call First-Degree Psychopathy—absent other pathologies, individuals present ultramild to mild psychopathy in the prototypical brain best suited to thrive and survive, and dream and scheme. Individuals, themselves, would not recognize the source of their powerful evolutionary mandated dynamic inherent in their deceptive charms; for sure, they recognize their own glitter as it is self-evident (*res ipsa*)—they anticipate getting whatever they want by just being themselves—but in the process of the payoff, they miss the glue, that is, the reason why they are so good at getting what they want or surviving because it comes natural.

MODERATE "HUBRISTIC" PSYCHOPATHY

As researchers consistently have shown, psychopathy exists across a spectrum. The Brainmarks Paradigm hypothesizes the ordered or nonviolent ultramild to mild varieties—those that produce adaptive *neuropsychopathy*—as a natural brain condition to severe (disordered) gradations that produce violent, criminal types. My term for *moderate varieties of psychopathy*—more pronounced than adaptive neuropsychopathy—is *hubristic psychopathy*. (*Hubris* is defined as an overbearing arrogance woven into the fabric of personality—and, of course, the brain—characterized by misusing people, relationships, or power as routinely observed in politics, celebrity, business, or otherwise, to victimize prey for sexual stimulation, or easy marks for financial abuse, or philandering escapades.) The recent philandering exploits of professional golfer Tiger Woods, "living a lie" in his words, from televised comments, 2010, is a salient example of arrogance-laced hubristic psychopathy. (Also, it is interesting to note that by suppressing his well-documented moderate gradations of psychopathy, Woods is not performing up to his championship standards. If muscles do indeed have memory—exemplified by Tiger's swing and putting—perhaps conscious attempts to mitigate his well-known philanderer's psychopathy adversely has affected his game. While interesting, the jury is still out on how long this condition will mark his game.) In addition to Tiger Woods, poster boys for hubristic psychopathy have personality characteristics of Bill Clintonesque persona characterized by lies and deceit in relationships with acquaintances. Notably in Clinton's case, the publicized antics with Paula Jones, Jennifer Flowers, and Monica Lewinsky amounted to lies, lies, and more lies.

Hubristic psychopaths will not kill you, but they will disgust and shock some when all facts are disclosed. An adolescent of moderate psychopathic gradation who places feces in the school locker of a rival is a disturbing example. Hubristic psychopathy shows that not all psychopaths are violent, not by a long shot, but they are masters of deception typified by compulsive lying and deceptive practices, and earmarked by political, financial, and relational dirty tricks over and above adaptive varieties of deceptive practices. In the popular culture press, it was not without reason that Richard Nixon was referred to as "Tricky Dick" or Bill Clinton as "Slick Willie."

In spectrum psychopathy, as the gradation dial of strength moves beyond moderate or hubristic varieties, darker designs of personality emerge, such as a stepping stone to cold-blooded violence. The moderates in the middle will seldom if ever display physical violence *per se*, but they may display verbal abuse and become architects of toxic relationships built upon compulsive lying and deceit. Yet, these "moderates" seldom are incarcerated; they are too smooth and powerful to be unsuccessful. The more the moderation dial moves toward more severe gradations, the more likely violence and perhaps sexualized violence emerge.

Paul Babiak (Babiak & Hare, 2007) refers to hubristic psychopaths as "psychopaths in suits," acknowledging deceptively smooth operators in corporate America who "smile in your face, and stab you in the back" all the while lying compulsively and stealing whatever they want, as observed by "wealth manager" Bernard Madoff who swindled investors out of a reported $65 billion, never once publicly showing remorse. Serially, he "killed" his investors' financial futures. Sadly, one of his sons recently committed suicide.

Professor Robert Hare, PhD, and colleagues are perhaps the researchers most responsible for 21st-century understanding of spectrum psychopathy. In presenting psychopathic traits delineated in Hare's pioneering work (2003), we present the factors of 20 measurable items from Factor 1 traits (Interpersonal) to Factor 2 traits (Social Deviance) from his checklist. Brainmarks contends a person who scores less than 30 on Hare's PCL-R (2003) displays mild gradations of adaptive neuropsychopathy as quantitative proof that this version of psychopathy exists.

Traits of Psychopathy Measured in Hare's Psychology Checklist

Factor 1 Traits: Interpersonal/Affective Expression

1. Glibness/superficial charm
2. Grandiose sense of self-worth expressed as pompous arrogance
3. Pathological (compulsive) lying
4. Cunning and manipulative
5. Lack of remorse or guilt
6. Shallow affect (lack of emotional depth)
7. Callousness and lack of empathy
8. Failure to accept self-responsibility

Additional Factors

9. Promiscuous sexual behavior
10. Criminal versatility

Factor 2 Traits: Social Deviance

11. Need for stimulation and proneness to boredom
12. Parasitic lifestyle (living off others)
13. Poor behavioral controls (unpredictability; never learning from mistakes)
14. Early behavioral problems
15. Lack of realistic, long-term goals
16. Impulsivity
17. Irresponsibility
18. Juvenile delinquency
19. Early exposure to criminal justice system
20. Many short-term marital relationships

A WAKE-UP CALL TO NAÏVETÉ

A brain supercharged with the chemistry of *ultramild to mild gradations of psychopathy* would be a brain lightly seasoned by self-entitlements and narcissism. In more moderate gradations, however, the person would have *robust* traits and characteristics of an engaging and charming person on the surface, yet in reality be a slippery (glib), unreliable, and fundamentally *parasitic* person—one soon to drain away time normally spent with friends and family. Financial resources soon will be drained as well. He is out to shatter your life almost beyond repair. Why? Because he can—he feels justified by doing all he can *as the special person he perceives himself to be*; yet, in reality, he is a person who never should have been trusted in the first place. Adolescents learn often painfully that most parents are equipped with a highly functioning PFC that allows them to have spotted his type early on from their own experiences with psychopaths, but did they listen? Will they learn?

PSYCHOPATHY: ABLE TO DISARM THE ALARM

On the surface, however, the mild to moderate psychopathic person seems entirely trustworthy and maybe "hilariously funny" as he performs like an accomplished comedian to win us over—signaling the beginning of *deception*—the cardinal trademark of psychopathy. (This charade is so highly successful that it almost never "sets off" our internal warning detector—the *amygdala*—that exists to alert us to creepy people, or from detecting someone capable of hurting us; clearly a person to get away from.) As spectrum psychopaths—meaning all gradations of psychopathic personalities—are *natural charmers*, they are astute at silencing the amygdala; they have no idea most likely what the amygdala is. That amounts to strike one against "psychopathy detection."

If a relationship ensues (if he targets you, it means he lavishes you with his considerable skills intent on creating a one-sided relationship sure to follow), it is going to be a stormy one—an affair filled with *fights and make-ups* as he displays a growing narcissism and, in full bloom, a *grandiose sense of self-worth*. (Often, in the young and naïve, this display of extraverted personality is often misread as confidence, when it is really arrogance.) That amounts to strike two.

Soon, "prey" are caught up in and overwhelmed in a bundle of lies, a particular predilection of psychopathy, due to feeling entitled—feeling justified in conning and manipulating—because he is so special and those he targets are not, they are "bottom feeders." (If his targets put up with his shenanigans, it only *proves his accuracy in assessment* so he continues to pile on more deception and abuse.)

As he proceeds to weave more elaborate webs of deception, he displays a callous disregard for the feelings of prey by displaying a *shallow affect* (displaying, in reality, a lack of emotional depth, another trait that is misread).

He is incapable of love, incapable of commitment, and incapable of being a reliable and loving parent.

Lack of remorse or guilt for doing whatever he feels like doing is always justified in his mind, including many ongoing sexual liaisons. (Sexual variety satisfies his insatiable desire for stimulation to mitigate boredom; sexually, he often demands more sadistic acts, including *ménage a trois*, bondage, and anal sex.) Fault lies in other people who are beneath him; they deserve exactly what he gives them and his proof: they keep taking it. That's strike three and the one preyed upon may never find his or her way home. The victim is completely under the spell of the psychopath and will be emotionally, if not physically, damaged for life.

MORAL DEPRAVITY

English physician J. C. Prichard (1835) viewed psychopathy as "a form of mental derangement in which intellectual faculties were unaffected, but moral principles of mind were depraved or perverted." Furthermore, he viewed psychopathy as a personality disorder "consisting of a morbid perversion of natural feelings, affections, inclinations, temper, moral dispositions, and natural impulses without any remarkable disorder or defect of interest or knowing and reasoning faculties, and particularly without any insane illusions or hallucinations." Obviously, Prichard embraced the negative symptoms of extreme psychopathy.

Therefore, the violent sexual psychopath is impaired morally, affectively (emotionally), and sexually, but not intellectually. (The connotation of the

word "moral" in the 19th century denoted more of a psychological implication rather than an ethical one.)

FEMALE PARTNERS OF SPECTRUM NONVIOLENT PSYCHOPATHS

Consensual sex partners to spectrum psychopaths (moderate varieties)
may or may not leave, even when sexual abuse or general spousal abuse
become chronic, verified, and well-publicized. On occasion, psychopaths
can show restraint but not for long. Even serial killer Ted Bundy's girlfriend
raised her young daughter in the apartment she shared with Bundy. While
the girlfriend often was subjected to "kinky sex," Bundy never harmed
her daughter as far as anyone knows.

Might actress Sandra Bullock wish she had not been so naïve in believing
her tattooed psychopathic lover? Similarly, it took eight years for Mary Jo
Buttafuoco to leave her husband, Joey, after his underage sexual paramour,
Amy Fisher, shot her in the face on the stoop of the Buttafuoco home.
In her book, *Getting It Through My Thick Skull* (2009) she tells all—why
she stayed, what she learned, and what millions of people involved with
sociopaths (her term) need to know.

On her Web site, Mary Jo describes the experiences of her husband,
Joey Buttafuoco, an obvious (res ipsa) moderate psychopath, whose affair
with Amy Fisher, "The Long Island Lolita," eventually led to Amy's
attempted murder of Mary Jo:

> My ex-husband, Joey, denied the affair, admitted the affair, went to jail,
> got out of jail, got caught soliciting a prostitute, went back to jail, got
> out of jail, got divorced (from me), plead guilty to insurance fraud in
> California, went back to jail, got out of jail, got remarried (I won't
> even go there!), violated probation and went back to jail, got out and
> made a porno tape, so far. (From her website)

Within the cocoon of psychological abuse often leading to violence
mixed with perverted sexuality, coercive males report a focus on casual
sexual relationships with women. They report a strong sex drive without
regard for partner intimacy that often is "short and stormy"; they display
authoritativeness, show less empathy and more hostile masculinity,
prefer sexual variety and uncommitted sex; they view dating as sexual opportunities. All the while, they deceive female prey as committed
lovers.

Women who stay with spectrum psychopaths are suspected of displaying
characteristics of Dependent Personality Disorder much like *codependent*

spouses—females who stay with abusive alcoholic husbands and women who profess love for serial murderers often marrying incarcerated sexual predators (such as Ted Bundy and Richard Ramirez) who remain behind bars for life. The women must know deep down they never will be allowed to touch their romanticized husbands.

With a brain "factory sealed" by nature for survival, gender-wise, could it be that females are capable of doing *anything* for love, while males are capable of doing *anything* for sex? Might this strategy move the species forever forward, capturing and duplicating the next generation of brains? Regarding the creation of a new brain, does it really matter whether it is for love or for sex? Regardless, the sapient-brained species wins.

Now, we move forward to an analogy of gradations of psychopathy in personality as shards of glass.

SHARDS OF GLASS

In light of the Brainmarks view of order versus disorder across the dial of spectrum psychopathy, the following model is a proposed revision of Cluster B personality disorders *based on psychopathy, not psychopathology, as differentially diagnosed in the DSM*. Imagine characteristics of spectrum psychopathy—across gradations from order as neuroadaptive (ultramild to mild gradations) to disorder of severity in personality disorders— configured into a pane of glass. If dropped, this psychopathy pane of glass would shatter into hundreds of pieces. Now imagine one shard of glass represents *narcissism* mildly expressed in an otherwise normal brain, a larger shard representing moderate narcissism, and the largest and most jagged shard representing severe narcissism typified by grandiosity of self-love (self-absorbed arrogance) observed in Narcissistic Personality Disorder (NPD). The normal (mild) shard, the larger (moderate) shard, and the largest and most jagged (severe) shard came from the same pane of glass representing psychopathy. From Salekin, Rogers, Ustad, and Sewell (1998), NPD is defined and characterized by a pervasive pattern of grandiosity, need for admiration, and lack of empathy and appears to have a stronger relationship to male psychopaths than female psychopaths. NPD is due to psychopathy, not psychopathology; the reason being *narcissism is not a source of subjective distress* as required by DSM personality disorder diagnostic criteria. Far from it, narcissists feel empowered with turbocharged entitlement. Did Edward Hyde feel distress?

The same scenario presents itself in *histrionicism* observed in female gender-specific behavior—one shard being mild psychopathy expressed as female histrionic behavior, widely observed in the stereotypical attractive and seductive female; the moderate shard marked with robust histrionicism;

and still another larger jagged shard indicative of full-blown Histrionic Personality Disorder (HPD). According to Salekin, HPD is characterized by traits reflecting pervasive attention-seeking behaviors that include inappropriate sexual seductiveness and exaggerated or shallow emotions—and appears to have the strongest relationship to psychopathy in female samples. It should be obvious that narcissism and histrionicism across all gradations—mild, moderate, and severe—are beneficial in popular culture. Add beneficial psychopathic traits to camera-friendly faces and a "hot body" and money starts to accumulate. *Res ipsa* evidence is not hard to find in *celebrity pop culture.* Across sports, movies, business, and politics—really across all occupations—millionaires and pop culture icons have cashed in on their mild to moderate traits of beneficial psychopathy.

Borderline: Low Gradations of Psychopathy?

The most interesting psychopathic shards—small, medium, and the largest and most jagged—belong to borderline and antisocial characteristics of personality. In the DSM's diagnostic features,

> the essential features of Borderline Personality Disorder (BPD) are:
>
> - pervasive patterns of instability of interpersonal relationships,
> - instability of self-image, and affects,
> - marked impulsivity (spending money, sex, substance abuse, reckless driving, and binge eating), and
> - chronic feelings of emptiness. (APA, 2000)

Also,

> [I]ndividuals make frantic efforts to avoid real or imagined abandonment (as) they are sensitive to impending separation, or rejection, and environmental circumstances. They believe abandonment means they are "bad." Their frantic efforts to avoid abandonment may include impulsive actions such as self-mutilation or suicidal behaviors. . . .
>
> [T]hey display inappropriate, intense anger or difficulty controlling anger (e.g., frequent displays of temper, constant anger, and recurrent physical fights).

Recalling the subject of this heading: *psychopathy as glass shards analogy,* what would it mean for a person to be diagnosed as mildly borderline? Might it be an impulsive, low-esteemed, quick-to-temper individual who is sensitive to being rejected or abandoned by peers resulting in a desperation to hold on to others for "security"? They may stalk others

FBI TEN MOST WANTED FUGITIVE

Racketeering Influenced and Corrupt Organizations (RICO) - Murder (19 Counts),
Conspiracy to Commit Murder, Conspiracy to Commit Extortion, Narcotics
Distribution, Conspiracy to Commit Money Laundering; Extortion; Money Laundering

JAMES J. BULGER

| Photograph taken in 1994 | Photograph Age Enhanced in 2008 | Photograph Age Enhanced in 2008 |

Aliases:

Thomas F. Baxter, Mark Shapeton, Jimmy Bulger, James Joseph Bulger, James J. Bulger, Jr., James Joseph Bulger, Jr., Tom Harris, Tom Marshall, Ernest E. Beaudreau, Harold W. Evers, Robert William Hanson, "Whitey"

DESCRIPTION

Date(s) of Birth Used:	September 3, 1929	**Hair:**	White/Silver
Place of Birth:	Boston, Massachusetts	**Eyes:**	Blue
Height:	5'7" to 5'9"	**Complexion:**	Light
Weight:	150 to 160 pounds	**Sex:**	Male
Build:	Medium	**Race:**	White
Occupation:	Unknown	**Nationality:**	American

Scars and Marks: None known

Remarks: Bulger is an avid reader with an interest in history. He is known to frequent libraries and historic sites. Bulger may be taking heart medication. He maintains his physical fitness by walking on beaches and in parks with his female companion, Catherine Elizabeth Greig . Bulger and Greig love animals. Bulger has been known to alter his appearance through the use of disguises. He has traveled extensively throughout the United States, Europe, Canada, and Mexico.

CAUTION

James J. Bulger is being sought for his role in numerous murders committed from the early 1970s through the mid-1980s in connection with his leadership of an organized crime group that allegedly controlled extortion, drug deals, and other illegal activities in the Boston, Massachusetts, area. He has a violent temper and is known to carry a knife at all times.

REWARD

The FBI is offering a $2,000,000 reward for information leading directly to the arrest of James J. Bulger.

CONSIDERED ARMED AND EXTREMELY DANGEROUS

ADDITIONAL INFORMATION

• Contact an investigator

If you have any information concerning this person, please contact your local FBI office or the nearest American Embassy or Consulate.

August 1999 Poster Revised September 2008

(FBI wanted poster for James J. "Whitey" Bulger. From http://www. fbi.gov/ wanted)

in semi-desperation but are not, on the whole, typically violent; they are, however, sensitive and frustrated, and feel retched when ignored or rejected. Might low gradation psychopathy be an indicator of borderline characteristics of low-gain neuropsychopathy?

Act of Terrorism - Domestic Terrorism; Unlawful Flight to Avoid Confinement - Murder

JOANNE DEBORAH CHESIMARD

Aliases:
Assata Shakur, Joanne Byron, Barbara Odoms, Joanne Chesterman, Joan Davis, Justine Henderson, Mary Davis, Pat Chesimard, Jo-Ann Chesimard, Joanne Debra Chesimard, Joanne D. Byron, Joanne D. Chesimard, Joanne Davis, Chesimard Joanne, Ches Chesimard, Sister-Love Chesimard, Joann Debra Byron Chesimard, Joanne Deborah Byron Chesimard, Joan Chesimard, Josephine Henderson, Carolyn Johnson, Carol Brown, "Ches"

DESCRIPTION

Date(s) of Birth Used:	July 16, 1947;	**Hair:**	Black/Gray
	August 19, 1952	**Eyes:**	Brown
Place of Birth:	New York City, New York	**Sex:**	Female
Height:	5'7"	**Race:**	Black
Weight:	135 to 150 pounds	**Nationality:**	American
NCIC:	W220305367		
Occupation:	Unknown		
Scars and Marks:	Chesimard has scars on her chest, abdomen, left shoulder, and left knee.		
Remarks:	Chesimard may be living in Cuba. She may wear her hair in a variety of styles and dress in African tribal clothing.		

CAUTION

Joanne Chesimard is wanted for escaping from prison in Clinton, New Jersey, while serving a life sentence for murder. On May 2, 1973, Chesimard, who was part of a revolutionary activist organization known as the Black Liberation Army, and two accomplices were stopped for a motor vehicle violation on the New Jersey Turnpike by two troopers with the New Jersey State Police. At the time, Chesimard was wanted for her involvement in several felonies, including bank robbery. Chesimard and her accomplices opened fire on the troopers, seemingly without provocation. One trooper was wounded and the other was shot and killed execution-style at point-blank range. Chesimard fled the scene, but was subsequently apprehended. One of her accomplices was killed in the shoot-out and the other was also apprehended and remains in jail. In 1977, Chesimard was found guilty of first degree murder, assault and battery of a police officer, assault with a dangerous weapon, assault with intent to kill, illegal possession of a weapon, and armed robbery. She was sentenced to life in prison. On November 2, 1979, Chesimard escaped from prison and lived underground before being located in Cuba in 1984. She is thought to currently still be living in Cuba.

REWARD

The FBI is offering a reward of up to $1,000,000 for information directly leading to the apprehension of Joanne Chesimard.

SHOULD BE CONSIDERED ARMED AND EXTREMELY DANGEROUS

If you have any information concerning this person, please contact your local FBI office or the nearest American Embassy or Consulate.

FBI wanted poster for Joanne Deborah Chesimard. (From http://www.fbi.gov/ wanted)

Typified by low adaptive neuropsychopathy, might moderate BPD varieties be populated by stalkers and real troublemakers eager to get back at others for being slighted at life's banquet table? Additionally, might the severe and jagged shards be populated by the jagged lives of

FBI TEN MOST WANTED FUGITIVE

Unlawful Flight to Avoid Prosecution - First Degree Murder (3 Counts), Arson of an Occupied Structure

ROBERT WILLIAM FISHER

Photograph taken in 1999	Photograph taken in 1997

Alias:
Robert W. Fisher

DESCRIPTION

Date(s) of Birth Used:	April 13, 1961	**Hair:**	Brown
Place of Birth:	Brooklyn, New York	**Eyes:**	Blue
Height:	6'0"	**Complexion:**	Light
Weight:	190 pounds	**Sex:**	Male
Build:	Medium	**Race:**	White
Occupations:	Surgical Catheter Technician,	**Nationality:**	American
	Respiratory Therapist,		
	Fireman		

Scars and Marks: Fisher has surgical scars on his lower back.
Remarks: Fisher is physically fit and is an avid outdoorsman, hunter, and fisherman. He has
a noticeable gold crown on his upper left first bicuspid tooth. He may walk with an
exaggerated erect posture and his chest pushed out due to a lower back injury. Fisher is
known to chew tobacco heavily. He has ties to New Mexico and Florida. Fisher is believed
to be in possession of several weapons, including a high-powered rifle.

CAUTION

Robert William Fisher is wanted for allegedly killing his wife and two young children and then blowing up the house in
which they all lived in Scottsdale, Arizona in April of 2001.

REWARD

The FBI is offering a reward of up to $100,000 for information leading directly to the arrest of Robert William Fisher.

CONSIDERED ARMED AND EXTREMELY DANGEROUS

If you have any information concerning this person, please contact your local FBI office or the nearest American Embassy
or Consulate.
June 2002 Poster Revised January 2005

**FBI wanted poster for Robert William Fisher. (From http://www.fbi.gov/
wanted)**

killers, serial killers, and serial rapists who are full of rage for feeling so
inadequate?

Returning to DSM diagnostic criteria, "borderlines may switch quickly
from idealizing other people to devaluating them, feeling that the other
person does not care enough, does not give enough, is not there enough."
According to Salekin (1997), BPD is characterized by traits reflecting

Unlawful Flight to Avoid Prosecution - Murder

CINTHYA JANETH RODRIGUEZ

Photograph taken in 2008   Photograph taken in 2008

Aliases:
Cinthya Janeth Castellanos Rodriguez, Cinthya Janeth Castellano, Cinthya Castetellanos, Castellan Cintya Rodriguez, Cintya Rodriguez Castellanos, Cinthya Rodriguez, Cinthya Janeth Rodriquez

DESCRIPTION

Date(s) of Birth Used:	August 20, 1982	**Hair:**	Black
Place of Birth:	Mexico	**Eyes:**	Brown
Height:	5'4" to 5'8"	**Sex:**	Female
Weight:	160 pounds	**Race:**	White (Hispanic)
NCIC:	W314280817	**Nationality:**	Mexican
Occupation:	Unknown		

Scars and Marks: None known.
Remarks: Rodriguez was living in the U.S. illegally, and may have fled to Mexico.

CAUTION

Cinthya Janeth Rodriguez and her brother-in-law, Arturo Montes De Oca , are wanted for the alleged kidnapping and murder of Rodriguez's boyfriend. On March 14, 2008, the victim left work and returned to the apartment he shared with Rodriguez in Corona, California. The victim's vehicle was discovered the following morning with blood stains in the rear passenger seat and blood splatter around the interior and exterior of the vehicle, and the victim's brother received ransom calls from the alleged kidnappers. On March 19, 2008, a grave site was located approximately 15 yards from De Oca's apartment in Moreno Valley, California, and the victim's body was discovered.

A state arrest warrant was issued in Riverside County, California, on April 23, 2008, after Rodriguez was charged with murder. She was charged federally with unlawful flight to avoid prosecution and an arrest warrant was issued by the United States District Court, Central District of California, on April 28, 2008.

SHOULD BE CONSIDERED ARMED AND DANGEROUS

If you have any information concerning this person, please contact your local FBI office or the nearest American Embassy or Consulate.

FBI wanted poster for Cinthya Janeth Rodriguez. (From http://www.fbi.gov/wanted)

"black-and-white" thinking and instability in relationships, self-image, and behavior and appears to have a modest relationship with psychopathy, regardless of gender.

Given the overlap of psychopathic personality traits with each other, there appears to be a momentum to *categorize subtypes of psychopathy into four types* that can be verified empirically: namely, psychopathy that may be characterized as narcissistic, antisocial, borderline, and histrionic as personality disorders.

Antisocial

In the DSM's diagnostic features,

> the essential feature of Antisocial Personality Disorder (APD) is a pervasive pattern of disregard for, and violation of, the rights of others that begins in childhood, or early adolescence and continues into adulthood. This pattern has been referred to as *psychopathy* [according to Brainmarks's and countless other perspectives, this is entirely *incorrect*], or sociopathy [which is *correct*], and dyssocial [which is also *correct*]. (APA, 2000)

Deceit and manipulation are central themes in APD.

> For the diagnosis to be given, the individual must be 18 years of age and must have had a history of some symptoms of Conduct Disorder before age 15 years. . . . the pattern of antisocial behavior continues into adulthood where they fail to conform to social norms with respect to lawful behavior; they may repeatedly perform acts that are grounds for arrest such as destroying property, harassing others, stealing, or pursuing illegal occupations. They may repeatedly lie, use an alias, con others, or *malinger* (an intentional con related to exaggerated physical or psychological symptoms motivated by external incentives to avoid military service, work, obtaining financial compensation, evading criminal prosecution, or obtaining drugs).

Recalling the *mild psychopathy* shard, what would it mean for a person to be diagnosed mildly APD? What about an impulsive, quick-to-temper individual, blind to the rights of others, who makes one bad decision after another with little regard for consequences to self or others and *ends up in the juvenile justice system*? If APD does feature psychopathy, he feels empowered by his petty criminality. Also, might parental modeling of antisocial behavior lead to the development of a petty criminal from a young age? Youthful offenders seldom may be violent, but as they grow into adolescents with bigger bodies and matching tempers fueled by testosterone, violence may erupt. To have APD, the person must feel subjective distress; *clearly the psychopath does not*.

Might a moderate antisocial shard be populated by prepubescent kids with juvenile delinquency records and other real troublemakers on the verge of becoming violent, with severe antisocial shards being populated by what appropriately may be called "sociopaths, dyssocials, and antisocials"—unsuccessful criminals with histories of ignoring social and ethical mores, yet *highly influenced* by antisocial parenting? It appears that severe antisocials (of the DSM-inspired personality disorders) fill most of the bunks in our prison population. *And, although they may on the surface share some psychopathic cluster traits, they are seldom psychotic or truly psychopathic.* Therefore, most antisocials in prison are antisocial criminals, not pathological psychopaths. Psychopaths seldom are caught. They are too slippery for that; they eventually may make mistakes and get caught in their grandiose schemes like financial pathological psychopaths Bernard Madoff, Allan Stanford, and Shalom Weiss.

I conclude this section with the following observations: DSM Cluster B personality disorders now may *shift away from pure psychopathologies to pathological psychopathies in delineating criminal minds that commit sexually motivated violence.* The shards of glass metaphor—in which psychopathic personality "shatters" into borderline, histrionic, and narcissistic characteristics—has held up astonishingly well under peer review. In the Brainmarks Paradigm, *they are all analogs of psychopathy with the usual suspects (characteristics) of deceptive practices, and in violent gradation, extreme dirty tricks typified by intermingled sexual perversity and violence.*

The brain is a near perfect organ for survival protocols thanks to fertile cortices of resilience in the face of conflict and competition by displaying characteristics of narcissism, entitlement, and astounding adaptabilities— the *tripartite of neuroadaptive psychopathic brainmarks.* We will likely survive into old age if we can survive puberty and adolescence during which time the owners of adolescent brains must adapt and adjust to the pressure cooker of modern middle schools, high schools, and a society run by conniving adults who are deep into deceptive practices themselves engineered by their PFC ripe with cognitive strategies of manipulation to gain advantage.

Often, adolescence is a developmental stage characterized, from the parental perspective, by making *one bad decision after another,* while from the adolescent perspective, "it's just what happened." When pressed by parents for a straight answer of accountability, the best that can be given is often a tearful "I don't know!"

In sum, regarding academic, intellectual, and forensics explanations, Brainmarks's paradigmatic shift away from conventional DSM criteria shows interrelated ways of explaining emotion, mood, thinking, and behavior relative to normalcy, abnormalcy, criminality, and psychopathy, and to the extreme gradations of violent sexual psychopathy as a violent and irreversible personality disorder. By what amounts to a brain marked by neuroadaptive (ultramild) psychopathy, the brain is ultimately a neuroadaptive organ of chemistry and cortices geared toward *adaptability and survivability, marked by dreaming and scheming, thriving and conniving.* Is it a coincidence that this apparently congenital condition fits descriptive criteria for spectrum psychopathy? We make a compelling argument over the next three chapters that brains are *outfitted by nature for adaptability and ultimately survivability* via Evo-Devo dynamics. Also, rather than neuro-psychopathy, other terms will no doubt emerge for characteristics that fit perfectly this psychological condition long recognized, described, and researched only as a disorder.

CORTICAL BRAINMARK REGIONS

Within the brain, the MLS and the PFC (shown at the top of the following page) are two cortical regions characterized by influential chemistry often engaged in hotly contested battles regarding rewarding pursuits versus the restraint or second thoughts mitigating those pursuits. The midbrain *per se*, a small narrow region located directly below the limbic system, functions similarly to a pilot light for physical movement (in the red nucleus) and for production of the neurotransmitter dopamine (DA). The main function of these two regions—midbrain and limbic systems, or MLS collectively—is the production of DA to ignite nearby and scattered dopaminergic receptors throughout the brain and illumination of pathways of pleasure and reward within the limbic system *per se* and extending to other regions, including the frontal lobes. Their ability to work in concert is our rationale for combining the two regions into one: the MLS.

Dopaminergic neurons (neurons whose principal activator is DA) are plentiful in the MLS, extending into PFC regions as part of two converging superhighways of chemical DA brainmarks (1) the mesolimbic pathway of the MLS *per se* connecting to (2) *the mesocortical* of the PFC *per se*; both regions connect to the reward and pleasure pathways and regions of *sexuality, eroticism, fantasy, and possibly sexual perversion.*

Knowledge of powerful chemical pathways and discrete cortical regions of the brain along a spectrum (or continuum) from mild to severe gradations demonstrates three practical protocols in educating our next generation of forensic psychologists:

- The highly rewarding *role of deception in the brain* as an evolutionary strategy of survival (keeping secrets, cover-ups, manipulating outcomes, or lying to get anticipated rewards or avoiding detection) has been shown to have substantial survival potential
- The pivotal *role of the gradations of neurochemistry upon discrete cortical regions, and*
- The vital role of "parenting out" moderate gradations of psychopathy in individuals becoming parents themselves.

It seems the more prefrontal a person becomes, adaptive psychopathy is balanced with empathy; hence, we suggest that empathy is largely a prefrontal manifestation of survival, while narcissism and entitlement are largely MLS manifestations until PFC regions become fully mature.

NEUROPLASTICITY: WIRING AND REWIRING

Given the brain's natural ability to rewire itself—*adaptive neuroplasticity*—thereby laying down new connections, such as parent-taught values, respect for another's feelings (empathy), and taking responsibility for one's actions (accountability), natural tendencies toward narcissism, entitlement, and deception *can either be exacerbated or mitigated* depending on the connectivity (maturity) of the PFC, which is the last tollbooth for adult accountability. This is what I refer to as the 5.08 centimeters that defines the so-called Generation Gap, or the approximate distance between MLS dominance and PFC dominance in sapient brains.

Au Natural Con

At its core, the traditional *hypothetical construct of psychopathy* refers to a theory of personality deception driven by bulletproof entitlement and self-absorbed narcissism, and punctuated by an abundant adaptability. These psychopaths masquerade as loving and caring individuals on the surface, yet unbeknownst to others fooled by the ruse, display a controlling *personality dynamic of deception*. They are intent on manipulating their prey in a variety of contexts and in a variety of ways (often sexual) and in severe gradations showings zero empathy and zero conscience. *Sounds rather like Jekyll becoming Hyde.*

Robert Hare maintains that psychopaths are *intraspecies predators* who charm, manipulate, intimate, and use violence in extreme gradation to control others and to satisfy their own selfish needs. Lacking conscience and empathy, they take what they want and leave what they please as they arrogantly violate social norms without the slightest grain of regret (Hare, 1993). *Psychopaths invent reality to conform to their needs.*

In the 21st century, the infusion of psychopathy into personality is considered a brain condition and, in most clinical and experimental quarters, a verifiable personality disorder. As such, it characterizes individuals who experience *no remorse or guilt* from conventional theories of conscience, yet know exactly what they're doing and feel magnanimously justified for accomplishing it in a well documented condition of *grandiose entitlement.*

The construct of psychopathy has been recognized historically with a long history of clinical, forensic, and research protocol over the past 20 years (Millon, Simonsen, Birket-Smith, & Davis, 1998). Characteristics of psychopathy have long been theorized to occur *across a continuum* (or our preferred term, gradations from mild to severe across a spectrum); hence, our reference throughout these pages to *spectrum psychopathy*. Until researchers have more to go on (and they are studying the syndrome daily), severe gradations of spectrum psychopathic personality are hypothesized to be manifested from a variety of related influences *with biology being the strongest*. The Brainmarks Paradigm presents descriptive criteria, carefully researched data, and self-evident anecdotes, supporting spectrum psychopathy as a tool for interdisciplinary practitioners to study personality, habits, and patterns of survival in normal brains (mild neuroadaptive versions) versus brains marked by severe psychopathy evident at horrific crime scenes.

A LITTLE PSYCHOPATHY GOES A LONG WAY

A little psychopathy goes a long way, while high-gain gradations prove to be toxic, producing violent antisocial behavior. It is impossible to dispute that some gradations of entitlement, narcissism, and deception are required to survive in a world of "head to head competition among rivals for food, love, people, and jobs."

Might drug and alcohol addiction in young adolescents be an obvious condition that makes successful parenting practically impossible? In addiction, psychopathy is known to deepen in effects, and in the process, deception multiples. Addicts become more tragically deceptive and may resort unexpectedly to violence.

SAPIENT BRAINS APPEAR EQUIPPED TO SURVIVE

From at least the 18th century and certainly into the 20th century, behavioral science has appeared at times to be on the threshold of admitting publicly that psychopathic characteristics of ultramild varieties might be exactly what the brain required to survive and that psychopathy, therefore, was a natural brain condition. Neuroscientists with an evolutionary perspective agree that the brain comes equipped to survive. What better strategy for thriving and surviving than to have a brain characterized by self-interest and feeling bulletproof in which case lies and deception have proven over and again to be beneficial in survival?

APRÈS MOI, LE DELUGE AND SCHADENFREUDE

In gradation, moderate psychopathy appears to best be described as an either-or condition. *Either* it poses real threats to congeniality and cooperation of individuals living in normal communities, *or* it really benefits individuals to find successes when paired with other traits such as good looks and talents. For example, moderate psychopaths—as parents or adults—may author cowardly poison-pen anonymous letters that extol Christian virtues, while trying to shame others for human mistakes or immaturity. They present themselves as concerned citizens and often hold responsible positions as teachers, administrators, and community leaders; they may coach community kids in youth sports or work at major universities. Yet, beneath finely crafted personas, they cowardly plot and scheme with venomous pride anonymously attempting control and manipulation of others. There is survival value and tremendous satisfaction in bringing down competitors while covering up their own identities.

Moderate psychopaths do not make silly human mistakes as they are far too cunning for that. Extremely refined psychopathic personalities such as O. J. Simpson or Scott Peterson, for example, often display something equivalent to *animal magnetism*—the trite euphemism for *charisma*. They know exactly what they are doing, driven by grandiose entitlement; they feel justified for doing it. By our individual histories, we all have a pretty good idea what we can get away with.

Operant Conditioning: An S+ Reward for Psychopathy

If natural psychopathy is not enough, when deception and lying lead to positive consequences (for example, an adolescent gets what he or she wants against the wishes of parents), deceptive practices become reinforced by experience (known as a reinforcing S+ in behavioral psychology) and rapidly become part of one's behavioral *modus operandi* (MO). When children get away with "murder" why would they stop? Getting away with lies through cover-up positively reinforces deceptive practices. No wonder lying and other forms of deception are so hard to reverse. If they worked once, they will work again and again. In extreme varieties of spectrum psychopathy, and with the good looks of a model, handsome spree killer Andrew Cunanan (killer of designer Gianni Versace and others) appeared to be gay as a ruse to manipulate wealthy benefactors to his financial benefit. (Many investigators believed Cunanan only appeared to be gay as it benefited him in obtaining money from older male benefactors). Cunanan wrote a prescient one-line inscription in his yearbook building up an image of *panache: Après moi, le deluge* ("After me, the storm!"). Those who knew him from high school embraced the persona of a charming kid, not a deceptive monster. In spectrum psychopathy, beneath the glib, superficial charmer is a deeper psychological dynamic characterized by deceptive practices; *deception does in fact pay.* Beneath Cunanan's polished veneer, however, a lack of emotional attachment resided, such as the following:

- Insincerity
- Compulsive lying
- Lack of empathy for others
- Jubilation in *schadenfreude*—happiness at another's expense (troubles they may have initiated by an anonymous poison pen letter, for example)
- Righteous indignation

As shown over millennia, crime and deception often pay, and pay very well as observed almost daily in financial white-collar crimes. In such crimes, violence is seldom part of the pretzel, but deception and deceit act as clubs and knives.

Is it possible that success from lying, deception, and entitlement are emotionally comparable to aphrodisiacs and are just as addicting? Wait and see what the DANE brain contributes to this answer in Chapter 9.

REFERENCES

APA (American Psychological Association). (2000). *Diagnostic and statistical manual of mental disorders* (DSM-IV-TR). Washington, DC: American Psychological Association.

Babiak, Paul, & Hare, Robert. (2007). *Psychopaths in suits: When psychopaths go to work* (2007). New York: HarperCollins.

Blair, James, Mitchell, Derek, & Blair, Karina. (2005). *The psychopath: Emotion and the brain.* New York: Wiley-Blackwell.

Buttafuoco, Mary Jo. (2009). *Getting it through my thick skull.* Deerfield Beach, FL: Health Communications.

Craig, Robert J. (2005). *Personality-guided forensic psychology.* Washington, DC: American Psychological Association.

Hare, Robert D. (1993). *Without conscience.* New York: Guilford Press.

Hare, Robert D. (2003). *Psychopathy checklist–revised technical manual* (2nd ed.). Toronto: Multihealth Systems.

Jacobs, Don. (2007). *Mind candy: Who's minding the adolescent brain?* Plymouth, MI: Hayden-McNeil.

Jacobs, Don. (2009a). *Brainmarks: Headquarters for things that go bump in the night.* Dubuque, IA: Kendall Hunt.

Jacobs, Don. (2009b). *Psychology of deception: Analysis of sexually psychopathic serial crime.* Dubuque, IA: Kendall Hunt.

Jacobs, Gregg D. (2003). *The ancestral mind.* New York: Viking Press.

Kalechstein, Ari, & Van Gorp, Wilfred G. (Eds.). (2007). *Neuropsychology and substance use.* New York: Taylor & Francis.

Kantor, Martin. (2006). *The psychopathy of everyday life.* Westport, CT: Praeger.

Lynch, Zach. (2009). *The neuro revolution: How brain science is changing our world.* New York: St. Martin's Press.

Millon, Theodore, Simonsen, Erik, Birket-Smith, Morten, & Davis, Roger D. (Eds.). (1998). *Psychopathy: Antisocial, criminal, and violent behavior.* New York: Guilford Press.

Nasar, Sylvia. (1998). *A beautiful mind: The life of mathematical genius and Nobel laureate John Nash.* New York: Touchstone.

Raine, Adrian. (1993). *The psychopathology of crime: Criminal behavior as a clinical disorder.* New York: Academic Press.

Raine, Adrian, & Sanmartin, Jose. (Eds.). (2001). *Violence and psychopathy.* New York: Kluwer Academic.

Salekin, R. T., Rogers, R., Ustad, K. L., & Sewell, K. W. (1998). Psychopathy and recidivism among female inmates. *Law and Human Behavior, 22,* 219–239.

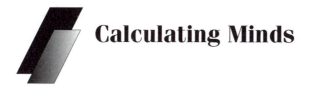

Chapter 5

Calculating Minds

Today, issues surrounding the scientific theory of evolution or evolutionary developmental biology—collectively known as Evo-Devo—have no logical reason whatsoever of being controversial. Synthesizing new research from the 1980s forward into molecular genetics, biological, and epigenetic growth patterns all confirm that *living tissue changes*. What does all this "evolutionary talk" have to do with criminal minds capture in 21st-century neuroscience? It has a lot to do with how "calculating minds" develop and survive.

—Don Jacobs (2010), *res ipsa* observation

INTRODUCTION: SIMPLE AND CHANGEABLE BEAUTY OF SCIENTIFIC THEORY

What makes scientific *theory* so simple and so changeable? According to Kenneth Miller (2007) in *Finding Darwin's God*, evolution is both a theory and a fact. As a theory, it has been denigrated and misunderstood from the day Darwin allowed the contents of *Origin of Species* (1859) to spill into published pages, thereby sending his life's work into the atmosphere of public opinion and peer review. Through it all, and over 150 years later, the theory and fact of evolution augmented by new perspectives from genetics and Evo-Devo is the backbone of modern biology. However, even this could change.

In the real world of science, in the hard-bitten realities of lab bench and field station, the intellectual triumph of Darwin's great idea is total. The paradigm of evolution succeeds every day as a hardworking theory that explains new data and new ideas from scores of fields. High-minded scholarship may treat evolution (and it should) as just another scientific idea that could someday be rejected on the basis of new data, but actual workers in the scientific enterprise have no such hesitation—they know it works as a historical framework that explains both present and past. (Miller, 2007, p. 165)

That's the simple and changeable beauty of scientific theory. Theory in the form of paradigms is not carved into stone tablets. With fresh scientific insight, theory may change until it becomes as sure as gravity— *indisputable and rock solid.* More scientists than not agree that new research into genetics and modern Evo-Devo theory is rock solid. However, many citizens from all walks of life are still unsure, or dodge the issue completely (as I did for almost 30 years); some contend that evolution is just speculation, dead wrong, or evil, while others aligned with a scientific pedigree summarily agree "as a scientific theory, it's a really good one."

Maybe it is time to get over all of the histrionicism of Darwin's good idea and move forward into the wonders of 21st-century neuroscience. This can done by observing a lingering fact: Natural scientists have documented that *living is a natural biological process that embraces modification, variation, and change.* That is evolution in a nutshell.

Modification

Ironically, *modification, variation, and change* can be applied to another less understood construct known as *psychopathy.* When neuroadaptive psychopathy (or simply, neuropsychopathy) is joined to the hip of Evo-Devo, it can be wrapped around a compelling theory to explain *how individual brains come equipped by a coalition of genes and neurochemistry to thrive and survive,* while more moderate versions of psychopathy can spell real trouble for our species. But first, let's talk about a lightning rod.

In the past and continuing into the 21st century, this *natural biological process of change through modification* has been, and continues to be, a lightning rod for those who simply are ill-informed, or those laden with personal beliefs and emotional agendas far afield from natural *cause and effect*—the twin pillars of science.

First off, let's straighten out one of the most misunderstood evolutionary *faux pas* straight away: Mammals with sapient brains (*Homo sapiens*) who sit atop the food chain *did not descend from apes or monkeys,* but Darwin never said we did. Like racial and religious discrimination and fanaticism in Western Hemisphere societies, evolution has been plagued by fanatics, radicals, and perhaps garden-variety moderate psychopaths, as well as those who *simply are misinformed* and misinterpret scientific theory and spread falsehoods as though they were urban legends.

Evo-Devo: Eventually, We All Die Trying

Let's take the pathway that evolution is a theory, and a really good one. Fundamentally, the theory of Evo-Devo is about three biological and genetic processes amenable to modification in living tissue, namely, the following:

- *Heredity.* Heredity injects genetic traits into familial gene pools passed on in traits that progeny inherit generation after generation.
- *Natural selection.* Natural selection is a biological dynamic that favors *helpful traits* staying in the gene pool geared toward *survival of the fittest.*
- *Descent by modification.* This developmental dynamic explains adaptability resulting in astounding variety in biological tissue of related species.

The square peg of biological Evo-Devo never was intended to fit the round hole of theology, creationism, or any other variation. One requires *biological pedigree*, while the other is sustained by *rigorous, often passionate, belief systems.*

In the 21st century, natural dynamics of Evo-Devo are robust and found everywhere in nature. Because the process is remarkably slow and tedious, however, it is hard to comprehend such staggering ramifications in one's lifetime. Following are instances of speedy varieties:

- A disgusting worm in pupa (its "changing room") morphs into a beautiful butterfly.
- A stolen appendage regenerates back to life in a few weeks after a sea crab's legs are separated from its body by the talons of a predatory bird.
- Our birthdays chronicle how we age and change in physical and mental ways; we started off limber, vital, and young and end up in our 80s stooped, wrinkled, feeble, and likely somewhat demented.

When genetically selected for long life, old-timers still get wrinkled and stooped nearing 100 years of age as bodily tissue wilts and brain tissue dements, but genetic "good luck" allows some to continue aging, while others die trying. Again, evolution is not a menace to celestial, theological, philosophical, or teleological debates; it is about a *natural, biological process observed in living tissue and documented in bones.*

SAPIENT BRAINS: ALONE, NATURALLY

Sapient brains are alone atop the food chain. But that was not the case during our remote evolutionary past. In the early history of anthropological paradigms (taxonomies), the focus on finding missing links presupposed a straight line of species development such as from ape to man. From the early 20th century to the latter decades of the century, a taxonomic shift occurred that lead directly to our modern taxonomies of *genera in multiple and separate ancestral lines.* Species were assigned to branches of a tree instead of existing across a single continuum. Finding cousins replaced the obsession of identifying missing links.

Using sophisticated technological advances to date the age of rocks, scientists could tag archeological finds with accurate geological time-lines. Alive 3.2 million years ago, for example, *Australopithecus Afarensus* ("Lucy") was discovered to be a tree-dwelling species more chimpanzee-like than human. But, finding her bones, almost a complete set in fact, told anthropologists she was indeed special. Climbing out of her home in the trees, they discovered *she stood upright and walked like a human.* From Lucy's 3-million-years-ago time frame forward, *specialization was selected for* species with lower body legs used for bipedal locomotion, allowing further specialization of upper torso arms, freed up for refined motor abilities. These skillful traits—walking upright, arms and hands free for hand and eye coordination—eventually characterized the Neanderthal's tool-making abilities 3 million years later. Nearing the 21st century, further discoveries in tagging ancient DNA samples disclosed a startling fact. In 1996, scientists discovered that Neanderthals' DNA was far removed from our own, suggesting they were a different species. However, a smart and deceptive rival to Neanderthals loomed nearby. This rival displayed an advanced calculating mind that opened the door to the Neanderthals' extinction. That competitor—Cro-Magnon—was the precursor to modern *Homo sapiens.* This smart competitor was characterized by a brain-friendly diet, including proteins from both meat and fish, and a knack for organization and communication. With the exit of the Neanderthals, we now are alone atop the food chain with only ourselves to prey upon—for no other reason than we want to.

What conclusions about sapient brains may we draw from this quick evolutionary sketch? Physical activity of any kind—certainly walking, running, jumping, throwing, and climbing—operates as brain nutrients that press the brain into rapid proliferation (via *adaptive neuroplasticity*)— that concept that what fires together wires together. This is especially true in brains augmented by a diet rich in proteins. Physical activities, language acquisition, communication, and social bonding in families led directly to culture and the evolution of the fully human social mind. When considering how far our sapient brains have developed since the time of Lucy, physically challenging activities augmented by skills acquisition by learning how new things work, sapient brain development is truly mind blowing.

BELIEFS TRUMP SCIENCE

Why would opponents of Evo-Devo (and its sidekick, evolutionary psychology) try to make evolution more or less than it is? The answer is deceptively simple: it is the sole reason why *beliefs* trump *science.* So, beliefs exude more powerful influences over behavior than facts?

Yes. Here's a compelling example: smokers know beyond any reasonable doubt that habitually smoking those disgusting coffin nails will eventually kill them, so why not make the simple and healthy decision to just quit? Reason: they don't want to. Harmful addiction aside, they have developed an *emotional connection,* deep in the cortices of the MLS, to the cylindrical tubes of nicotine-laced poison. The sensation that the nicotine produces becomes integrated into personality like a living appendage—smoke rings in the brain if you will; it becomes part of the living tissue of the brain at receptor levels. Just try telling a smoker otherwise; they get defensive and nasty, very quick. It is like trying to tell a moderate to severe psychopath to stop fantasizing about sex—it is not going to happen.

Apparently, our treasured beliefs become connected to emotion and reside in the brain and, at one end of the spectrum of human experience, are lodged in the hippocampus of the MLS, while theory and science are joined in the PFC's synapses of reason and logic. Deciding what to do usually involves a cortical and chemical ricochet between three brain regions— cognitive brainstorming comes from the uppermost *dorsolateral prefrontal cortex* (DLPFC); next comes possible edits from emotional feedback due to the *ventromedial prefrontal cortex* (VMPFC); finally, action follows from a decision from *orbitofrontal cortices* of the prefrontal cortex (OFPFC). Interestingly, the orbitofrontal region of the frontal lobes is located just below and directly between the eyes—the place life hits us the hardest at times.

Earth's Fossils: A Matter of Record

The study of evolutionary biology began in the mid-19th century (1850s) with research into the Earth's fossil record suggesting diversity among living organisms. In the intervening years, evolutionary biologists (and increasingly, evolutionary psychologists) developed and tested theories to further explain cause and effect in species-wide variation—variation so striking it is *res ipsa* observable in side-by-side comparisons by anyone who cares to notice.

By empirical methods alone, scientists were summarily convinced that organisms did change over time. But change from what source? This implies descent from a prior condition, that condition being common ancestors. Over extended periods of time, the fossil record documented this evidence beyond question—that is stone cold fact, not theory. Biological evidence has transformed evolution into *a biological lab and fossil-gathering field science*—a kind of *forensic fossil science*. As everyone knows, life, at times, becomes violent when species compete to survive; therefore, fossils may suggest similarities to crime scenes.

In the early days of evolutionary theory the mechanism driving species' change and diversity remained unclear. Then, almost simultaneously, the theory of natural selection was independently proposed by Darwin and fellow naturalist Alfred Wallace. *Natural selection*, a neuroadaptive process, determines biological variation in light of helpful traits becoming more common in genes (*genotype*—one's inherited genes) in deference to harmful traits showing up as *phenotypes*—observed characteristics—that would not encourage species to thrive and survive.

Advantageous traits, therefore, are more likely to be repeated. Natural selection is the biological process that drives and reinforces helpful traits—characteristics that increase chances of survival—by passing on helpful genes to succeeding generations through familial gene pools. Therefore, Evo-Devo can be summed up as descent through modification of living tissue, guided by natural selection, driving the engine of development over time. Might characteristics of spectrum psychopathy be a favored trait in sapient-brained survival? In contrast to natural selection, another genetic possibility, *genetic drift,* is a pure chance, an evolutionary roll of the dice. It is a toss-up whether or not a given trait will be scattered into one's gene pool, yet it is another way to explain biological diversity.

How could naturalistic and developmental aspects of species survival be outrageous or blasphemous to anyone? To borrow a college campus "map of buildings" metaphor, cherished belief systems can reside in one building on campus—the theology building—while theory and science can reside in another—the science building. They are connected by walkways. Students freely walk across campus to receive instruction in both, one, or neither. One discipline—Evo-Devo—demonstrates how species biologically thrive and survive, while the other extols the virtues of being favored in creation by a supreme being, and how personal choices determine, in part, one's address for eternity.

Life is too grand (and too short) to put every divergent idea into a cognitive whirlpool for the sake of winning an argument (who's right or who's wrong?). Ultimately, it wastes living time. What of substance over millennia has been accomplished by all the bickering?

As descent by modification aligns with biological sciences in living organisms, it does not apply or fit anywhere else in modern discourse, nor should it. It is a gene thing. It is a double helix, Crick and Watson, DNA thing. It is what allows evolutionary psychology to, tangentially, become a branch of neuroscience and part ways forever with the gothic novelist Sigmund Freud, on the one hand, and pop psychologists on the other.

Developmental modifications produced in any one generation (or over many) are indeed minuscule; but, differences accumulate over long spans of time (millennia) and show substantial and observable modifications in a given species—a process that can result in the *emergence of an entirely new species.* That process is a logical outcome of natural modification in biological development. Life cannot survive and thrive without change. Imagine infants retaining their small and underdeveloped bodies and brains well into their 20s. Change is absolutely necessary because there is always a next phase in development.

Physiological similarities among species suggest that all known species are descended from common ancestors developmentally "sculptured" through the biological process of *gradual divergence.* This is the crux of Evo-Devo. Therefore, over many generations, adaptations occur through a combination of successive, small, and often random changes that tend to encourage variations best suited for survival.

Because we are living in a natural environment with competition at every turn, humans need as many biological advantages as possible to survive and thrive or we die trying, just like the dinosaurs. Ultimately, Evo-Devo is nothing more than a neuroadaptive, biological process of genetic inheritance that constantly introduces common or rare variations (gene mutation or genetic recombination) producing astounding variety. This does not, nor should it, threaten cherished beliefs.

DARWIN'S DILEMMA

In 1859, upon publication of *On the Origin of Species,* the fossil record was poorly understood; Darwin said as much himself: "Lack of transitional fossilization is the most obvious and most grave objection against my theory." Even Darwin acknowledged his own theory as theoretical. In the

21st century, the fossil record of evolutionary change is evolution's *most compelling and affirming argument*. In fact, *Archaeopteryx*, representing a classical transition between dinosaurs and birds, appeared in 1861 just two years after *Origin's* publication date (1859). Many more transitional fossils have since been discovered; they are considered examples of the abundant evidence of how major groups of species are *tangentially related* and documented in transitional fossil remains.

The real story leading up to publication of his good idea at age 50 showed that he was hesitant and seemed afraid to publish his landmark comparative biology book. He held on to what his research told him from more than 20 years of gathering samples of beetles and everything else he could catalog. Darwin's greatest fear was the *misinterpretation of his findings*, which is exactly what happened. Again, sapient-brained mammals did not evolve from apes or monkeys, a preposterous and dead-wrong interpretation. In fact, we evolved *away* from them, a fact that should be great news to those still fuming over the mere mention of the most misinterpreted word in the history of linguistics. As a recipient of a theology degree, Darwin once considered the ministry, but being a naturalist was his passion, so he followed his emotional connection. More than any one single factor, however, was the loss of his daughter at age 10; this singular event moved him to such grief that the gamble of unleashing his theory could be tolerated. How could grief from his writings be more palpable than the loss of his beloved child? This one event changed the Darwin name forever.

Yet, even in Darwin's lifetime, the gamble proved to be a worthy one. Scientists overwhelmingly accepted the scientific validity of *Origins*; and elements of Evo-Devo have become the central organizing principle of biology in the 21st century, driving research and providing a unifying explanation for the diversity of biological life on Earth.

Evolution also documents the importance of brain nutrients: good nutrition, physical activity, bonding through socialization—components that promote healthy offspring that grow even stronger in loving families. In the process, good genes passed on generation after generation continue to survive and thrive in those individuals. In the end, life finds many ways to survive—the success or failure of which ultimately is documented and preserved in the Earth by anthropologists and archeologists.

Upon his death, Darwin was entombed in Westminster Abby next to Sir Isaac Newton. Newton and Darwin are universally considered by scholars and educated members of the general public to be two of the most influential men in history of human thought. But, "Less than half of the U.S. public believes that humans evolved from an earlier species" (Miller, 2007, p. 167).

EVO-DEVO, EVOLUTIONARY PSYCHOLOGY, AND
ADAPTIVE NEUROPSYCHOPATHY

In the distant future I see open fields far more important than research. Psychology will be based on a new foundation, that of the *necessary acquirement of each mental power and capacity by gradation*. Light will be thrown on the origin of man and his history. [Jacobs: If I may, "capacity of gradation" is precisely the point of the "mental power" of psychopathy for the sake of survival.] (Darwin, 1859, p. 438)

The quote above forecasts what has been hidden in plain sight over millennia. We can only scratch our heads in collective amazement: How could we have we missed it? One plausible answer for not making the connection—that psychopathy is a neuroadaptive process linked to survivability—might be a palatable negativity amounting to a "halo effect" that continues to swirl around anything remotely associated with evolution; a fact not lost on evolutionary psychology, a struggling academic relative to Evo-Devo and neuropsychology.

First, to set the stage for the conclusion of this pivotal chapter; let me offer an example, prefaced by a question: In the struggle to thrive and survive, which of the following individuals would most likely survive?

- Would it be Lex, a person filled with narcissism and grandiose entitlement, who ultimately cares about no one but himself? He hides his true feelings under an engaging veneer using deception and lying—that is, a high-performance calculating mind—to manipulate outcomes or to manufacture convincing cover-ups.
- Or would it be Rex, who is filled with empathy for the trials and tribulations of fellow humans? He goes out of his way to help others to ease the tears and fears of living. He sacrifices time and attention to help others. He gets easily distracted from his routine life when he sees others mistreated or maligned. He is a crusader for humanity.

Asked another way, who is the most vulnerable in a dangerous society characterized by competition and the absolute need to adapt to survive? Recall that Rex puts himself last and the interests of others first. Recall that Lex displays only superficial interest in others, while secretly targeting others as prey by a carefully crafting a persona of deception intended to manipulate outcomes to his advantage.

The answer is *res ipsa* evident. Lex is the person most likely to thrive and survive into old age. Lex displays characteristics of both adaptive versions and moderate versions of spectrum psychopathy. This is true, of course, unless he makes an uncalculated error and becomes an unsuccessful and, as a result, incarcerated psychopath.

Like everyone else, and over my entire career spanning 25 years as a psychology professor, I had been trained to perceive psychopathologies, such as depression and anxiety, and more profound dysfunctions, such as personality disorders, as a "must fit" to diagnostic criteria within the pages of the DSM. But missing from this academic training was the fact that principles of evolution, back in the 1970s, were considered a serious misstep if taken seriously that might threaten employment. By 2000, I started to wonder whether some of the characteristics of traditionally viewed disorders of the DSM were not disorders as much as they were *neuroadaptations*, mandated by survival strategies, genetically wired within the brain for competitiveness. Up against Evo-Devo and on balance from the new 21st-century tools of criminal mind analysis, the connection of all three—Evo-Devo, evolutionary psychology, and spectrum psychopathy— form the idea of neuroadaptability that hatched the Brainmarks Paradigm of Adaptive Neuropsychopathy.

Only appearing to care about others arms individuals with a deceptive ruse hiding darker intentions of gaining advantage (or getting ahead) by manipulation and subterfuge. Who is more likely to survive? Is it a predator willing to cover up or naïve prey who never see what's coming? Look no further for examples than normal children and adolescents. Do they appear to have calculating minds? How narcissistic and self-absorbed do they appear? Five-year-olds have to be taught to share their toys, especially boys. Adolescents wear their narcissism and entitlement as tribal badges. From 2-year-olds to 21-year-olds, behavior from calculating minds— what we have come to call psychopathy of ultramild to mild gradation— can be observed and documented everywhere as *res ipsa* evidence of its existence.

As I previously mentioned in the introduction, assigning students to write personal biographies—my longest running assignment—proved to be influential in the development of my paradigm. (See autobiographical essays placed at the end of each of the four parts of this book.) Calculating minds, filled with manipulation, lying, and deception, were common themes in the biographies:

- How they lied to parents and other adults about what they really do within the protective veil of their peer tribes versus the version they told parents
- How two-faced friends spread lies to bring down rivals

- How they *emotionally survived* some of the most horrific treatment imaginable intended to destroy fragile self-esteem at the hands of bitter rivals

PARENTING-IN AND PARENTING-OUT

When considering parenting adaptive neuropsychopathy, we are faced with more questions than answers:

- Must moderate conditions of neuropsychopathy be parented-out somewhat in late childhood to adolescence? Will firm and consistent discipline guard against the brain developing more robust versions of psychopathy?
- Is good parenting consistent with an inoculation against developing more strength of psychopathic gradation? Might learning to get away with lies, ironically, make psychopathy a positive personality trait? By results of deception, might adolescents get really good at deception with the payoff of getting their way?
- How many troubled teens—deep into addiction, lying, stealing, elopement from school—ultimately must be turned over to agencies after stressed out, fed-up parents give up on their own children?

Many questions abound, but few solid answers emerge while parents, doing their best, wait and see what works with their progeny. Undoubtedly, we will learn a great deal more over the next 10 years with regard to the best parental strategies for managing neuroadaptive psychopathy and how best to parent-out moderate psychopathy. This process will become a fertile ground for researchers to help parents make vital decisions in parenting.

It appears from anecdotal evidence alone—our *res ipsa* evidentiary argument—that adolescents can get so entrenched in tribal kinship, punctuated by psychopathy among high school peers, they may have really rough times growing into their PFCs—adult version of sapient brains. Parents and school administrators must stand resilient with courage to show adolescents the way back and must not crush them with wrong-headed policies.

Why would young adults (20 to 30 years of age) with brains naturally wired with narcissism and entitlement (and perhaps coddled as the favorite child) desire to change circumstances in adulthood? They have learned *de facto* to be charming cons; presumably, they feel better equipped to survive in highly competitive milieus armed with calculating minds deep into deception than doing an about-face and telling the truth. *Telling the truth requires maturation in learned stages of development as the PFC gains in strength.*

Because of the genetic wiring of mild psychopathic sapient brains, enhanced by the tribal influence of older peers, young adolescents are shown by peers how deception and lies can lead to acceptance and popularity (thriving and surviving in the halls of Hormone High). In this way, parent and child are dangerously disconnected—as some bad decisions are inevitable—transforming adolescence into one of the most stressful phases of life for parents.

Coincidentally, the connectivity of spectrum psychopathy to elements of Evo-Devo appears as a nice paradigmatic fit to core premises of evolutionary psychology. According to Buss (2005),

- Manifest behavior depends on underlying psychological mechanisms, information processing housed in the brain, in conjunction with the external and internal inputs that trigger activation. [Jacobs: If I may, this information processing must be a "dynamic mechanism" strong enough to mold personality characteristics as insulation against loss and failure—a genetically loaded dynamic as strong as neuroadaptive psychopathy.]
- Evolution by natural selection is the only known causal process capable of creating complex organic mechanisms. [Jacobs: If I may, this premise suggests a complex construct (such as species-wide neuropsychopathy) genetically wired into brains as survival agenda.]
- Evolved psychological mechanisms are functionally specialized to solve adaptive problems that recurred for humans over evolutionary time. [Jacobs: If I may, psychopathy solves adaptive problems of living through the strategies of survival by deception evidenced in narcissism, entitlement, manipulation, and lying with cover up that become architects of success through "deceptive practices."]
- Selection designed the information processing of many evolved psychological mechanisms to be adaptive and influenced by specific classes of information from the environment.
- Human psychology consists of a large number of functionally specialized evolved mechanisms [Jacobs: If I may, spectrum psychopathy]; each sensitive to particular forms of contextual input that is combined, coordinated, and integrated with each other to produce manifest behavior.

ADAPTIVE PERSONALITY TRAITS
IN EVERYDAY PSYCHOPATHY

It is our theoretical perspective—Brainmarks—that ultramild to mild psychopathy has evolved in neurochemistry and modularity of the brain via developmental mandates as neuroadaptive constituents of brain evolution.

Psychopathy of Everyday Life

In *Psychopathy of Everyday Life*, Kantor (2006) makes a similar contention that psychopathy of the "everyday variety" (his term) deceives others by carefully crafted deception and thrives *just below the radar of criminality;* to me, it is *res ipsa* evidence of its species-wide inoculation. It makes sense to suggest that neuropsychopathy is in every sapient brain. However, Kantor stops short of connecting spectrum psychopathy with Evo-Devo *as a natural brain condition mandating survival.* Our notion of neuropsychopathy is written between the lines in Robert Hare's book *Without Conscience: The Disturbing World of the Psychopaths Among Us:*

> Sub-criminal psychopaths are every bit as egocentric, callous, and manipulative as the average criminal psychopath; however, intelligence, family background, social skills, and circumstances permit them to construct a *façade of normalcy* and to get what they want with relative impunity. (1993, p. 113)

It is clear from current theoretical and research-oriented literature that *unsuccessful psychopaths* are the ones who attract the most attention from researchers; being unsuccessful, they end up warehoused in prisons and mental hospitals (wrongly, as there is no known therapeutic intervention for psychopathy). Safely confined, clinicians meet with them and file reports that rival those generated by *personality traits of the highly successful ones*—that is, the ones who are thriving and surviving.

Clinicians may never meet the ultrasuccessful psychopaths, who in many-splendored ways bilk hundreds of investors out of millions of dollars before being imprisoned as occurred with wealth managers Bernard Madoff and Alan Stanford. Or, through deception by the con of lying— their genetic gift from psychopathy—actively participating in the following everyday activities (suggested by Kantor, 2006), often punctuated by outrageous successes and influences:

- Cheating on taxes, if they pay them at all
- Billing insurance carriers for services not actually rendered
- Being professional "hired guns" who can argue just as easily for one side as the other, thereby reaping big paychecks

- Preaching as religious televangelists who use fear of eternal damnation as a means to a rich and lavish lifestyle, admonishing followers with the proviso: God wants his children to be rich!
- Using highly questionable business or marketing practices as a hedge to profiteering, such as Anheuser-Busch sponsoring fraternity parties and Drink Responsibly advertising
- Using deception as professional politicians, lawyers, doctors, therapists, coaches, accountants, chief executive officers, and managers, while masquerading as legitimate, so that lies or intimidation underlie procurement of a deal, service, or piece of legislation
- Profiteering, the source of which can be traced to traits of psychopathy
- Appearing "too good to be true" on the surface, yet secretly spreading hurtful gossip or rumors about neighbors
- Telling half-truths to appear more trustworthy or honest
- Cheating on a spouse
- Mistreating children, peers, and pets
- Acting as sexual lotharios (or adolescent Don Juan characters), feigning love in return for sexual favors only to abandon prey when a pregnancy occurs
- Abusing substances and repeatedly lying about it
- Pursuing self-absorbed lifestyles made possible by media celebrity
- Acting as femme fatales—attractive and seductive females—who cry sexual assault with individuals who can pay to keep her quiet
- Penning poison letters anonymously wherein self-righteous indignation is masked by Christian principles

THE LATE ARRIVING PFC AND CONSEQUENCES

What genetic process might the brain engineer internally to stop the advance toward moderate gradations of psychopathy into young adulthood, especially in reference to rearing children? The answer is the maturation of the orbitofrontal prefrontal cortex within the frontal lobes of the brain.

REFERENCES

Bowler, Peter J. (2003). *Evolution: The history of an idea*. Berkeley: University of California Press.

Buss, D. M. (Ed.). (2005). *Evolutionary psychology handbook*. Hoboken, NJ: John Wiley & Sons.

Buss, D. M. (2005). *The murderer next door: Why the mind is designed to kill.* New York: Penguin.

Darwin, Charles. (1859). *On the origin of species.* London: John Murray.

Hare, R. D. (1993). *Without conscience.* New York: Guilford Press.

Kantor, Martin. (2006). *The psychopathy of everyday life.* Westport, CT: Praeger.

Kirschner, Marc, & Gerhart, John. (2005). *The plausibility of life: Resolving Darwin's dilemma.* New Haven, CT: Yale University Press.

Miller, Kenneth R. (2007). *Finding Darwin's god: A scientist's search for common ground between god and evolution.* New York: Harper Perennial.

Raine, Adrian. (1993). *The psychopathology of crime.* New York: Academic Press.

Raine, Adrian, & Sanmartin, Jose. (Eds.). (2001). *Violence and psychopathy.* New York: Kluwer Academic.

Zimmer, Carl. (2009a). The ever evolving theories of Darwin. *Time Magazine,* February 12.

Zimmer, Carl. (2009b). *The tangled bank: An introduction to evolution.* Greenfield Village, CO: Roberts and Company.

Chapter 6

Res Ipsa Loquitur

As a natural brain condition—behavioral characteristics and per-sonality proclivities that comprise an adaptive neuropsychopathy—speaks for themselves.

From anecdotal evidence alone—what we observe every day in behavior from sapient brains is self-evident that personality characteristics of what we have come to call "psychopathy" is species-wide. Endogenous chemistry acting upon the central nervous system produces a chemistry of adaptive *neuropsychopathy*—a congenital brain condition that inoculates sapient brains with powerful chemicals as mood brighteners, psychological and deceptive practices, required for survival.

—Don Jacobs (2010), *res ipsa* observation

INTRODUCTION: SPECTRUM PSYCHOPATHY THROUGH HISTORY

One place to start in the long historical accounts of behavior associated with spectrum psychopathy can be thematically connected to Aristotle's student, Theophrastus, whose circa 300 BC *The Unscrupulous Man* essay describes modern characteristics of this brain condition:

The Unscrupulous Man will go and borrow more money from a creditor he has never paid; when marketing he reminds the butcher of some service he has rendered him and, standing near the scales, throws in some meat, if he can, and a soup-bone. If he succeeds, so much the better; if not, he will snatch a piece of tripe and go off laughing.

RES IPSA EVIDENCE

When sapient brains who are in the research sciences observe other sapient brains from all walks of life who display certain habits and patterns of personality—routinely and repetitively in everyday interaction—what must this be saying to even the most casual of observers? Even more so, what must this tell those of us dedicated to criminal minds analysis in the investigative and behavioral sciences? In this book, an important feature of applying Brainmarks's principles to criminal minds analysis is *to give credence to commonly observed experiences in behavioral repertoires.* As a general principle, it matters what people do and say. When things matter, proof from scientists comes later.

Essentially, this was what occurred behind the data collection from *The Criminal Personality Profile* (1970s) questionnaire by then-FBI agents John Douglas and Robert Ressler. By discovering the backgrounds and mind-sets of violent criminal offenders (*known offender characteristics*)—responses directly from the horses' mouths, so to speak—information emerged as the first step in creating a reliable database for the early conceptualization of forensic investigative science. When the same or similar responses were gathered from later offenders, shared characteristics became significant in both profiling and apprehension.

A centuries-old legal doctrine from common law—*res ipsa loquitur*—created an inference of negligence. Still in use in the 21st century, the doctrine is applied to matters of law that do not have to be explained beyond *obvious facts.* The doctrine was first observed in *Byrne v. Boadle* (1863). Plaintiff Byrne was struck by a barrel of flour falling from defendant's second-story window. The court's presumption of *res ipsa loquitur* was that the barrel of flour falling out of a second story was in and of itself sufficient evidence for the presence of negligence. As a corollary, what we commonly see every day in behavior that continues in others repetitively should speak volumes to what really is going on. In the Brainmarks Paradigm, we look to the brain for answers. Neuroscience tells us that cascades of powerful underlying chemicals are at the sources of behavior abetted by *neurocognitive mapping* (that is, powerful thinking maps of behavior) and furthermore by an active imagination. These conditions, in turn, give form and substance to behavior. In this way, *res ipsa loquitur* translates to behavior speaking for itself as significant in sapient-brained criminal minds. As powerful chemistry is known to lie behind behavior, might it in gradations be beneficial to shield us against giving up on life? We suggest that the natural brain condition of adaptive neuropsychopathy is a beneficial inoculation against caving in to despair from the stresses and strains of living in a highly competitive society. In a real sense, this should be comforting news to parents who need a bit of cheering up as they attempt to raise self-absorbed teenagers who are deep into deceptive practices.

RES IPSA: AN APPLIED SCIENCE OF EVERYDAY EXPERIENCES

Legal jurisprudence has its own version of academic applied science, that being *case law* used to build arguments and theories of law in cases tried in court and in federal *statutes* that determine standards of culpability. Likewise, law has its own version of courtroom science—the acid tests of *preponderance of the evidence* requiring more than 51 percent certainty of guilt to convict in civil cases, and the more rigorous *beyond a reasonable doubt* criteria requiring more than 90 percent certainty of guilt to convict in criminal cases. Therefore, *res ipsa* evidence is *an applied science of behavioral commonsense and frequency.* Scientific paradigms and principles follow *res ipsa* evidence in institutional or laboratory research protocols obtained by narrowly defined variables that can be quantified—measured, compared, and reported—in journal articles. This produces what we can call hard science. However, not all human behavior, especially criminal-inspired behavior, can be so wrapped around laboratory experimentation. Forensic investigative science of criminal minds is really an *applied field science of crime scenes* that calculates what likely happened in reverse to the causes— why this victim and not another, and the habits and patterns of the person who ultimately is responsible.

As an applied science of observing what happens in actual behavior seen every day marks the brain in ways that may be quantifiable and, therefore, applied to large population groups. However, for many experiences of living, life is too slippery for empirical validation. *When we see it every day, however, it must be significant.* Science perks up its ears to investigate *res ipsa* evidence with its own special tools. As previously mentioned, the best tool to quantify psychopathy across the continuum is already in use. The best evidence that ultramild to mild versions of psychopathy and moderate gradations exist is in the scores obtained in Robert Hare's brilliant tool, The PCL-R (2003). High scores below 30 can be arranged from high to low, suggesting moderate versions of psychopathy, while lower scores verify the beneficial variety of neuropsychopathy. We suspect that anyone who takes the PCL-R will have scores indicating the entire continuum of psychopathy. Interestingly, Hervey Cleckley affirmed one of Brainmarks's contentions "that the brain condition of psychopathy is highly resistant to suicides," in fact, they practically never occur, while in APD, suicides occur more frequently.

In related examples of *res ipsa* efficacy, we can say with confidence that DA liberation is *res ipsa* proof of cocaine's ingestion and its effect on sapient brains' dopaminergic receptors; likewise, a cocktail laced with GHB is *res ipsa* proof of a date rape allegation in a predatory rapist's arsenal of dirty tricks; also, a pot smoker's demeanor is *res ipsa* proof of the liberation of endogenous anandamide on receptors; and so on, *ad infinitum*.

Similarly, sapient brain neuroanatomy and neurochemistry produce characteristics and traits that have been shown to offer, and continue to offer, the best chance for survival in a conflicted world of movers and shakers amid stab-you-in-the-back contentious competition. Pedagogically, as I evolved my own thinking on how best to teach *criminal forensic psychopathy* versus criminal psychology (technically, a big difference), the interdisciplinary merging of Evo-Devo influences, evolutionary psychology paradigms, and modern views of spectrum psychopathy produced, in concert, the Brainmarks Paradigm. It follows that a compelling body of science will come from what was, at first, *res ipsa* evidence. This, no doubt, will be the case with *neuroadaptive psychopathy*. What follows is childproof and adolescent-proof as *res ipsa* evidence of neuropsychopathy—nature's inoculation against suicide.

Childproof

The playpen of neuroadaptive psychopathy shows self-absorbed, narcissistic young children getting attention by highly effective temper tantrums. A tantrum is defined as "a fit of bad temper, or a violent demonstration of rage or frustration for not getting one's way." As teeth erupt, biting is a form of a tantrum where children bite other children, parents, caretakers, pets, or themselves—anyone or anything that dares contradict self-absorbed narcissism. Human bites can be dangerous. Some children must be expelled from nursery school because of uncontrollable biting and temper tantrum meltdowns; so must adolescents be sent to boot camps and juvenile detention because of assaultive behavior.

Could it be that most theories of why children bite or display meltdown temper tantrums are based on old-school paradigms? Why do such disruptive and assaultive behaviors seem so prevalent? Following are a few instances of antidotes for biting from child psychologists; in light of the Brainmarks Paradigm, we must ask, "Are you kidding?"

- Young children (1–4 years of age or slightly older) are merely frustrated communicators. So, "just ignore the bites and tantrums," a clinician advised, "and everything works out. Just let them vent their frustrations, they will eventually stop."

- Develop "sign language" says another clinician with children immersed in the "terrible twos." They only know about 50 words! Sign language?
- Give hugs to stop meltdowns? (Not unless you don't mind being bitten!)
- Offer food. Are you kidding? Children using this strategy are destined to be obese and to become food obsessed.
- Offer a cognitive incentive (a bribe) to redeem later in exchange for good behavior now. The problem is that toddlers and kindergarteners are not particularly cognitive yet. Cognitive restructuring is largely a farce as has been shown repeatedly in addiction studies.
- Speak calmly to biters or tantrum throwers, or laugh it off. Are you kidding?

Adolescent Proof

As a group, who is more self-absorbed, narcissistic, and self-entitled than adolescents? We would be hard pressed to find any others, perhaps addicts, whose psychopathy runs deeper.

Puberty unleashes cascading chemicals and hormones into the central nervous system to prepare sapient brains for sexual maturity. Turbo-charged testosterone unleashes a *torrent of DANE brain-driven entitlement* with behavioral acts requiring no permission from parents or society. Entitlement and narcissism reinforce each other and connect to behavior—sex, drugs, and dangerous behavior—known to liberate highly "stimulating, sexualizing, and jazzing chemistry." In puberty, self-absorption gains momentum in teenage behavior featuring self-medication in drugs, impulsivity, and bad choices. Without constant stimulation, teenage angst, depression, and low-self esteem seem destined to be observed.

Brainmarks contends that Evo-Devo agendas lie behind ultramild to mild psychopathy as a beneficial chemical gift to life; adaptive neuropsychopathy represents the *natural way of survival* regardless of millennia time frames. Every single person who has ever lived into adolescence and young adulthood has his or her own stories of surviving against overwhelming odds. Recently, many residents of the Katrina disaster survived days without food, water, or sanitation, while grieving over the loss of loved ones yet to be placed in body bags.

Young Adult and Adult Proof

Traveling back in time to the 19th century, shortly after giving birth, Mary Wollstonecraft developed puerperal poisoning and died 10 days later. She left behind a daughter, also named Mary, who would never know her. The daughter would grow up to have an affair with a married man, Percy Shelley. Mary Shelley would survive the deaths of three of her four children. Later she would write the semi-autobiographical *Mathilda,* a novella with the theme of father-daughter incestuous love. A few years later she almost died of a miscarriage and in the same year lost Percy, her beloved husband, at sea. She lived alone for almost 30 years before dying of a brain tumor at age 53. As a teenage girl, Mary Wollstonecraft Shelley wrote *Frankenstein.* Other than a congenital brain condition inoculating her against sadness, despair, loss of children and her loss of her husband, what could have saved her life filled with tragedy? A brain marked by the chemistry of survivability—neuropsychopathy—is our answer.

In the 21st century, with all we know, scientists continue to be baffled by inconsistencies in a well-known semantics charade. Historically, it was predictable that two highly political organizations—the American Psychiatric Association (APA) and the World Health Organization (WHO)—would leave academics, clinicians, scientists, educators, and students confused over *diagnostic criteria* used to define, categorize, and diagnose violent criminal minds by a charade of *clinical taxonomies*—

- Psychopathy
- Sociopathy
- Antisocial
- Dyssocial

Experimental neuropsychology refers to the use of cutting-edge clinical research utilizing high-resolution brain imaging (neuroscans) and reliable psychometrics, such as the PCL-R (2003) so that neuroscientists are not so summarily confused. Hard evidence from research does not confound *forensic neuropsychologists* who pay little attention to the inaccuracies evident in ongoing *qualitative differences* among psychopathy, antisocial, and dyssocial terminology in the *DSM* and in *The International Classification of Diseases,* 10 ed. (ICD-10). It is a long-running semantics issue that must end in the early decades of the 21st century.

Twenty-first-century research literature supports a spectrum psychopathy pedigree for violent, remorseless killers who display zero empathy or conscience. In contrast, the terms sociopathy and dyssocial are reflective of social influences and pop culture *zeitgeist;* although welcome in social discourse, both terms are misleading and unnecessary; they are successful in muddying the waters of diagnostic clarity. So-called interchangeable terms prove to be confusing. It is beyond time for forensic investigative scientists to wake up and smell psychopathy inherent in sapient brains that produced both normal minds and criminal minds.

- Why wouldn't a smart, heavy-brained species have survival criteria prewired into the brain?
- Why wouldn't a PFC be required to shepherd parents through the years most influenced by an adaptive neuropsychopathy in their children?
- Why would brains not come factory-wired with a neurochemical and cortical advantages in neurochemistry that produce deceptive practices?
- Random, dumb luck alone is not evolutionarily mandated because it does not favor survivability.

DECEPTIVE PRACTICES AND POLITICS

In no corner of American life is Theophrastus's Unscrupulous Man more at home than in political areas. In fact, many opinion-editorial columnists in major news organization around the world would argue that *deception is a synonym for politics.* Who could argue? What goes on behind the closed doors of policy making has spawned a genre of books exposing such deals with the devil. For sure, every administration has had it watershed moments of deceptive practices, none better documented than in Theodore White's *Breach of Faith: The Fall of Richard Nixon* (1975). "All nations live by myths," wrote Theodore White, "and nowhere are myths more important than in America." From the publisher's jacket notes, his idea continues to resonate:

This was what the Nixon crisis of 1973–1974 threatened as the nation realized that the myth of their President as a man of law had been betrayed—that equality before the law might now become a fiction; that Vice-President Agnew was a grafter; that the national intelligence agencies had slipped from control; and that, for the first time in their history, a President would have to be removed. (White, 1975)

DECEPTIVE PRACTICES: THE AMERICAN DREAM
OF HOMEOWNERSHIP

Another example of deception at the very heart of the American dream is found in the shenanigans by the cartoonish-sounding mortgage guarantors, Fannie Mae and Freddie Mac. As of 2010, the bailout mortgage twins had cost taxpayers approximately $125 billion. Since both were bailed out of financial ruin in 2008, they have become even more important in the U.S. obsession with homeownership. Shouldn't they have become less important? Less important, that is, if government administrators are truly making efforts to reverse bad financial ideas. Shamefully, without Uncle Sam, it appears citizens would not have a private market for housing, as government support of the mortgage giants—companies who guarantee 9 of 10 new mortgages—is the leading contender in the current U.S. financial crisis.

According to Sarah Quinn, a PhD candidate at the University of California–Berkeley, Fannie and Freddie come from a long line of government programs dating back to the Great Depression, followed by the New Deal's Federal Housing Administration, a measure intended to stimulate mortgage lending. Researching these programs, she states, "the point was to camouflage, hide, or understate the extent to which the U.S. government actually intervened in the economy." Mae and Mac might act respectable, like Dr. Jekyll on the surface, while really operating as the deceptive Mr. Hyde.

Instances of deceptive practices in the highest offices of U.S. government continue to march on. Recall the image of President Bill Clinton, vigorously wagging his finger at the American public on television, as he remarked to a nationally televised audience, "I did not have sex with that woman—Ms. Lewinsky!" *Political forensics showed otherwise.* As darlings of popular culture media, both "Tricky Dick" Nixon and "Slick Willie" Clinton were considerably talented at prevarication and political dirty tricks.

REFERENCES

Byrne v. Boadle. (1863). Court of Exchequer. 2 H. & C. 722, 159 Eng. Rep. 299.

Cooke, D. J., Forth, A. E., & Hare, R. D. (Eds.). (1998). *Psychopathy: Theory, research, and implications for society.* Dordrecht: Kluwer.

Dabney, Dean A. (2004). *Criminal types.* Belmont, CA: Thomson.

Ewing, C. P., & McCann, J. T. (2006). *Minds on trial: Great cases in law and psychology.* New York: Oxford University Press.

Forth, A. E., Newman, J. P., & Hare, R. D. (Eds.). (1996). *Issues in criminological and legal psychology*: No. 24, International perspective on psychopathy (pp. 12–17). Leicester, UK: British Psychological Society.

Hare, R. D., & Neumann, C. N. (2006). The PCL-R assessment of psychopathy: Development, structural properties, and new directions. In C. Patrick (Ed.), *Handbook of psychopathy* (pp. 58–88). New York: Guilford Press.

Hindle, Maurice. (1818/1992). Introduction to *Frankenstein* by Mary Shelley. New York: Penguin Books.

Kiehl, Kent A., & Buckholtz, Joshua W. (2010). Inside the mind of a psychopath. *Scientific American Mind*, September–October.

Samaha, Joel. (1999). *Criminal law* (6th ed.). Belmont, CA: Wadsworth.

Simon, R. I. (1996). Psychopaths, the predators among us. In R. I. Simon (Ed.), *Bad men do what good men dream* (pp. 21–46). Washington, DC: American Psychiatric Publishing.

Simon, Rita James, & Mahan, Linda. (1971). Quantifying burdens of proof—A view from the bench, the jury, and the classroom. *Law and Society Review, 5*, 319–330.

Verona, E., Patrick, C. J., & Joiner, T. E. (2001). Psychopathy, antisocial personality, suicide risk. *Journal of Abnormal Psychology, 110* (3), 462–470.

White, Theodore H. (1975). *Breach of faith: The fall of Richard Nixon*. New York: Atheneum.

Chapter 7

Trapdoor Spiders

It is worth noting that the historical link between psychopathy and violence is not peculiar to Western psychiatry. Indeed, psychopathy is a disorder that apparently occurs in every culture, and the *potential for violence* usually is considered symptomatic of the disorder.
—Raine and Sanmartin (2001, p. 7)

INTRODUCTION: DIRTY TRICKS

The trapdoor spider plays a dirty trick on its prey. First, the predatory spiders construct silken "trip lines" around their trapdoors to detect prey. Ready on a moment's alert to leap out from beneath trapdoors constructed of leaves and soil held tight by silk, the spiders hold the underside of the door with tarsi claws until vibrations from the trip lines signal an intruder. About 120 known species of these nocturnal serial killers exist. As nature provides the original pattern for deceptive practices that extends to all species great and small, residing at the top of the food chain, sapient brains have excelled in highly creative, as well as down-and-dirty tricks—a subject we now address in the modern venue of political dirty tricks. Then, toward the middle and end of this chapter, we address qualitative differences between two serious personality disorders and the modern evolution of criminal profiling.

In U.S. political history of the early 1970s, the term "dirty tricks" as well as the inside meaning of the word "plumbers" became forever memorialized in the aftermath of the break-in at the National Democratic Party headquarters inside the Watergate Hotel in Washington, D.C. It became clear in three articles of impeachment that President Richard M. Nixon attempted to use the Central Intelligence Agency (CIA) to halt the FBI investigation of possible criminal behavior and abuse of power (instances

Nature provides the original pattern for deceptive practices that enable killers from the deadly trapdoor spider to human serial murderers like Ted Bundy, Michael Ross, and Jeffery Dahmer. (Courtesy of Stanislav Macík)

of *hubristic psychopathy*—my term) personified by Nixon's men on the Committee to Re-elect the President (CREEP).

- Were they responsible for a plethora of illegal "dirty tricks"?
- Were illegal funds used to pay for crimes and misdemeanors by those closest to the president?
- Did a sitting president cover up personal knowledge of the dirty tricks?

Ultimately, the mounting evidence confirmed that illegality, in fact, had been perpetrated and covered up, sending Nixon into resignation as the 37th president of the United States.

Political dirty tricks—including lies, deception, illegalities, secret slush funds, payoffs, and cover-ups—pale in comparison to the *sexually violent and psychopathic version of dirty tricks* that characterize the horrific crimes committed by violent human predators. The presence of violence mingled with perverted sexuality converging in *pathological psychopathy* is the subject of this chapter, and secondarily, how extreme psychopathy differs qualitatively from the DSM's stance on Antisocial Personality Disorder (APD). Truly, the crimes associated with violent dirty tricks bring out the worst in human predatory behavior.

President Richard Nixon boards a helicopter after his resignation on August 9, 1974. (National Archives)

PSYCHOPATHY AND SEXUALITY

The relationship between *violent pathological psychopathy and sexual offending* has been empirically established, but is little understood (Meloy, 2002). The construct of *spectrum psychopathy*—a psychological theory characterized by a *variety of deceptive practices masquerading as normalcy*—has been theorized to be caused by a mixture of related influences, *with biological endowment being the strongest.* The construct has a long history of clinical reliability and, since the 1990s, more precise forensic application because of forensic investigate research protocol (Millon, Simonsen, Birket-Smith, & Davis, 1998).

This resurgence of psychopathy into national discourse primarily is due to the pioneering research of Robert Hare, PhD, author of *Without*

Conscience: The Disturbing World of the Psychopaths Among Us (1993, 1999), a professor at the University of British Columbia, and associates, who followed in the pioneering wake of Hervey Cleckley's landmark book *The Mask of Sanity: An Attempt to Clarify Some Issues about the So-Called Psychopathic Personality* (1941/1988). Interestingly, Cleckley, an MD and psychiatrist, co-wrote with Corbett Thigpin *Three Faces of Eve*, a pop culture look at multiple personality disorder (now, dissociative identity disorder). The book became a hit movie upon its release in 1957 starring actress Joanne Woodward as "Eve White," "Eve Black," and "Jane." The movie earned the actress the Academy Award as Best Actress for her performance. This movie is one from a long list of stories associated with clinically aberrant behavior. It appears Hollywood has a love affair with psychopathy.

A psychiatric disorder, once characterized as *moral insanity* (from Latin *manie sans delire,* or the French *folie raisonnante*), psychopathy is theorized to be composed of *aggressive narcissism* (Meloy, 2002) and chronic *antisocial behavior* (Hare et al., 1990). Violent sexual psychopaths, indeed, are a breed apart; they are markedly different from any human personality disorder of the sapient brain variety on Earth, and certainly *qualitatively different than the DSM-inspired APD.*

Perhaps a common dictionary definition best characterizes what unsuspecting persons encounter when they are confronted by the cowardly and emotionally vacant monster hiding behind a "mask of sanity":

> Psychopathic personality disorder is an emotionally and behaviorally disordered state characterized by *clear perception of reality* except for an individual's *social and moral obligations,* and often by the pursuit of *immediate personal gratification in criminal acts, drug addiction, or sexual perversion.* (*Merriam-Webster*)

CRIMINAL PERSONALITY AND NCAVC

Analyzing personality for habits and patterns has long been considered a hot topic in law enforcement's attempt to capture society's most elusive and violent predators. Investigators in the 1990s wondered whether *pathological psychopathy* as defined in extreme gradations of a violent cold-blooded criminal personality defined the predators they were after, or was the DSM-inspired APD more accurate? Might KOCs help stitch together the answer residing within society's most outrageous serial Grim Reapers? *Criminal profiling was invented to answer these concerns, and for the most part, it has.*

Continuing our discussion from an earlier chapter regarding the rise of criminal profiling, what follows is a brief historical account of the continuing importance of KOC from FBI files. This history provides the fabric of criminal personality characteristics that we have identified historically as Psychopathic Personality Disorder (PPD)—an irreversible and violent condition and *not* as it turns out, similar in important ways to APD, not by a long shot.

FBI'S BEHAVIORAL SCIENCE UNIT

In the same decade that Samenow was conducting his pioneering research into criminal personality, John Douglas (1977) became a member of the FBI's new Behavioral Science Unit. Teaching *applied criminal psychology* at the FBI Academy in Quantico, Virginia, his audience was composed of FBI agents and police officers from across the nation. Subsequently, Douglas created and managed the FBI's *Criminal Profiling Program* and later became unit chief of the *Investigative Support Unit* of the FBI's National Center for the Analysis of Violent Crime (NCAVC).

Traveling across the continent to instruct police officers and detectives in the latest FBI criminal apprehension techniques (dubbed "crime schools"), Douglas and fellow agent Robert Ressler began interviewing incarcerated violent sex offenders to determine personality characteristics, gathering data that never before had been quantified. This study produced *inductive evidence* that established a database of habits, patterns, parental influences, social and incarceration histories, and mental health factors, including addiction that could be applied to the larger populations of incarcerated criminals. Although *deductive logic* based on educated guesses—the method of Holmes—provided starting points, when enhanced by *res ipsa* evidence from targeted samples, confirmed by KOC, *empiricism framed in paradigms* emerged. The result of this singular endeavor—Criminal Personality Profiles—resulted in Douglas and Ressler's book *Sexual Homicide: Patterns & Motives* (1988). Soon after, their *Crime Classification Manual* (Douglas & Ressler, 1992) was published. Clinical forensic psychologists as expert witnesses and *forensic amicus curiae* as well as forensic neuropsychologists armed with brain scans were just around the corner as new products for 21st-century forensic investigative science.

In 1995, following retirement from the FBI, Douglas gained international fame as the author of a series of books tracking serial killers. This information was considered to be some of the most insightful written about the minds, motives, and operation of society's most elusive predators seeking thrills accomplished through deception and finalized by violent dirty tricks.

Evolution of Vi-CAP

The FBI foursome of Teten, Mullany, Douglas, and Ressler were responsible for the *accuracy* that now is commonplace in criminal profiling. In 1973, they needed one blockbuster case to draw attention to criminal profiling as a viable investigative tool. (A similar case would be played out on a worldwide stage six years later when John Douglas and fellow FBI agent Roy Hazelwood would proffer an accurate profile of the serial killer of young black youths in Georgia [*Atlanta Child Murders,* 1979–1981]). Using an extremely accurate profile, Atlanta resident Wayne B. Williams was identified as the serial murderer. He is now on death row.

Before that seminal event, in 1973, a young girl was abducted as she slept in a tent near her parents in the Rocky Mountains. The FBI-inspired profile declared the abductor to be a young white male, likely a Peeping Tom, who sexually mutilated victims to harvest body parts as souvenirs. The accuracy of the profile led to the arrest of David Meirhofer, a local 23-year-old single male who was a suspect in a similar case. Although Meirhofer killed two victims, versus the numbers he might otherwise have killed, he became recognized as the first psychopathic serial killer to be captured thanks to an accurate profile.

Showing the evolution of this new investigative tool, criminal profiles once were called psychological profilers and later psycho-behavioral profilers in the movie *Silence of the Lambs.* According to FBI standards, a killer must kill three or more victims with cooling off periods in between to correctly be called a serial killer.

Intermittently, in 1974, homicide detective Robert Keppel used profiling methods to aid in the capture of serial killers Ted Bundy and Gary Ridgway, the Green River Killer (the identification of which placed so much stress on profiler John Douglas that he developed a viral infection almost costing him his life). Specifically, the profiling team of Douglas and Ressler became well-known among the early founders of criminal profiling. In the early 1980s, Ressler and Douglas interviewed 36 incarcerated serial killers as part of their coast-to-coast crime schools. They succeeded in discovering parallels between criminal *mens rea* as a sexually driven motive often coupled with horrendous, often toxic parenting, in highly dysfunctional families. Douglas and Ressler were the first to interview, study, and apply what they gathered from convicted serial sexual predators, creating the *organized* and *disorganized* typologies still in use in the 21st century.

Ressler, Douglas, Hazelwood, and others were instrumental in starting up the Violent Criminal Apprehension Program (Vi-CAP) consisting of a *centralized computer database* of information on unsolved homicides.

Knowing the nomadic lifestyle of serial killers who kill a string of strangers with no apparent motive, *similarities in personality* began to arise as well as *victimology* and MO—the step-by-step procedures leading to the kill. The goal of Vi-CAP is to watch for pronounced similarities even though they occur across different jurisdictions and across the nation. Ressler retired from the FBI in 1990 and is the author of best-selling books on sexually psychopathic serial killers. He remains active on lecture circuits providing insight into criminal minds to students, new FBI agents, and police officers.

The perfect *segue from criminal psychology into forensic psychology* came from this rich tradition of reliance on both *inductive* (applying the methods of science) and *deductive reasoning* (speculative logic) connecting *mens rea*—a criminal mind—with criminal behavior (*actus reus*), merging at horrific crime scenes. Recall that where psychology and law interact, forensic psychology is right in the middle of the proceedings. When victimology, MO, and signature (that is, the *cri de coeur*, the "cry from the heart," or the emotional justification for the crime) are infused into the investigation, the chase is on in what becomes a strategic chess game of wits between the good guys and the bad guys.

DSM'S MISFIRE: ANTISOCIAL PERSONALITY DISORDER

Toward the close of the 1990s, it became the consensus of researchers that the roots of violent psychopathy were due to a *severe, underlying personality disorder.* It was considered pervasive enough to be conceptualized as the most severe example of *spectrum psychopathy* with a diagnosis of an irreversible personality disorder.

Ironically, the DSM-IV-TR (APA, 2000)—the bible of clinical psychologists—does not differentiate between psychopathy and APD; in fact, the word psychopathy is mentioned only once under APD and is not listed at all in the glossary. Instead, diagnostic criteria for APD is listed and often confused with the construct of spectrum psychopathy, and of course, violent sexual psychopathy—this chapter's reference to trapdoor spiders. As the APA publishes the DSM, it is conceivable that turf wars would emerge between researchers whose data consistently show a definite *qualitative difference* between psychopathy *per se* and antisociality *per se*. They are not the same disorder, not by a long shot.

QUALITATIVE DIFFERENCES IN PERSONALITY DISORDERS

Criteria for violent psychopathy represent a 180-degree gradation away from nature's strategy of thriving and surviving through endogenous neurochemistry and hormones lying behind survivability; this adaptive version is accomplished by radiant (in contrast to grandiose) narcissism and entitlement along with deceptive practices—lying, manipulation, and cover-up—surefire ways to constantly gain competitive advantages. In our view, *adaptive neuropsychopathy is beneficial and is the ace up the sleeve of species longevity and survivability.*

In trapdoor spider version, a severe personality disorder exists and is a perversion of neuroadaptive psychopathy; violent sexual predators display a lifelong *rapacious mind* characterized by violent predatory behavior. As indicated below, criminal minds marked with severe gradations of spectrum psychopathy are *qualitatively different* and far removed from representing the apparently intended brilliance of species with sapient brains.

Listed below are the major qualifying differences between DSM criteria for personality disorders, which are not consistent with PPD. We use the exact lexicon in the DSM's personality disorder criteria: "Only when personality traits are inflexible and maladaptive and cause significant functional impairment or subjective distress do they constitute Personality Disorders" (DSM-IV-TR, APA, 2000, p. 686). This definition of DSM personality disorders (such as Narcissistic, Borderline, or Antisocial) entirely misses the mark relative to PPD.

First, from ultramild to mild chemical gradations of adaptive neuropsychopathy, and its umbrella of learned deception intended to manipulate outcomes, the condition is *highly flexible and highly adaptable* as it is in severe forms with PPD. Adaptability is characteristic of psychopathy across the spectrum, accounting for advantages in neuroadaptive survivability, and in severe gradations required by necessity for the development of a new tool of capture—the criminal profile—to apprehend society's most elusive predators. Showing highly refined ways of con-artistry, successful con artists continue to dream and scheme, and thrive and connive. They are not inflexible nor are they maladapted—they flourish in their scheming and dreaming as brilliant con artists. In severe cases, Ted Bundy presented a deceptively engaging persona (a psychology major, then law student on his way to a thriving career in politics). No one but his prey encountered the real and extremely violent Ted. Months after his capture, former attorneys who knew Bundy said publicly, "You've got the wrong guy!"

If gradations of psychopathy were inflexible and maladaptive, which they are not, it would not serve the brain as a *neuroadaptive agent* in thriving and surviving. The adaptive version does; in contrast, in severe gradations, it may take 30 years of hunting the human predator before capture. So, criminal profiling was invented to mitigate this fact. Serial killer John Wayne Gacy presented himself as an outstanding and involved citizen as chapter president of his town's National Organization of Jaycees; he deceived others by the appearance of supporting his community by employing youthful workers, many of whom ended up buried in the crawlspace of his modest home.

The list of violent psychopathic personalities (especially of the FBI's organized typology addressed in Chapter 3) contains similar deceptions of individuals who appear to be engaging and socially adept, while deceiving others out of reputations or their lives because of the animal cunning and magnetism of pathological psychopathy.

Second, psychopaths across the spectrum are not functionally impaired, nor do they experience subjective emotional distress. Far from it, they feel a *grandiose sense of entitlement*—a free pass for life to do whatever they chose all the while feeling guiltless and remorseless in the process; they know that deep down their targeted prey had it coming. This psychopathic mind-set amounts to the complete phenomenological opposite of the DSM's definition of personality disorders; antisocial criminals may be saturated by subjective distress knowing that capture means more hard time. In actuality, the antisocial individual may feel real regret for committing the crime, knowing incarceration will interrupt his treasured lifestyle. In contrast, psychopaths remain guiltless, free from the burden of conscience, and free to kill again even if it means an abrupt halt due to "doing time".

Although the antisocial criminal often has a career punctuated by long stints of incarceration, psychopaths often have long undetected careers, in some cases, spanning 30 years before apprehension as occurred with the Green River Killer, Gary Ridgway, and others.

BRAKES ON CRIMINALITY: THE PFC

In normally wired PFCs, the region becomes the default setting for mitigating or restraining inappropriate behavior woven into action from the emotional and reward centers of the MLS—perhaps the prime activation center for chemical psychopathy.

The adult brain with strong PFC control trumps the dangerous impulsivity of the adolescent-oriented chemistry of the MLS. According to neuroscans of the brain, brainstorming—that is, creating cognitive ideas and then mulling them over—occurs primarily in the dorsolateral prefrontal cortex (DLPFC) inside the frontal lobes. Adding an additional layer of feelings about possible options includes the ventromedial prefrontal cortex (VMPFC); deciding and choosing behavioral action, "just doing it" is the function of the orbitofrontal prefrontal cortex (OFPFC).

If psychopathy resulting from brain chemistry can be plotted across a spectrum and is "wired" by gradation into sapient brains from birth, the only sure way to mitigate or lessen impulsivity, narcissism, entitlement, deception, and lying is by the precocious development of the PFC and then, by degrees, its full maturity. By age 25 to 30, adult responsibility emerges as the way our central nervous system learns to make solid decisions from experience, consequence, and responsibility for actions.

To be sure, when crime scene investigators and profilers do not understand sapient brains, they really do not understand criminal minds. They fail to account for how powerful psychopathy can be in directing behavior into endless scenarios of serial lying and deception, hence our insistence on interdisciplinary training in 21st-century forensic investigative science.

Deviant Sexual Fantasies inherent in Pathological Psychopathy

Although it is true that both psychopathic and APD individuals habitually perform acts that are deceitful, hurtful, conning, or manipulative for personal profit and pleasure, a strong and compelling argument exists to differentiate the major difference between *pathological psychopathy and antisocial psychopathology*. In contrast to the antisocial criminal, the pathological psychopath is characterized by possessing deviant sexual fantasies earmarked by the sexual obsession and eroticism that drive sexual homicides. Interestingly, these perverse fantasies may have roots in ultramild to mild psychopathy as evidenced by the *rich imagination of children before they reach puberty—that is, the sexualization of sapient brains*. Children are notorious for creating imaginary friends and telling parents things that did not really happen, further proof of the central importance of fantasies in spectrum psychopathy, which is *res ipsa* evident in early development.

Severe neurological glitches suggested by *blunt affect* (the expressionless face) or *histrionic affect* (inappropriate facial expressions such as smiling at sad news when an expression of sadness would be appropriate) signal the requisite lack of positive regard for anyone—a kind of *misanthropic psychopathy*—the hallmark of pathological psychopathy readily seen in the crimes of Susan Smith, Richard Ramirez, and John Wayne Gacy.

Although psychopaths account for about 15 to 20 percent of the total prison population, they nonetheless count for more than 50 percent of violent crimes. In tracking violent criminals, learning to see Mr. Hyde— the true character beyond deceptive persona of Dr. Jekyll—is the challenge of modern interdisciplinary forensic investigative scientists.

According to Jose Sanmartin, "Psychopaths have a peculiar, striking affect disorder—superficial pleasantness, facile lying, and the capacity to kill in cold blood. In some cases, cold blood best captures what is most characteristic about the violent psychopath" (Raine & Sanmartin, 2001). Based on a study that appeared in the *Bulletin of the Menninger Clinic* (Meloy, 2002), the following behavioral characteristics are known to lie behind gradations of *spectrum psychopathy*:

- It is well known by researchers and clinical forensic psychologists that psychopaths do not emotionally bond to mates as normally observed in committed relationships. Instead, *sexual victimization* is the overriding intention, while mate and parental responsibilities are marginalized or ignored. In his early attachment research, John Bowlby labeled such individuals "affectionless" (1944). The MO of psychopaths with their own children is documented—they abandon numerous children of self-absorbed sexual liaisons so that moms are left alone in single-parent, broken homes. One of the first clues that relational bonding will never be consummated with a psychopath is the red flag of constant bickering and verbal (possibly physical) tirades with jealousy a constant theme. Also, sexual behavior gradually becomes *more sexually perverse*, often by preferential demands for anal intercourse.
- Although not initially shown or suggested in demeanor, psychopaths eventually display a callous disregard for the rights and feelings of others. If social bonding suggests the ability to *empathize*, both are lost on the psychopath. An extreme (and violent) example of callousness is *pathological sadism* where pleasure is derived from a victim's suffering and degradation.
- Psychopaths attempt to control, not affectionately relate to, others; therefore, it is predictable that psychopathy and sexual sadism would be positively correlated. Criminal sexual sadists prefer anal intercourse, a sex act that dominates and controls another from behind to further dehumanize victims; this is directly opposite the preferred sexuality of normal adults, where face-to-face intimacy stimulates emotional exchange.
- Interdisciplinary research over the past 50 years confirms that *psychopaths* as a group are sensation-seekers. They often engage in dangerous activities in adolescence. This characteristic likely is due to peripheral autonomic understimulation or hyporeactivity. This biological predisposition predicts early onset, violent criminality in

adults. It provides incentive for forbidden and risky sexual adventure so appealing to the brain of violent sexual psychopaths, with serial rape and pedophilia as examples.

- *Grandiosity*, evident in the inflated sense of self-worth in psychopathy, and the fuse to entitlement, is the banner (and red flag) of pathological narcissism. *Entitlement* is the deep-seated feeling that psychopaths have the right to take whatever they desire from victims (sexual burglary), including their lives. A grandiose sense of self-worth is defined as showy, ostentatious, pretentious, and ultimately, a deceptive ruse designed to attract attention to one's self, or to demonstrate how much smarter the psychopath is in comparison to everyone else in the room. There is no give-and-take, only take, in the orbit of psychopathy; therefore, psychopaths continually manipulate others as accomplished *compulsive liars.*

Predictably, a wide chasm exists between the psychopath's real-life failures reported (imagined or exaggerated) as successes. Grandiosity, entitlement, and compulsive lying project the desire for control—observed eventually in sexual abuse of girlfriends to the abduction and violent sexual sadism characterized in sexually psychopathic serial crime. *Sexual predation is inherent in the construct of pathological psychopathy*. In violent sexual psychopathy, researchers expect to identify the following characteristics in serial offenders:

- Low levels of anxiety and autonomic hyporeactivity
- Chronic emotional detachment (and lack of empathy)
- Sensation-seeking
- A fearless demeanor
- Hiding a manipulative, controlling nature
- Focus on deception and compulsive lying
- Criminal versatility
- Lacking guilt or remorse
- Shallowness of affect (often manifested as blunt affect or inappropriate affect)

Novelist Patricia Cornwell states in her book *Portrait of a Killer: Jack the Ripper Case Closed*:

These people are extraordinarily cunning and lead double lives. Those closest to them usually have no idea that behind the charming mask there is a monster who does not reveal himself until—as "Jack the Ripper" did—right before he attacked his unsuspecting victims. *Psychopaths are incapable of love.* When they show what appears to be regret, sadness, or sorrow, these expressions are manipulative and originate from their own needs and not out of any genuine consideration for another creature. Psychopaths are often attractive, charismatic, and above average in intelligence. While they are given to impulse, they are organized in the planning and execution of their crimes. While they continue to harm others right up until they are captured, upon incarceration there is no cure. (2002)

PROFILING SEXUAL PSYCHOPATHY

The art and science of criminal profiling is most useful to criminal investigative scientists when the crime scene reflects a perpetrator with a profound degree of sexual (pathological) psychopathy. The justification for the efficacy of profiling the sexually perverse criminal with psychosexual deviance is evident in unknown subjects (UNSUBs) who display severely flawed characters absent altruism and restraint (or conscience), with distinct emotional apathy toward victims.

According to Holmes and Holmes (2002), and verified by FBI statistics, criminal profiling is the most accurate tool and offers the best chance of targeting the probable offender relative to the following crimes:

1. *Sadistic Crimes (often involving torture)*
   According to Dr. Richard Walter, a forensic psychologist at Michigan State Penitentiary, the "three Ds" of *sexual sadism* are the manifestation of psychosexual dysfunction observed in the protocol of *dread, dependency, and degradation* forced on victims. Breaking the victim's *will to resist by sadistic torture* as well as breathing life back into the victim with the express purpose of prolonging rape, torture, and degradation as long as possible is a benchmark. When death comes too rapidly or by accidentally delivering a deathblow, the sexual sadist feels cheated and may brutalize the body further with overkill or necrophilia.

2. *Evisceration*
   Jack the Ripper–styled crime scenes best exemplify *evisceration-type crimes* characterized by disembowelment or removing the entrails or organs of another in slaughterhouse fashion with the total destruction of mind, body, and soul of the victim.

3. *Postmortem Slashing and Cutting*
   Stopping short of evisceration, postmortem slashing and cutting alternatively referred to as *overkill* denote sexual crimes within

the context of repressed anger, rage, and hostility observed in mutilation-type crimes, such as the first known serial psychopath Jack the Ripper. Sexual impotence or genital deformity of the UNSUB is often suspected.

4. *Pyromania*

   A malicious fire-starter according to the DSM is a person who experiences "tension or affective arousal" before setting the fire and has "fascination with, interest in, curiosity about, or attraction to fire" and receives "pleasure, gratification, or relief when setting fires, or when witnessing or participating in their aftermath." The DSM stops short of using the words "becomes sexually excited" as a fire-starter, but this aspect cannot be ignored with evidence from pathological psychopaths who were fire-starters long before launching careers in serial crime, including David Berkowitz, "the Son of Sam."

5. *Lust and Mutilation Murders*

   Sexual crimes involving mutilation of the genitals, breasts, or evisceration of internal sexual organs (or other organs) as trophies create the

Some pathological psychopaths were fire-starters long before launching careers in serial crime, including David Berkowitz, "the Son of Sam."(AP Photo)

clinical forensic picture of the lust and mutilation murderer driven by rage, impulsivity, and lack of conscience or remorse typical of pathological psychopaths.

6. *Rape*

Through the years, researchers and criminal investigators have variously analyzed rape as a crime of power, control, and degradation, but in serial crime such as serial rape and serial murder, strong sexual context of rape is present. When the UNSUB's *signature* (or emotional connection to the crime) is uncovered, it shows strong elements of sexual dysfunction and deviant cognitive mapping often marked by an obsession or addiction to violent pornography.

7. *Satanic and Ritualistic Crimes*

Crimes involving satanic worship often are ritualistic in process showing marked sexual dysfunction (as in the sacrifice of virgins, vampirism, and blood-drinking) and obsession with a sadistic view of life.

8. *Pedophilia*

The obsession and compulsion to commit sexual acts with children or underage teenagers (the DSM's term is "prepubescent child, generally age 13 years or younger") has long been observed as severe disorder in the DSM, and those convicted of such crimes are among the most reviled criminals (even by the prison population). The DSM defines a pedophile as a person who "must be age 16 years or older and at least 5 years older than the child." So-called pedophilic pornography contains a plethora of sexually arousing activities of pedophiles that purport that sex has "educational value to the child or the child was sexually provocative indicating his/her desire for sexual pleasuring." The deviant cognitive mapping of pedophiles is confirmed by their devotion to deviant Web sites, photographs, and literature recovered at the residences of pedophiles.

Because of the heinous nature of serial crimes indicated above and the societal unrest engendered by serial rapes and murders—*rapacious crimes*—human predators must be captured and incarcerated for life. There is no treatment.

REFERENCES

APA (American Psychological Association). (2000). *Diagnostic and statistical manual of mental disorders* (DSM-IV-TR). Washington, DC: American Psychological Association.

Caspi, A., McClay, J., Moffitt, T. E., Mill, J., Martin, J., Craig, I. W., Taylor, A., & Poulton, R. (2002). Role of genotype in the cycle of violence in maltreated children. *Science, 297* (5582), 851–854.

Cornwell, Patricia. (2002). *Portrait of a killer: Jack the Ripper case closed.* New York: G. P. Putnam's Sons.

Douglas, J. (with Olshaker, Mark). (1995). *Mind hunter: Inside the FBI's elite serial killer crime unit.* New York: Pocket Books.

Douglas, J. (with Olshaker, Mark). (1999). *The anatomy of motive.* New York: Pocket Books.

Holmes, R. M., & Holmes, S. T. (2002). *Profiling violent crimes: An investigative tool* (3rd ed.). Thousand Oaks, CA: Sage.

Meloy, J. Reid. (2002). The "polymorphously perverse" psychopath: Understanding a strong empirical relationship. *The Menninger Foundation Journal*, 66(3).

Miller, Bruce E., & Cummings, Jeffrey L. (1999). *The human frontal lobes: Functions and disorders.* New York: Guilford Press.

Millon, Theodore, Simonsen, Erik, Birket-Smith, Morten, & Davis, Roger D. (Eds.). (1998). *Psychopathy: Antisocial, criminal, and violent behavior.* New York: Guilford Press.

Mladinich, Robert. (2001). *From the mouth of the monster: The Joel Rifkin story.* New York: Simon and Schuster.

Patrick, Christopher J. (Ed.). (2006). *Handbook of psychopathy.* New York: Guilford Press.

Raine, Adrian, & Sanmartin, Jose. (Eds.) (2001). *Violence and psychopathy.* New York: Kluwer Academic.

Turvey, Brent E. (2002). *Criminal profiling: An introduction to behavioral evidence analysis* (2nd ed.). New York: Elsevier.

White, Theodore H. (1975). *Breach of faith: The fall of Richard Nixon.* New York: Atheneum.

Autobiography of Sabrina's Life: Invincible

Today, I am a stable and responsible 28-year-old female who is attending college to pursue my bachelor's degree in teaching while raising four children; might I add that only one of the four is my own daughter.

I have proudly received my AA in general studies and an AAS in social work/substance abuse. I am looking forward to a career dealing with adolescents in the field of teaching, counseling, or social work. I fully understand that these fields do not consist of very high salaries, but to me, there is more at stake than money. One of the main reasons I want to become a school counselor is to teach students they need to be mindful of obligations, responsibilities, and consequences; that their actions and behaviors can take a tremendous toll and change their lives drastically.

Why do teenagers act out in destructive ways? It is a question that many parents and teachers want the answer to, but there is no clear answer. Maybe it is something in their environment; maybe it has to do in how they are raised; or maybe it's just in their genes? Some teenagers are just plain mean and aggressive, with no feelings of remorse. Some get tired of the abuse and the victimization of their peers or parents and lash out after holding in resentment. I guess others just have a big ego. They get obsessed with themselves and think they are invincible. Some are deprived of love and gratification as though violence is their way to get attention. Then there are teenagers who just want to fit in and be a part of something, or someone, because *they lack the affection from their parents*; you can say that is my story. I am who I am because of my family, my friends, and my tragic experiences.

Now to my story: My parents divorced when I was 11, a crucial time for a female to have stability and the attention of both parents; they divorced because my father was an alcoholic who had many affairs and was physically abusive to my mother. Regardless of what my father did, he was everything to me and I always blamed my mother because she never showed us any kind of love or affection. Our family was separated and my older brothers got to stay with the funny, affectionate and ambitious daddy of mine. That's where the resentment started!

We had to move to a new house, new school, and new neighborhood; I hated every part of it. So my six-grade year I remember bullying girls, talking back, and acting out. I always had good grades, but I was always in some kind of trouble, getting the nickname "Little Trouble!" Gangs were also very prominent in my junior high school years. So I decided to be a part of a new family. My initiation was to fight one of my best friends. Why? Because I was convinced "she was a loser," so my new friends decided. I beat her so severely that she withdrew and moved to another school. After that, I was popular and known as a bad ass. Nobody better mess with me! The drugs, partying, and being sexually promiscuous followed. Even after all this, I made it to high school where I met my off-and-on-again boyfriend of five years. He had always been in trouble, but he finally got his act together his senior year and graduated from Sea Corps.

The next year I graduated and he decided to enlist in the Army Reserve. We had a mutual agreement that we would temporarily break up until he came back. But while he was gone to boot camp I met up and fell in love with an old friend from junior high. *He was the most profitable drug dealer in our hometown.* He wasn't doing so hot in the beginning of 2003, his father, cousin, and a few other "mules" (drug runners) had been busted so he convinced me to finally do what he said he would never let me do—a drug run for him! I got busted in May 2003. At the age of 21, I ended up in prison for trafficking drugs from Mexico.

In the next month, while awaiting trial, I received a letter from my sister-in-law that my high school sweetheart had overdosed and passed away. I literally went crazy! How? Why? He was doing so well I thought. He was in the army. I found out from his mom that he had acquired some white heroin, thinking it was just cocaine! He fell asleep and never woke up! The hardest thing was never being able to say goodbye. That drastically changed my view of addiction. I believe you were supposed to do drugs, not let the drugs do you! How could this happen to such a strong individual; someone who turned his life around and wanted better for himself! I still wish I could ask him, Why?

That wasn't the only tragedy I experienced while incarcerated. I was sentenced at the end of August 2003, to 18 months with 3 years supervised release. I would soon be heading to the Women's Federal Prison in

Ft. Worth, Texas. While waiting to be transferred I called home to let my family know that they had moved me once again to a different county, and while talking to a family member they informed me that my grandfather had been murdered. My grandparents had moved to the border town of Del Rio, Texas, to be closer to my father who had skipped bond and moved to Acuña Coahuila, Mexico, to avoid being arrested for dealing drugs. My older brother had also been deported for burglary of a habitation and domestic violence. My brother had always had trouble with the law and had a problem with inhaling paint. He had been addicted for years before his arrest; he served six years in all. This time it wasn't paint that he was using to get high; his addiction had moved from a cheap high to a more expensive drug, that being crack cocaine. On one of his rampages to get drugs, he tried to steal my grandfather's wallet. My grandfather, who was also an alcoholic, wasn't having it and he picked up a kitchen knife and tried to scare my brother off. My brother in his drug-induced state says he was just defending himself and stabbed my grandfather more than seven times! He was sentenced to 15 years in a Mexican prison. Mexican law requires you to do half your sentence. He would have been released last year but he committed another murder while in prison.

What can a person lose because of drugs? How about your lover, your best friend, your family and their trust. How about your freedom, but most important of all, your very own LIFE! I lost three very important people in my life in a very short time period because of addictions. My high school sweetheart because he loved to party. My brother because he always felt like he had to be on a drug to numb his feelings. My grandfather because of his drinking problem and ego. Thankfully, I didn't lose my life. I think back now and I am so grateful that I was incarcerated at that time. Had not the prison walls protected me, would I still be alive?

Unfortunately, that wasn't enough to make me turn my life around. I was released from prison in the fall of 2004. I remained clean and straight for a while but soon my bad habits and temptation came to haunt me. I had it in my mind that I should enjoy my life and my freedom! I was on probation when I gave a dirty U.A. [urine analysis] that tested positive for cocaine. I knew I would be incarcerated again so I decided to run from the law and stay out as long as I could. In December 2004, I found out I was pregnant. I was in disbelief; in utter denial, I couldn't grasp the idea that I was actually pregnant! I told my baby's father, but kept it from everyone else. I knew if my friends discovered I was pregnant they would give me hell about using drugs, drinking, and clubbing. I was three months pregnant when I finally got apprehended by the "long arm of the law." I decided to go to Mexico to make some deals and drop off some money for a different dealer. Coming back through the border they ran my driver license and discovered I was wanted by the federal marshals. The judge was not very content with my actions at all. I had used drugs, stopped reporting, and thought I could travel to another country, all which violated my supervised release! He decided to sentence me to 10 months in jail, which was the maximum for violating my probation! My world came crushing down yet again. Why didn't I just "cave in"? In the judge's own words he bickered, "I'm sorry, but I can't trust you to stay clean while you're pregnant." Again my bad decisions led me back behind the walls of FMC Carlswell, but this time I wasn't alone.

While in prison, I was fortunate enough to be able to apply for a prison program called M.I.N.T.; which stands for Mothers Infants Nurturing Together. This program would allow me to relocate to a half-way house and have my daughter with me until my release date. I finally got it through my thick skull what I had been doing to myself. I decided to leave all the immaturity behind and focused solemnly on my baby's future. In what words am I going to explain to my daughter that she was born under Federal Prison Custody? I had nothing to offer her. I had acquired my high school diploma behind bars but now it would be even harder to get a decent job, let alone a good paying career. I took every parenting and developmental class I could attend during my stay at the VOA and decided to not let any barrier keep me from acquiring the knowledge to do something positive with my life.

We were released January 9, 2009, with two years left on probation, which I completed successfully. I started my family with my baby's father and we decided to move away from our beloved hometown, which is only filled with drama, drugs, and temptation. I believe moving away was the best decision I have made in my life. My husband is a self-employed truck driver who works hard every day to provide for his family and my sister's children. (Their parents divorced and they left them with us and as yet have made no effort to take them back. Two of them are teenagers and this course has helped me understand them and taught me how to talk and encourage them to better their lives.) I believe everything happens for a reason, and there is a reason why God let me fall when I did. Addiction is a killer! It kills the mind, the heart, and the soul of not only the user but also the people who love them the most.

I am who I am today because I chose to stop my collection of bad habits such as addiction to drugs and hanging around the wrong crowd. I decided to make a difference and even though I made many mistakes after my daughter came into this world there is nothing that I wouldn't do for her. If I was to keep living that destructive lifestyle, where would my child be today? I am who I am because of my family, my friends, and my past experiences. I learned to think and acknowledge that no matter what your circumstances are, you can make a change for the better. I no longer feel invincible, just blessed.

SABRINA'S BRAINMARKS

The brain is the organ of addiction; it is one of the vulnerabilities of living exclusively in the MLS as adolescents. Without parental supervision, what should one expect? Being consumed in a lifestyle of peer tribes can breed tragedy. Yet, Sabrina, like Rachel, did not cave in. In some cases, becoming a mother forces reflection and focus upon the slowly developing PFC; and like a string of interconnected fireworks, an explosion of growth occurs toward adult resolve. Rachel's and Sabrina's autobiographies are startling and compelling res ipsa evidence for nature's powerful invincibility—the beneficial and adaptive version of neuropsychopathy—against "caving in" to despair, humiliation, and sadness. They are both in college pursuing their dreams.

Part III

Order Becoming Disorder

awr-*der*   normal biological ordering in architecture and chemical connectivity in sapient brains best suited to survive and thrive

dis-**awr**-*der*   disorder and dysfunction in the natural ordering of sapient brains observed in severe gradations of psychopathy known as pathological psychopathy expressed in clinical diagnosis as psychopathic personality disorder

Introduction to Part III: Being Whatever He Needs to Be

According to the Brainmarks Paradigm (Jacobs, 2009), adaptive neuro-psychopathy is a natural by-product of the architectural neuroanatomy and cascading chemistry inherent in sapient brains. It has long been known that enzymes "wash" synapses clean, preventing chemical buildup of neurotransmitter chemistry so every chemical makes its most demonstrative mark felt—nothing is wasted in the brain. If neuropsychopathy is a natural brain condition, are all infants by implication, born psychopaths? No, not exactly. Brainmarks contends that all sapient-brained species have nature's gift of a beneficial neurochemical fountainhead of affect and mood-brightening chemistry that provides psychological armor by way of excitatory "jazzers"—that is, endogenous chemistry that showers the brain with life-affirming chemistry. This measure is a preventative against caving in to despair from such conditions as physical and sexual abuse, toxic doses of negativity, and humiliation, as well as to psychophysiological stresses associated with growing up amid all known conditions of marginal, incompetent, and toxic influences, such as complete and consuming chaos of war, natural disasters, and "toxic" parenting. The glue of this neuro-adaptive condition might be just what a young brain needs—determination and resilience—a tarpaulin of protection continues into transitions of prefrontal regions becoming dominant in the adult sapient brain.

Thus, by largely unknown causes, *pathological psychopathy* emerges—the sexually violent and predatory variety, a condition not far removed from "pornographic psychopathy," a reference to the accompanying sexual perversity observed as though the perpetrator is making his own hard-core movie to document his crimes (which is often the case). By degrees, the condition stretches across pre-pubescence into young adulthood, emerging as the vicious and irreversible Psychopathic Personality Disorder (PPD). Unlike Antisocial Personality Disorder (APD), Oppositional Defiant Disorder (ODD) and conduct disorders diagnosed in pubescence *are not necessarily precursors to pathological psychopathy*; however, they are indicative of the DSM's Antisocial Personality disorder (APD).

The only clue we may have to those with moderate to severe gradations of psychopathy who systematically revel in deception is the incredible ability to adapt on-the-fly to any condition allowing the charade to continue. In the time it takes to draw in one breath, the psychopath's seamless transition has materialized from *one thin disguise to another*. He is as masculine as he needs to be, as feminine, as seductive, as transparent, as confrontational, as apologetic, as understanding, and as professional. Then, as quick as a lightning strike, the ruse may shift yet again to another persona, all for advantage, control, and deception. In the process, Edward Hyde masquerades underneath Henry Jekyll. Where do they learn how to do this so effortlessly? How can they be so convincing? Is it perfected in family milieus? Toxic parenting within dysfunctional families is our next stop.

Chapter 8

Toxic Recipes

Many people feel uncomfortable applying the term "psychopath" to children. They site ethical and practical problems [with this label] . . . but clinical experience and empirical research clearly indicates that the raw materials can and do exist in children. Psychopathy does not suddenly spring, unannounced, into existence in adulthood. The precursors of the profile first reveal themselves early in life.

—Robert Hare, (1993, p. 157)

ANTECEDENT CAUSATIONS

From the Federal Bureau of Investigation's (FBI's) known offender characteristics (KOC), family dysfunction, addiction, and red flags of criminality, well documented from the mouths of monsters themselves, give insight into the pretzel of *antecedent influences*. It is somewhat safe to presume that negative parent-child relationships and peer-upon-peer influences *per se* would exacerbate preexisting conditions of the chemical and biological sapient brain. Like a mistreated pup, children are observed to cower as *res ipsa* evidence of abuse.

Still, can exogenous influences, by themselves, be the sole or even a 51 percent tangential cause of this violent and cold-blooded personality disorder producing society's serial Grim Reapers? At present, the best answer is to side with nature, biology, and genetics. Family and peer influences alone do not seem powerful enough by themselves to produce psychopathic criminal minds. We would be remiss not to suggest that some influential factors may exist from peer and family influences.

At present, coconspirators to biological causation of pathological gradations of psychopathy are physical brain traumas to cortical tissues, addiction to hard-core and perverted pornography, and loveless "toxic"

It is somewhat safe to presume that negative parent-child relationships and peer-upon-peer influences *per se* would exacerbate preexisting conditions of the chemical and biological sapient brain. But can they, by themselves, be the sole or even a 51 percent tangential cause of this violent and cold-blooded personality disorder producing society's serial Grim Reapers? (PhotoDisc, Inc./ Getty Images)

parenting—the subject of this chapter. But even these traumatic conditions are clearly standing on thin ice. *Nature still holds the sledgehammer for spectrum psychopathy* in our view.

With our current knowledge of criminal minds, the most toxic of parental influences imaginable, even when compounded by addiction to the most violent hard-core porn, by themselves, seem inadequate to produce society's most lethal predators; *especially, when credence is given to the chemistry of adaptive neuropsychopathy.* From student biographies alone, I have read 25 years' worth of examples describing how students have survived the most horrific experiences imaginable to arrive on campus groomed from head to toe wearing their new backpacks and ready to make something of their young lives even in light of toxic influences. Rachel, Sabrina, Lauren, and Cassidy prove sapient brains can survive and thrive almost any abusive condition.

Additional biomarkers of psychopathy, other than powerful brain chemistry activated in discrete regions of the brain already addressed, someday will be teased apart—such as might be accomplished from the human genome project. *Yet, effective parenting must never be diminished in importance; nurturing and supportive and responsibility-building parenting has res ipsa evidence of its significance in children's lives all over the planet.*

PARENTING-IN AND PARENTING-OUT STRATEGIES

It has long been a premise of the psychology of parenting that to be a nurturing parent some behavioral standards and thinking must be "parented-in," such as wholesome values, attitudes, and morals through example enhanced by firm line-in-the-sand discipline. As traditional parenting goes, what children most need is a steady recipe of applied self-control, sharing and caring for another's feelings, a strong dose of honesty, and a bundle of values that illustrate how to take the "high road" in life. In this way, various *core values* universally interpreted as important for socialization must be parented-in, which often is accomplished by the long-suffering resilience of parents who are confronted with ever-changing developmental stages of progeny. The zenith of all stages—the most emotionally combustible years—comes as no surprise. In late pre-pubescence and in adolescence, parents are universally concerned with the fact that the only perspective their progeny relate to and fully engage is their own. (This condition of self-importance seems now be a natural carryover from adaptive neuropsychopathy.)

Parenting-in wholesome goals and values must continue, argue the experts, unabated into adolescence, during which time challenges seem to multiply with additional conundrums observed in magnified dramatic escapades exacerbated by deceptive practices.

- What are parents to do with adolescents who continually gravitate to the rituals of their own tribe (peers) and are collectively immersed in risky behavior? Might parents notify anyone who cares to listen by going so far in print as to make a notion in their offspring's high school annual: "Make good choices." Is this more to absolve themselves from the fear they may not be doing as much as they should?
- How many times do parents seldom get straight answers from their bright-eyed and otherwise lovable offspring?
- Are they ever doing what they claim they are doing with peers when under parental radar?
- Do parents realize the reality of "being raised" by their own adolescents up against the standards of peer tribes? Will parents listen? Or, will they choose to ignore the reality of highly influential peer tribes on adolescent behavior?

Brainmarks suggests that in addition to parenting-in shared values of society, community, and church by drawing lines in the sand, parents should consider parenting-out some conditions that, if left unabated, may persist and grow in gradational strength into middle and late adolescence. Following Brainmarks, the one condition that appears the most necessary to parent-out in gradation is the congenital wiring of the brain wrapped around narcissism, entitlement, and lack of empathy for others. Such personality proclivities foster deception and lying, inching closer in gradation to characteristics of moderate psychopathy. *Complete lack of empathy for others seems a cardinal trait of moderate psychopathy.* Fired up by powerful endogenous chemistry, the shielding chemistry of psychopathy intertwined with territoriality and obsessive compulsivity from the brainstem and by mood brighteners from the DANE (dopamine-norepinephrine) brain, anticipation of reward from the midbrain limbic system (MLS) and the hippocampus is triggered. Thus, chemically armed, we go out into the world to "make our own way."

In moderate gradation, the "signal strength" of the chemistry of psychopathy is stronger than adaptive gradients. This robust condition produces red flags of concern when behavioral evidence from adolescent behavior suggests lack of remorse, lack of empathy, and lack of conscience. Is it too late to recapture children with these conditions?

The final obstacle in effective parenting by Brainmarks's logic is to parent-out stronger gradations of psychopathy to pave the way for the transition into engagement by the prefrontal cortex (PFC). *Moderate gradations of psychopathy seem to retard the emergence of PFC dominance.* With PFC dominance thus accomplished, the brain becomes receptive to *responsibility tied to consequence*—the final blueprint of the adult brain. The effort to assist this pivotal event likely will extract a considerable amount of energy from parents who hopefully will remain resilient and patient. (Interestingly, it appears that adaptive neuropsychopathy paired to a fully mature PFC defines best-case scenario for resiliency, determination, and patience in young adulthood.)

Psychopathy Appears Early and Stays Late

Infants have a long developmental growth curve ahead and constant close-up and engaged parenting is required for survival. Every need is met, often by anxious parents, who are trying desperately to be good parents. Other parents, soon to be addressed, are 180-degree opposites as toxic parents who fail offspring daily and often in magnanimous ways. With every need met by loving parents, infants are observed as thriving.

All it takes for even more attention is the slightest whimper; parents come running. A congenital brain condition of adaptive neuropsychopathy ensures that young children are inoculated by the resilient chemistry needed to survive. As puberty explodes with hormones and neuro-chemistry of sexuality and erotic fantasy, the effects of psychopathy may multiply in strength to more moderate gradation. How close does this bring adolescent sapient brains to sexualized dirty tricks? Without pre-frontal regulatory control of the PFC, what kind of decisions are they likely to make? How close will adolescents get to the criminal justice system?

Adaptive Neuropsychopathy in Childhood

Every parent knows children are notoriously selfish and prone to temper tantrums. "Mine!" says the four-year-old who erupts in a high-pitched scream when a competitor (playmate) tries to take possession of his or her cherished toy. What parents are observing—starting from the "terrible twos" straight through puberty and beyond—is the natural brain condition of adaptive neuropsychopathy highlighted by narcissism, entitlement, and lack of empathy. What else could it be? Also, children have to be constantly reminded to share. It is not a big leap in logic—more like a half-step—to contend that self-absorbed children and adolescents are hedonistic attention-seekers. Otherwise, they may not get their share of the attention.

Adaptive Neuropsychopathy in Nursery School

Nursery school is a playpen for evidence of ultramild to mild adaptive neuropsychopathy. Children require constant supervision to keep the little darlings from terrorizing each other. *Here we find the biters, scratchers, and hitters who display the most resilient and robust characteristics of entitle-ment:* "This is mine!" Some are so extreme in acting out (out of control) that they have to be removed from child care.

Adaptive Neuropsychopathy in Elementary and Middle School

Ask any elementary or middle school teacher which one component of her day takes up the most time and concentrated effort. The standard answer is the *immature and self-absorbed behavior of students.* Deep in the emotional brain (MLS), older children still crave attention that once was theirs; they will get attention by disturbing class on a regular basis, if necessary. The bigger kids get attention by *bullying*—a direct effect from the brain that highlights both control and manipulation, driven by self-absorbed narcissism and entitlement.

Neuroadaptive Psychopathy in High School

Puberty is the demarcation—the line in the sand—that presents the potential for the development of more moderate conditions of psychopathy, or in contrast, less moderate conditions, by parents chipping away still more at gradations of this adaptive version of neuropsychopathy straight into young adulthood. Twenty-first-century high school principals and counselors observe dangerous behavior in teenagers that did not exist in the lifetimes of the children's parents. Look no further than the tribal ritual of sexting images from camera phones. "Are you kidding?" ask baffled parents. What were they thinking? It is shocking that nudity of underage kids is archived in cell phones, not to mention on the Internet.

The adolescent tribe mentality, pervasive in the halls of Hormone High, where students feel bulletproof and entitled to participate in some of the most outrageous and risky behavior imaginable, is becoming more commonplace, more transparent, and more dangerous. This condition can be hypothesized to be connected directly to conditions of narcissism, entitlement, and adaptability—the tripartite pillars of neuroadaptive psychopathy. It long has been postulated that whatever wires (connects) together, fires together in the cortices of the brain. It appears true with tribal peer groups' habits and patterns connected to adaptive neuropsychopathy in group behavior: whatever wires (connects) together, in fact, fires together in ways that magnify peer tribes.

As parents who are bathed in the adult responsibilities of the PFC continue to scratch their collective heads over endless examples of deceptive practices and adolescent-style dirty tricks from beloved teenagers, we now move into scary milieus of predatory (toxic) parenting that can, like huge icebreaker ships, potentially break down aspects of adaptive neuropsychopathy in its wake. Why would *affect disorders* (depression and anxiety) increase in puberty and adolescence? Why does *suicide* increase during this developmental phase? Has nature's protective armor failed? Has the PFC not made substantial connections in the frontal lobes?

PARENT-CHILD BONDING: ANOTHER LAYER ON TOP OF NEUROPSYCHOPATHY

Brainmarks contends that children and adolescents can survive fairly unscathed because of incompetent parenting—really bad parenting—punctuated by ambivalent discipline and emotional detachment. But, common sense alone would tell us that some children might be emotionally scarred for life by horrific parenting—what we call *predatory (toxic) parenting*—characterized by loveless, neglectful, and assaultive parenting through which children become afraid of their own parents. Drivers must pass a test of competency to acquire a license; should parents be required to pass some kind of an applied test of competency in raising their own children? According to the Brainmarks Paradigm, would negative parenting of this magnitude pollute the possibility that survivability—armed with the protective cloak of adaptive neuropsychopathy—be chipped away to the extent that blinding anger marks the brain inwardly (toward suicide) or outwardly (toward violence to others)? We simply do not know.

Neuropsychopathy Trumps Freud's Elaborate Defense Theory

When the Brainmarks Paradigm is contrasted to Freud's pseudo-science, differences between 19th- and 21st-century psychology become

Parents Raymond and Vanessa Jackson, shown here with their adopted, foster, and biological children, were convicted of aggravated assault and child endangerment after starving their four adopted children. Can such toxic parenting mark a child's brain for violence, or for suicide? (AP/Wide World Photos)

magnified. By Freud's estimation, children somehow must construct elaborate defense mechanisms against *self-hatred, anxiety, and anger*; such defensive maneuvering presented as *denial, rationalization,* and *regression*— so-called psychic devices one and all—erupted to deflect anxieties. Freud's overblown theory of *defensive maneuvering* ignored three central fixtures of sapient brains marked by adaptive neuropsychopathy: (1) the central importance of the brain itself and "pecking-order" importance of survivability inherent in sapient brains; (2) the power and superiority of endogenous chemicals and hormones cascading together in discrete regions of sapient brains for survival agenda; and (3) the progressive wiring due to maturing of experiences into regulatory control of the PFC. Neuroscience was an unknown commodity in Freud's *zeitgeist*.

Brainmarks proposes that if not for the protective cloak of adaptive neuropsychopathy, minimally skilled parents would routinely scar children thorough inadequate emotional expressions of love, caring, and nurturing. What would happen to progeny who were bullied consistently with verbal abuses and physical violence? It is well known that children from toxic homes often grow up with addictions related to chemical abuse as instances of *self-medication* to cover a growing sadness and despair. Self-medication with drugs, sex, and eating are predictable activities with scarcity of adaptive neuropsychopathy as a shield.

Emotional Nihilism

In our nomenclature, predatory *toxic parents* raise children who feel terrorized by their mere presence. Might blunt emotions in children on the surface act as a thin disguise of powerfully destructive emotions boiling and scheming below the surface? Effectively, toxic parenting logically would be counterproductive to neuroadaptive psychopathy. Without nature's natural psychological armor, the result may be the rearing of an angry antisocial criminal or, at the worst, a violent cold-blooded predator seething with anger and rage. We simply do not know enough about how spectrum psychopathy progresses (if it does) into the pathological version. By extension, it appears that some emotional response must fill the void in a person's mental life who feels unloved and unwanted. Questions beg for answers:

- Might anger and rage "rewire" adolescent sapient brains away from tender emotions and empathy for others?
- From emotional toxicity, can damage of the *neurological variety result* in the central nervous system as though repeatedly hit over the head by a club?

- Can toxic feelings lead to real physical damage in cortices of the brain?
- From toxic parenting experiences, might *emotional nihilism*—that is, viewing targeted prey and morality as meaningless and amounting to nothing—be permissible because existence is meaningless?

To follow "recipes" from toxic parenting scripts is to transform innocence and the promise of excelling in life and finding happiness into a self-loathing human predator, or an antisocial misfit. Might daughters raised by toxic parenting turn anger and humiliation *inward* with erosion of self-esteem and nature's gift of adaptive neuropsychopathy, while sons *lash out* at others with violence? Is the trapdoor spider uncovered?

KOC: Childhoods of Violence

In the late 1970s, the FBI's 57-page *Criminal Personality Research Profile* revealed the results of 36 incarcerated serial killers talking about their childhood influences. For the first time, investigators had insight into the horrific milieus of violent childhoods. In short, serial killers came to be observed as a function of *having been conditioned as violent criminals in severely dysfunctional homes characterized by toxic parenting.* In this regard, sins of omission (what parents failed to do) were just as glaring as sins of commission (what parents did do). The following answers were given to questions from the questionnaire; personal experiences reflected violence from traumatized childhoods. Although this list of characteristics does not offer the most compelling instances of why killers kill, the results did come directly from men who came from toxic parent-child milieus. The following 23 toxicity indicators are listed in no special order:

1. In the survey, 50 percent (half of the incarcerated offenders, or 18 men) had *mental illness* in their immediate family.
2. 50 percent of the subjects had parents involved in *some form of criminality.*
3. Nearly 70 percent (25 men) had a family *history of alcohol or drug abuse.*
4. 100 percent of the killers (all 36) had a history of *serious emotional abuse.*
5. 100 percent of the killers (all 36) had developed into *sexually dysfunctional adults,* unable to sustain a mature, consensual relationship with another adult.
6. From birth to age seven, recognized as an important time for *maternal bonding,* relationships between the killers and their mothers were uniformly cool, distant, unloving, and neglectful.

7. 100 percent (all 36) of the killers experienced *mental or physical abuse.*
8. From a young age, parents ignored 100 percent (all 36) of the offender's behavior and imposed few, if any, limits on behavior, leading to an *egocentric view* of the world.
9. More than 40 percent (14 men) received physical beatings.
10. More than 70 percent (25 men) reported "witnessing or participating in *sexually stressful events* when young" (sexual abuse, fondling, attempted rape, or rape).
11. 100 percent (all 36) of the offenders said *no sense of familial attachments* existed, resulting in feeling "lonely and isolated."
12. In 100 percent (all 36) of the offenders, from ages 8 to 12 years of age, "negative and destructive influences of earlier stages were exacerbated." No strong, influential adult rescued any of them.
13. Half of the offenders (18 men) had *absent fathers;* some died, while others became incarcerated. Some fathers left thorough divorce or abandonment during adolescent years.
14. More than 75 percent (27 men) reported *autoerotic fantasies* as preadolescents. Half of the offenders (18 men) reported *rape fantasies* occurring between ages of 12 and14.
15. In 100 percent of responses, the sexualized nature of crimes showed *every single subject was sexually dysfunctional.*
16. As a rule, the offenders as young adolescents experienced a confusing mix of compulsive masturbation, lying, bed-wetting, and nightmares.
17. Although some of the killers had high intelligence quotients (IQs), none performed well in school; *most hated school.*
18. In 100 percent of the responses (all 36), men directed energy to "negative outlets" that consumed them, such as drugs, vandalism, burglary, and pornography, because no positive stimulation existed.
19. In 100 percent of the responses (all 36), perverse, sexualized fantasies fueled the killers' murderous acts; all serial predators have underlying, unresolved sexual issues.
20. In 100 percent of the responses (all 36), the men reported extensive sexual fantasies, so that *victims become depersonalized* objects as though "evicted from their body," as one killer phrased it.
21. Sexual urges 100 percent of the time become *disconnected* from affection and tender emotion.
22. Sexualized, deviant *cognitive maps* stimulated perversity 100 percent of the time and pornography only temporarily satisfied, "forcing" offenders to confront live victims.

23. Precrime triggers or stressors in 100% percent of the cases existed that escalated rapidly into violence. Perception of a loss: a job, or money problems, or a vociferous argument, or the brutal urge to find another victim triggered violence. (Ressler, 1992)

What conclusions can we safely draw? A safe position—a position that does not infer too much without proof—is this: at best, such toxicity in family milieus is certainly contributory and must be factored into the pretzel of violence; at the least, it makes no significant difference. We must remember that psychopathic serial predators have few if any of the endearing traits we recognize as species *Homo sapiens*.

In the meantime, let's approach the parental component from another study's point of view.

VIOLENCE: LACK OF CONTACT COMFORT

Experimental psychologists Harry Harlow and wife Margaret Harlow began a series of studies in the 1950s showing the importance of tactile stimulation (touch) fostering normal behavior. The famous Contact Comfort studies (1962) extended into the mid-1960s at the University of Wisconsin provided the first experimental evidence that inattentive and dysfunctional mothering resulted in abnormal behavior, hence abnormal brain development. Moreover, inattentive and loveless mothering conditioned in the offspring the propensity for some forms of violence later in life.

One aspect of toxic parenting is inattentive, unaffectionate, and loveless mothering or fathering, which produces an emotional detachment from family milieu. As mentioned previously, milieu provides important social contexts of learning (such as the home and peer groups) that should encourage emotional connection, empathy, and social bonding.

Accordingly, Winnicott (1965) contends there is no such thing as an infant *per se*, meaning that maternal care merges into an infant's identity making mother and child emotionally inseparable. (Healthy development guides the child into maturity, thus allowing the natural bond to be broken; otherwise, the child would experience excessive "separation anxiety" from the mother.)

The Harlow study chose infant rhesus monkeys as subjects because, like human infants, they require long periods of emotional attachment to caregivers. The experimenters isolated the infants at birth in solitary cages that prevented touch of any kind, as well as attachment, or social bonding with the other monkeys.

Infants raised in isolation appeared singularly withdrawn as adults and engaged in self-mutating behavior (evidenced by pinching and biting themselves). Later, they channeled self-aggression into hostility—acting out inappropriately against others.

As infant monkeys grew up and became adult mothers, they were indifferent mothers. Similarly, male and female monkeys raised in isolation grew up to be unstable, brutal parents. Could these results reveal an early parental blueprint for raising dysfunctional kids?

Surrogate Mothers

In a related experiment, researchers placed a group of newborn infant rhesus monkeys in a cage with surrogate mothers—that is, "dummy" mothers—to test the mothering process from another angle. They constructed one mother from wire mesh and a heating lamp, and provided a bottle with a nipple for nourishment. They covered the other mother in soft terrycloth and gave no further accoutrements (i.e., no lamp, no bottle). The infants routinely chose the terrycloth-covered mother under a variety of conditions (such as being frightened by a loud noise). Even when hungry, the infants would cling to the cloth-covered mother while reaching across the wire mother for milk. This experiment verified the importance of "contact comfort" in the bonding experience between infants and mothers.

Before the Harlows' study, the dominant theory of parent-to-child bonding was the *cupboard theory of attachment*. This view held that infants bonded with their mothers because they provided nourishment as a flesh-and-blood "cupboard." After the Harlow results, touch and cuddling became significant factors in the understanding of how maternal and social bonding produced healthy, well-adjusted children. But, there's more. When experimenters replaced the wire surrogate mother with a cloth-covered surrogate capable of a rocking motion, the infant monkeys preferred the sensation of being rocked to the motionless terrycloth surrogate. Later, as young children, the rhesus monkeys raised with motionless cloth surrogates showed repetitive rocking movements. In contrast, the monkeys raised with the surrogate capable of rocking did not display abnormal rocking movements.

THE PSYCHOLOGY OF HTCR: HOLDING, TOUCHING, CUDDLING, AND ROCKING

The classic study by Harlow and others has convinced neuropsychologists that sensory stimulation before age two of the variety researched by the Harlows—holding, touching, cuddling, and rocking (HTCR) is necessary for normal brain development. When most of the HTCR nutrients are found to be lacking, what logically may be expected to occur in behavior? What a perfect time for brain imaging in neuroscans to step up and tell us. It is not a big leap in logic to contend that sensory enrichment through HTCR leads to changes in the branching of neurons, and possibly ion conductance, which lie at the heart of normal synaptic connectivity. The developing brain depends on sensory stimulation to such an extent that some researchers refer to *touch as a brain nutrient*. Rocking chairs may be the best neuropsych tool ever invented for the development of normal sapient brains.

Advanced Attachment Theory

In 1951, British psychoanalyst John Bowlby added a human touch to the Harlow findings in rhesus monkeys when he began a series of studies of homeless children in postwar Europe. He analyzed the mother-infant bonding process that led to his attachment theory of bonding. We can analyze the genetic determination of social bonding and its centrality to the normal development of the brain expressed through self-concept, personality, and behavior by analyzing bonding types:

- Type B bonding corresponds to being *securely attached*. Infants received optimal and consistent responsiveness from caregivers, and parents routinely comforted them in times of distress. They display considerable positive affect (emotions) and resiliency.
- Type A *avoidant attachment* corresponds to maternal insensitivity to infant's cues. Infants learn to distrust parental affection as a defense against being overwhelmed by fear or sadness. They tend to anticipate rejection and become hostile or angry. They show less resilience in times of distress.
- Type C *ambivalent-resistant attachment* produces unpredictability of emotional attachment. Such children become impulsive and helpless. Although normal, they tend to be clingy and insecure.
- Type D *disorganized attachment* occurs when parents become frightening to the child because of their own traumatic issues. Instead of providing security, parents become elicitors of fear. Children display anxiety, hostility, and anger.

According to researchers, Type B, securely attached, and Type C, ambivalent attachment, fall within what is considered the normal range without pathological implications. Type A, avoidant attachment, produces difficult children who may require professional counseling later in life; Type D is the prototype for the development of really dysfunctional kids. Might Type A be one blueprint for violent criminal minds?

Psychology of Movement and Bonding

The Cerebellum—HTCR Nutrients

The cerebellum, the three-lobed cerebral tissue behind the occipital lobe of the brain, coordinates balance and fine muscle movements. When an inebriated person fails a field sobriety test, it is the cerebellum that nails him. Flunking the test of normal balance and coordination means the effects of alcohol or other drugs anesthetized the cerebellum.

Not surprisingly, the cerebellum is the brain center most targeted when infants and small children experience sensory enrichment through HTCR. A litmus test for whether or not a given three-year-old child is receiving adequate HTCR is for mom or dad to playfully throw him up in the air (not too high!), as most parents do in play. If the child's eyes widen in fear, and he stiffens from head to toe, the implication is that the brain's motion center—the cerebellum—is somewhat dissonant to HTCR (unless, of course, this was the first time tossed in the air). If the child gleefully smiles and says, "Do it again!" we have some anecdotal evidence that the cerebellum is becoming finely tuned due to the enhanced development attributable to HTCR. As any parent knows, children playfully thrown in the air and caught love it and never want to stop. The author's experience is that when this occurs outside in the front yard in plain view of other children, a "me next" line soon forms. The same rationale holds true for swinging, sliding, jumping on a trampoline, riding a bike, or riding on the merry-go-round.

Kids love motion—running, jumping, spinning around, and falling down. Apparently, the brain requires motion for normal development. In a practical and beneficial way, youth sports enhance early parent-child interactive play. Noncontact sports, such as gymnastics, swimming, tennis, and, to a lesser extent, soccer and volleyball, seem especially beneficial. Because of the likelihood of head trauma from vicious blows to the head, the physical violence of football, rugby, and boxing can exacerbate pre-existing neurological damage (currently observed in the violent social behavior of Mike Tyson and the nearly incomprehensible interviews with former professional boxers such as Joe Frazier, Muhammad Ali, and Michael Spinks). Some authorities believe the cumulative effects of the head butt in soccer can lead to head trauma.

According to brain neuroscientist Dr. James Prescott of the National Institute of Child Health and Human Development, "when touch and movement receptors and their projections to other brain structures do not receive sufficient sensory stimulation, normal development and function [do not occur]." Dr. Prescott believes that understimulation can have devastating effects on emotionality later in life because of the cerebellum's involvement in complex emotional and bonding behavior.

The Central Importance of Mothering

Many developmental psychologists believe that the most important adult figure in early childhood development (up to age three) is the mother. A strong emotional sentiment that develops during this time is a sense of belonging and love, or lack thereof. In the 21st century, modern neuroscience believes moms are primarily responsible for wiring their babies' brains.

Evidence from incarceration interviews with serial offenders shows the relationship with antisocial mothering was uniformly cool, distant, unloving, and neglectful, and characterized by a lack of emotional warmth. Infants who eventually grew up to become serial killers never internalized maternal love from an early age. Internalizing abuse—sexual, verbal, mental, or physical—continually showed up in interviews with violent serial killers.

It is no wonder children grow up angry, oppositional, and defiant when they have emotionally absent mothers and often literally absent fathers. They received practically no behavioral limits. Might this condition produce a nihilistic introverted loner incapable of caring for and nurturing others?

Comprehending the world in egocentric ways characterizes the early developmental stages of childhood development evident in both normal and psychopathic children. As normal children develop, however, they become less egocentric and more empathetic—they can see the world from another's perspective. By contrast, the psychopathic adolescent becomes more egocentric. They often hide fragile egos behind arrogance and inflated confidence.

The renowned Swiss developmental psychologist Jean Piaget (1896–1980) demonstrated egocentricity with his famous Three Mountains experiment. The researcher seated children across a small table from a doll and asked them to judge a papier-mâché model of three mountains, as it would appear from the doll's perspective. Piaget selected the responses from a number of cards depicting different angles of the mountains in relation to the different perspectives around the table. Preoperational children (age two to seven) chose the picture of the mountain from their own perspective, not the doll's, an example of egocentric thinking. In contrast, the older, concrete operational children (age 7 to 12) most often chose the correct picture, the way the mountains looked from the doll's side of the table.

The lethal combination of *superficial normalcy* observed in many psychopaths, paired with emotional immaturity and egocentricity, with an increasing focus on sexual perversity, explains why sexual psychopaths are so dangerous. Apparently, strong, influential adult role models never emerged in the first seven years of life in the slowly "simmering" development of dysfunctional brain development.

DEVELOPMENTAL PSYCHOLOGY

A boy entering puberty needs a strong, stabilizing figure in his life; a boy needs a loving father. More than half of all serial killers studied (over 18 of the original 36 respondents) saw their fathers leave the home during this stage. Absent fathers produce anger, embarrassment, and, worst of all, loneliness during this stage. Isolated and lonely feelings from lifelong emotional scarcity characterize a salient feature of psychopathy.

Also damaging is the fact that preadolescent sexuality and fantasies do not connect to another person. Rather, at approximately 12 to 14 years of age, they emerge as autoerotic rape fantasies. A pronounced fascination with pornography, fetishism, voyeurism, and compulsive masturbation in mid-to-late adolescence may exacerbate perverse fantasies. Sexual psychopaths are immature and socially incompetent when entering adolescence; that is, they lack the social skills required to foster normal interpersonal relationships. They have many short-term relationships that end, according to their egocentric view, because of the other person.

Some "becoming" psychopaths who launch from this developmental stage feeling inferior remain painfully introverted and shy (Edmund Kemper types), but some appear extroverted with a gift of gab (Ted Bundy types), which masks their inner loneliness, deviance, and emotional desperation.

Deviant Sexual Fantasies

Deviant sexual fantasies spill over into the minds of adolescents on the brink of entering adult sexuality who are far from feeling like proactive, independent adults. Deviant sexualized fantasies further erode any hope

Ted Bundy—handsome, cultured, and previously a law student—presented a deceptively engaging persona. He confessed to some 30 murders. Bundy strangled and mutilated his victims, afterward sleeping with their corpses. While awaiting execution, he received thousands of fan letters. (AP/Wide World Photos)

of developing normal social and sexual skills with consenting adults, further exacerbating resentment and oppositional defiance for not having nurturing experiences from competent parenting.

According to Ressler, loneliness, isolation, and sexual daydreaming provide an emotional platform for cruelty to animals and other children, truancy, setting fires, fighting, and assaulting teachers. Later, as young adults, they are job hoppers and unstable in the workplace and under-achievers in school. This is further evidence of their greatest fear that others will discover their incompetence and feelings of inferiority. Later adolescence (14 to 18 years of age) produces compulsive masturbation, lying, promiscuous sex, and nightmares. Adolescent psychopaths sleep poorly and wake up chronically tired.

The possibility of acting out deviant fantasies becomes an obsession as these adolescents enter young adulthood. They perceive the world as a cruel place. With little restraint on oppositional deviant behavior in middle childhood, sexual themes of dominance, molestation, manipulation, and revenge fuel aggression and the need to act out. As young adulthood transcends the teen years, the time draws near to unleash rapacious behavior on deserving victims.

The nihilistic and egocentric mind-set of rapists and murderers allows them to depersonalize victims as objects to fulfill their sexual fantasies. Deviant cognitive maps set up neural pathways in the brain with tainted, sadistic, and rapacious sexuality.

Stressors (or environmental "triggers") provide the final push into *rapacious behavior*, preying upon others. The loss of a job, a relationship breakup, or financial problems can trigger the actualization of deviant fantasies. The straw that breaks the camel's back may be something minor in relation to what normal people adjust to in everyday life.

So-called "magical thinking" enters the mind-set of human predators diagnosed with paranoid schizophrenia, a psychotic thought disorder. For example, serial killer Richard Chase, the Vampire Killer, believed his own blood would turn to powder if he did not drink his victims' blood. Yet, as we have shown, the vast majority of serial predators are not mentally ill; they know exactly what they are doing.

BRAINMARKS OF SERIAL KILLER MICHAEL ROSS

A brain marked by biological templates toward behavioral tendencies of a violent nature, such as antisocial behavior or sexual psychopathy and perhaps exacerbated by toxic parenting, Michael Ross's brain displayed a low-functioning serotonin (5-HT) brain—absent a calm, cool, collected, and confident mind-set in the presence of a high-gain testosterone brain. Severe family dysfunction or longstanding abuse—physical, sexual, or verbal—also may contribute to dangerously imbalanced brainmarks. This brainmark was dramatically documented in the case of Cornell University graduate Michael Ross who claimed responsibility for murdering eight young women he encountered on his route to work.

In our brainwise terminology, Ross's brain can be hypothecated as marked with the following chemistry:

- Because of documented high levels of testosterone, Ross's sex drive hormone ignited an insatiable drive to sexually victimize women who presented physical markers—body type, facial features, and so on—that cued his well-defined sexual fantasies.
- Because of a low-gain 5-HT brain—indicative of a brain on edge and reflective of low self-esteem—his crimes could be assessed as perverse examples of self-medication.

- A low-gain dopamine brain could be hypothesized to squeeze every ounce of pleasure from victimization, while a high-gain dopamine could produce uncontrollable urges as orgasmic pleasure is anticipated.
- Exacerbated by years of deviant cognitive maps of thinking, a mix of biological tendencies (chemical templates) and social influencers resulted in garish violence against women. Diagnosed with sexual sadism, Ross compared his violent sexual urges to "living with an obnoxious roommate I could not escape."

While incarcerated for multiple homicides, he was given testosterone blockers (Depo Provera) on the recommendation of prison psychiatrists attempting to lower his surging testosterone levels—a measure mandated to protect female guards. By lowering testosterone, his low-gain 5-HT brain gradually became more normalized; he experienced some success as a writer—a documentarian of his sadistic crimes. The change was dramatic. No longer possessing a volatile mix of chemistry on diminished prefrontal regulatory control, he became a calmer inmate. Ross continued writing articles on his dramatic personality change, warning others of the danger of chemical imbalances. He felt normal—and remorse—for the first time in his life, yet he would not challenge the death penalty, a penalty he felt he deserved.

In conclusion, it is possible, even probable, that toxicity in family relationships exacerbates preexisting conditions in brain wiring and chemical conditions deep in receptors of the brain. However, it is unwise to point an accusatory finger at parents as the sole blame for creating conditions that produce society's most dangerous predators—sexually psychopathic serial murderers. There is always more to the story.

REFERENCES

Beilin, H. (1992). Piaget's enduring contribution to developmental psychology. *Developmental Psychology, 28*, 191–204.

Beilin, H. (1994). Jean Piaget's enduring contribution to developmental psychology. In *A century of developmental psychology* (pp. 257–290). Washington, DC: American Psychological Association.

Blum, Deborah. (2002). *Love at Goon Park: Harry Harlow and the science of affection.* New York: Perseus.

Brizendine, Louann. (2006). *The female brain.* New York: Morgan Road Books.

Brown, Nina. (2006). *Coping with infuriating, mean, critical people: The destructive narcissistic pattern.* Westport, CT: Praeger.

Douglas, J. (with Olshaker, Mark). (1999). *The anatomy of motive.* New York: Pocket Books.

Guthrie, Robert V. (2004). *Even the rat was white: A historical view of psychology.* New York: Pearson.

Hare, Robert D. (1993). *Without conscience.* New York: Guilford Press.

Harlow, H. F. (1962). Development of affection in primates. In E. L. Bliss (Ed.), *Roots of behavior* (pp. 157–166). New York: Harper.

Jacobs, Don. (2007). *Mind candy: Who's minding the adolescent brain?* Plymouth, MI: Hayden-McNeil.

Jacobs, Don. (2009). *Brainmarks: Headquarters for things that go bump in the night.* Dubuque, IA: Kendall Hunt.

Johnson, Steven. (2004). *Mind wide open: Your brain and the neuroscience of everyday life.* New York: Scribner.

Neufeld, Gordon, & Mate, Gabor. (2004). *Hold on to your kids.* New York: Ballantine Books.

Pron, Nick. (1995). *Lethal marriage: The uncensored truth behind the crimes of Karla Homolka and Paul Bernardo.* Toronto: Seal Books.

Raine, Adrian, & Sanmartin, Jose. (2001). *Violence and psychopathy.* New York: Kluwer Academic.

Ramsland, Katherine. (2006). *Inside the minds of serial killers.* Westport, CT: Praeger.

Ressler, Robert K. (1992). *Whoever fights monsters.* New York: St. Martin's Press.

Samenow, Stanton, E. (1984). *Inside the criminal mind.* New York: Crown.

Walsh, David. (2004). *Why do they act that way? A survival guide to the adolescent brain for you and your teen.* New York: Free Press.

Chapter 9

DANE Brainmarks

The most practical solution is a good theory.
—Albert Einstein (Zeidler, 1995, p. 1)

What exactly is orgasm? Almost everyone would agree that orgasm is an intense, pleasurable response to genital stimulation . . . {yet} there are many reports that other types of sensory stimulation also generate orgasm . . . there are documented cases of women who claim they can experience orgasm just by thinking—without any physical stimulation. Xaviera Hollander (1981), author of *The Happy Hooker*, said she experienced an orgasm when a police officer placed his hand on her shoulder.
—Komisaruk, Beyer-Flores, & Whipple, (2006, p. 3)

SURVIVING AND CONNIVING IN TWO HIGH-GAIN BRAINS

Obviously, orgasm is one of the most powerful chemically inscribed and chemically induced brainmarks of sapient brains. So, what does orgasm have to do with psychopathy? Merely to prove a delicate point, I would contend that both orgasm and psychopathy drive the strong likelihood of species survivability. In adaptive gradations of *neuropsychopathy*, this natural brain condition is theorized to produce *narcissism and entitlement*—defined as egotistical empowerment to gain advantages via deceptive practices. Trolling for sexual conquests and its payoff—orgasm—comes naturally to a narcissist who feels entitled to have sex with as many women as he can find. I suspect there is a strong correlation between psychopathy and sexual adventure (and criminal misadventure) across all gradations of spectrum psychopathy. In pathological versions, no one knows exactly where or how Paul Bernardo—the Scarborough rapist, aided by co-serial killer Karla Homolka, who killed young girls, including Karla's own

Jeffrey Dahmer, arrested in 1991, killed at least 17 young men and boys, strangling, dismembering, and cannibalizing them. (Eugene Garcia/AFP/Getty Images)

sister—obtained his particular sexual appetites with a focus on anal intercourse, fellatio, and obsessive-compulsive sexual dominance of Karla and his victims. Similarly, why did Jeffrey Dahmer prefer young males and necrophilia?

Why did Ted Bundy prefer college co-eds and necrophilia? Why did Ed Gein prefer older women and skinning his victims to produce trinkets made of human body parts? Why did he favor making himself a "girl suit" from his victims? Was producing the physical and psychological effects of orgasm in the finality of each crime the trigger behind it all? In the rush to prove power, control, and manipulation, as forensic investigative scientists we must never forget the sexual component behind violent psychopathic serial crimes.

Experiencing orgasm qualifies as one of the most pleasurable emotional and physical sensations known to sapient brains. Once discovered, why wouldn't adolescents seek to repeat the experience? Why wouldn't young males and females create deceptive practices and lie to parents regarding their whereabouts and who they really are hanging with?

Cognitive-dissonance scenarios allow teenagers to be with whom they want and get their way through deceptive practices, especially lying; over and over again, it has been shown that parents are prepared to believe anything. The cooperative connection of the DANE brain and its powerful chemistry is the evolutionary tool that represents the ultimate neuro-physiological payoff. Similar shenanigans account for the adult variety of deceptive practices observed in clandestine extramarital affairs. Adolescent and adult A-N-T-I-C-I-P-A-T-I-O-N of the payoff—that is, orgasm—comes from the same fountainhead of desire: the DANE brain. Like the mythical Pandora's Box, the high-gain DANE brain—comprising DA's pleasure molecules merging with NE's laser focus and motivation and testosterone's libido—unleashes an immensely powerful aphrodisiac-like tonic of cascading chemistry culminating in heightened mental awareness, motivation, and, above it all, *passion*—known to lie behind some of life's more intense sensations, thoughts, feelings, and fantasies.

In full efficacy (high gain), as a general excitatory tonic, the DANE brain can be defined as a "jazzer" and initiator brainmark, acting as a motivator and natural stimulant promoting wakefulness, energy, alertness, focus, and interest. Also, DA lies behind muscular motility, excitatory affect (mood accelerant and brightener) and generalized pleasure across physical and psychological spectra. On the sexual side, the DANE brain with a boost from testosterone lies beneath sexual passion, lust, eroticism, euphoria, and orgasm. Although it is an ingredient in the psychological experience of love, *DANE is qualitatively more lust than love.*

It is the DANE brain comprised of DA receptors and NE receptors, cascading together and others to be discussed later, that we contend lies beneath the characteristics and personality proclivities we observe collectively as adaptive neuropsychopathy. That is, are sapient brains marked with chemistry and chemical consequences—predictable pleasure sure to follow from behavioral cues—and thus wired for scenarios that anticipate its realization? Specifically, the high-gain DA brainmark—featuring dopamine in liberation—is known to lie behind some especially dangerous pursuits overwhelmingly tempting to teenagers. On the high-gain side, liberated DA lies behind euphoric moods, bulletproof sensibilities, and feelings of entitlement (it is not a big leap in logic to posit that entitlement would become more grandiose with a boost from testosterone). This fact is our number one argument—a strong and com-pelling argument—that DA and its sidekick NE, collectively DANE brain, comprise *chemical transmitters of neuroadaptive psychopathy* in the cortical

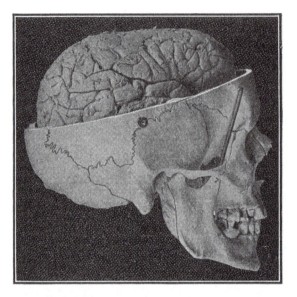

Are sapient brains indelibly marked with chemistry and chemical consequences—
predictable pleasure sure to follow from behavioral cues—and thus wired
for scenarios that anticipate its realization? (From Davison, Alvin. (1908). *The
human body and health: A text-book of essential anatomy, applied physiology,
and practical hygiene.* New York: American Book Company)

tissue of sapient brains. No doubt, other chemicals contribute, soon to be
addressed.

In contrast, on the low-gain DA side resides *anhedonia*—a draining of
energy and pleasure—often pronounced in puberty (observed in *adolescent
angst*), triggering possible self-medication, explorations into drugs, and
sexual impulsivity without thought of consequence. *Anhedonia*, unabated,
often leads to chronic underachieving, depression, and possibly suicide
ideation. This condition is 180 degrees away from thriving and surviving,
dreaming and scheming in the high-gain DANE brain. Chronically low
DA (pronounced in low DANE with accompanying low NE) results in
low energy and scarcity of motivation and focus—a life without passion.

In literature, Hester Prynne in puritan Boston was forced to wear the
scarlet letter "A" for her behavior (displaying a high-gain DANE brain
in committing adultery). In the movie *Pleasantville* the black-and-white
lives of the repressed and unemotional citizens (those denying high-gain
DANE brain) captured in the television sitcoms of the 1950s showed what
happens when DANE is activated—*passion is ignited with lust, sex, and
anger displayed in blazing full-color images.*

The DA Brainmark

By itself, dopamine (DA) *per se* is a neurotransmitter of chemical cascades in the mammalian brain, but also a precursor to the manufacture of norepinephrine (NE)—the chemical of focus and motivation, related in pharmacodynamics to adrenaline in the sympathetic division of the autonomic nervous system. Without sufficient DA, the sapient brain is characterized by diminished passion and lust for adventure with muted sensibilities. How erotic and pleasurable is our world when jazzed (powered) by DA pathways and enhanced, of course, by testosterone—genuinely our natural aphrodisiac!

There is nothing on Earth (or certainly in our cranium) like the high-gain DA brainmark. Sexually, it transforms young bodies into ticking time bombs: we may find another person so sexually desirable we might have sex in less than an hour after meeting them. (This is exactly what happened with Paul Bernardo and Karla Homolka, Canada's most notorious serial killers.) For fans of the movie *Body Heat*, 36 seconds is almost unbearable to sleazy lawyer Ned Racine as he prepares to break into the home of sexy Mattie Tyler Walker to express the raw energy of his high-gain dopamine brain. (Watch it on YouTube if still available.)

Yet, the downside is that low-gain dopamine (DA in scarcity) also affects muscular movements and coordination (observed in Parkinsonism) in addition to clinical depression, dysphoria (impoverished pleasure), and neuromuscular dopa-responsive dystonia (a neurological movement disorder characterized by muscle contractions causing twitching and repetitive movements, also prevalent in the neuromuscular movement-disorder Parkinsonism). Levodopa (L-dopa) is its synthetic precursor used to boost DA scarcity in treating Parkinson's disease.

Discovering DA

On the upside, how did we come to know the sexiest endogenous chemical on Earth? The birthplace in the discovery of this pleasure molecule would make a great marketing piece—the country is Sweden. In 1952, at a laboratory for chemical pharmacology, Arvid Carlsson and Niles-Ake Hillarp discovered this sexy catecholamine—a chemical category that includes NE and adrenaline. Soon, precursor amino acids *phenylalanine* and *tyrosine* were identified as necessary in the manufacture of DA.

As a music metaphor, if the Eagles' soft rock classic *Peaceful, Easy Feeling* best captures the essence of the inhibitory serotonin (5-HT) brainmark, then, in contrast, the driving guitars of Foreigner's hard rock *Hot Blooded* best captures the excitatory DA brainmark. Triggered by perception and expectation, excitatory and inhibitory chemical brainmarks produce their versions and gradations of affect and cognition in individual sapient brains. Which one dominates: excitatory or inhibitory? Environmental cues can act as preliminary stimuli: Would female nudity capture a male's attention? Does the male dopamine brain have *neuroadaptive hormone markers* geared toward sexuality and copulation? Evolutionarily speaking, you bet they do.

In contrast to dopamine and the DANE brain, inhibitory 5-HT receptors cocoon in clusters deep in the brainstem, PFC, and brain-wide to produce affect and mood consistent with feeling cool, calm, collected, and confident—characteristics of the high-gain 5-HT brainmark. When in liberation, reflective second thoughts and foreseeable consequences fire up as neuro-adaptive dynamics geared to adult survival. In contrast, dopamine pathways cocoon deep within the MLS and PFC, producing the high-gain dopamine brain—a stiff rival and competitor—a playground bully to all other brainmarks.

This region packs a powerful hedonistic punch as home to the vastly robust *mesolimbic dopamine pathway* (MLDAP). Regions include the thalamus, a major relay from MLS to the upper cortical regions; hypothalamus, a central region for monitoring blood chemistry and the endocrine gland system; and the midbrain (mesencephalon), which is located above (superior to) the brainstem and below (inferior to) the limbic system *per se*.

The *substantia nigra* of the midbrain is a major source of DA production, while the *ventral tegmental area* (VTA) is central to the rapid transit of DA's reward loops via the mesolimbic DA pathway connecting the VTA to the *nucleus accumbens* (NAcc) in the limbic system; in turn, the intersection of the mesocortical pathways to the mesolimbic connects VTA to the PFC. This fact alone explains how devastating addiction can be—the entire brain is hijacked by the superhighways of DA across mesolimbic and mesocortical pathways. Forensic investigative scientists must never forget this pathway lies behind addiction to sexually psychopathic serial crime and other sexually explicit crimes, including pedophilia. In this way, violent serial offending is more like a major drug addiction.

The pituitary gland orchestrates the *endocrine network of glands*, while the amygdala is an alerting and orienting fear "signaler," and the hippocampus is associated with learning and memory. It is hypothesized by Blair (2006) and others that the amygdala operates minimally in the brains of pathological psychopaths, effectually producing cardinal psychopathic behavior—that is, they act with impunity and without fear. Even in broad daylight, they may snatch a child from the front yard.

Behind sexual magnetism, DA—the molecule of machismo—is the mental sparkplug and prime mover of all things sexual. Because NE is made from DA, it has access to DA pathways and can exert a powerful influence by itself or in concert with DA. Additionally, two hormonal sidekicks of DA—testosterone and phenylethylamine (PEA)—will be addressed, respectively, as the hormone of aggression (testosterone) and the amphetamine-like hormone of attraction (PEA) to specific individual traits of a person.

Not only is the neurotransmitter DA important to mood states, passion, and personality magnetism, but in scientific and academic circles, DANE also provides the tripwire to *adaptation in evolutionary development* (Evo-Devo)—the backbone of all biological science. We are purposing the presence of DANE as chemical thrusters behind neuroadaptive psychopathy. Without two bodies attracted to each other and banging together with laser focus on a consistent basis, would the species survive and thrive? Who but progeny pass on our DNA?

The Adolescent Brain and DA Brainmark

What chemistry lies behind feeling bulletproof? Feeling invincible? Feeling entitled? Feeling *carte blanche* permission to engage in risky behavior? Leaping before looking into excitement and danger sounds like typical pubescent teenager behavior. The adolescent brain, turbocharged by the chemistry of puberty, delineates the full-bloom DANE brain soon to usher in the young adult brain. There is a big "if" here; that is, *if teenagers can survive the most dangerous brain of all*—both high-gain and low-gain versions of the same DANE brainmark.

Sizzle over Substance

When fully illuminated, almost no power on this planet can harness DANE brain *per se.* Just try to dissuade a teenage girl or boy from becoming completely immersed in each other's sexual charms. The high-gain DANE brainmark is behind all their shared chemical fireworks; their dreamy-eyed devotion soon will test patience and sanity all the way down to parents' last neuron, that is, in parents with the high-gain serotonin (5-HT) brainmark—a brain characterized as calm, cool, and connected enough to show resilience in parenting. Parents who reside largely in the adult version of the DANE brain may downplay adolescent behavior as "nothing to worry about; they're just kids." Interestingly, young parents in their 30s may share similar brainmarks with their adolescents as young moms may take a liberal stance on daughters mingling with older male peers. Also, young moms may dress like (and act like) their teenage daughters as though seeking acceptance from friends and peers of her progeny. They may flirt with their daughter's male friends, causing obvious friction between mother and daughter.

Young dads may dismiss the adolescent girlfriend-boyfriend thing as only "infatuation," not realizing they probably are already sexual with each other. Older parents, often characterized by the high-gain 5-HT brain—the characteristic "leadership brain"—might suggest birth control, knowing that even the best of kids have "half-baked" brains. DANE brain-smitten adolescents—even the best of the bunch—will continue to conceal behavior in deceptive practices to continue to get their chemical "fixes" from each other. They are good kids—*but kids nonetheless*—caught in the orbit of euphoria—the DANE brain pedigree of *sizzle over substance.*

The high-gain DA adolescent sapient brain provides the biggest challenge for parents; adolescents require direction and explanation of this most potentially dangerous brainmark. Adults in middle-age high-gain 5-HT brain still have robust memories of their own DANE brainmark and secretly may wonder how they survived into adulthood. They fear for their children's safety and well-being as they reflect on this exciting and riveting, yet impulsive and sexual, brainmark.

Addiction and the DA Brainmark

Addiction represents a chemical "rewiring" of dopaminergic cells of DA pathways within the MLS (via mesolimbic DA pathways and extending to prefrontal regions (via mesocortical DA pathways). Through compulsive use, drug addiction rewires DA pathways to the favored drug, such as to alcohol, nicotine, or a score of illegal drugs. In some brains, one use of an addictive chemical substance is enough to launch a major addiction. With use over time, dopaminergic neurons thicken and widen—I refer to this process as neurons becoming "fat and sassy" when describing the process of *adaptive neuroplasticity,* which is the ability of the brain to wire and rewire itself to favored chemical hits. Once dopaminergic neurons become fat and sassy, with consistent hits suggesting overuse, it may require years to "slim down" overused neurons. Beating an addiction amounts to neurons "rewiring" in reverse, as the brain essentially goes on a diet when denied its chemical fix.

Like a string of interconnected firecrackers, liberated DA in the dopaminergic VTA of the midbrain connects to the medial forebrain bundle (MFB), and finally to the NAcc of the limbic system and represents brainmarks of cascading pleasure molecules. From the powerful DA brainmark, it is easy to see why so-called drug rehab is often ineffective as addicted brains literally must become "lean" again, not "fat and sassy." *Addiction is truly a chronic relapse disorder.*

As the high-gain dopamine and high-gain norepinephrine brain represents most likely the dominant brain in adolescence because of the illumination of the MLS during puberty, it is easy to see how truly dangerous this developmental stage can be. The power of the DANE brainmark is well documented so that the frontal regions of the prefrontal cortex (PFC) truly become the last outpost to stop urges created by DANE pathways. What if PFC regions are immature, damaged, or not well connected? Might this condition continue to account for impulsivity and seemingly careless behavior so often observed in the adolescent years? Many families are littered with 40-year-old "adolescents" who never got around to growing up.

To modern neuropsychology, the high-gain DANE brain explains why adolescents "leap before they look" so often landing in the fire directly from the frying pan. What is more powerful than lust, sexual magnetism, and erotic fantasy? As the brain transitions to the DANE brain from any other pathways, including the highly prized high-gain 5-HT brainmark, we become mentally and emotionally energized in ways no other pathway provides in multiplex of mind. For example, in one instance, the liberated 5-HT brainmark can rivet our perception in a good book, and as quickly as turning a page, we embrace a lover with a fired-up high-gain DANE brain. She may have touched only the shoulder of her lover or he merely caught a whiff of her perfume.

It should be becoming obvious that the high-gain DANE brainmark lies behind neuroadaptive psychopathy as the brain most likely to survive. This is ensured by the owner of the brain being drenched in narcissism and entitlement that hatch deception, often using a charming demeanor to get whatever one wants. The default brain of every teenager on Earth appears to be some gradation of the DANE brain.

The Low-Gain DA Brain and Crime

The low-gain dopamine brain (DA scarcity *per se*) tends to produce *anhedonia* and conditions during which anger and frustration emerge. These conditions often are observed in the brainmarks of juvenile crime, which over time and experience may escalate into more violent, sexually psychopathic crime.

The chemical signature of clinical depression is manifested in behavior by low DA, low NE, and low serotonin (5-HT). Pharmacologically, the antidepressant Prozac works by "blocking reuptake" (liberating) 5-HT at synapse, releasing 5-HT to bind to chemo-receptors downstream from synaptic clefts. As the depressed person begins to feel better—calmer, more collected, and more confident—the DANE brain may rally to infuse a little pleasure and focus back into life. Later in young adulthood, low-gain DA and low-gain 5-HT brainmarks are exacerbated by a high-testosterone brain—the collective brainmarks for violence often observed in serial killers. Serial killer Michael Ross possessed such a brainmark, as most likely did fallen hero O. J. Simpson, widely held to be guilty but found innocent in court.

Four DA Pathways

DA is so central to the neuroadaptive architectural wiring of the brain four DA pathways exist to weave the magic of DA into synaptic clefts. In the *nigrostriatal pathway*, the *substantia nigra* of the midbrain *per se*, which provides the major source of DA in the mammalian brain, unleashes DA to the striatum, a component of the basal ganglia directing muscular movement. In this pathway, *muscular motility* is the upside of DA liberation, whereas Parkinsonism's muscular tremors result from dopaminergic scarcity. Also, this pathway is implicated in *tardive dyskinesia*, the irreversible neurological side effect of sustained neuroleptics medication (antipsychotics) designed to block D2 receptors in treating schizophrenia.

Therefore, across the DA spectrum, two major neurological disorders reside at the poles: (1) schizophrenia in excessive high-gain, and (2) Parkinsonism in excessive low-gain, punctuated by "a whole lot of shaking going on"—largely with bodies banging together in sexual unions—in between.

In the *tuberoinfundibular pathway*, dopaminergic neurons acting in the role of a hormone regulate secretion of prolactin from the anterior pituitary gland. *Prolactin* is the peptide hormone primarily associated with lactation; in breastfeeding, suckling stimulates prolactin production, filling the breast with milk as the hormones *oxytocin* triggers milk letdown.

It is fascinating to forensic neuropsychologists that testosterone, the hormone of aggression, is joined to the hip of pleasure molecules. Might individuals use violence to get what they want sexually? By the same token, might they engage in sex violently?

Orgasm Requirements

Still not convinced that the DANE brainmark lies behind the anticipation of reward-seeking behavior? Abundant evidence exists for the role of DA *per se* in stimulating orgasm and sexual pursuit, in general, so in terms of raw sensuality, two endogenous chemicals are necessary for sexual expression: specifically, physical orgasm, erection, and ejaculation *per se*, representing perfectly the yin and the yang of the brain—the *yin is inhibitory 5-HT* and the *yang is excitatory DA*. The best way to conceptualize the role of 5-HT in human sexual response is by its inhibitory control over orgasm, requiring progressive and sustained stimulation of the genitals and other erogenous zones of the body to overcome tonic inhibitory effects. In ejaculation *per se*, mediated by a DA threshold, premature ejaculation is due to 5-HT scarcity, while *anorgasmia*, the opposite condition—the inability to experience orgasm—is from liberated 5-HT blunting the excitatory effect of DA, a side effect observed in SSRIs (selective serotonin reuptake inhibitors) such as Prozac. Hence, orgasm and ejaculation depend on the *tonic balance between inhibitory and excitatory activators* in concomitant 5-HT and DA transitioning brainmarks. Every sapient brain activity except for simple reflexes runs through the cortices and chemistry of the brain.

So, the point is abundantly clear that life, certainly life energized and sexualized, as well as a life requiring motility and fine-motor skill movements, and finesse in sexual maneuvering would be lame without high-gain DANE winning against a worthy chemical inhibitor, 5-HT. Dopaminergic neurons populate the brainstem, the midbrain *per se*, the MLS, and the PFC.

The Mesolimbic DA Pathway

The third DA pathway is the mesolimbic DA pathway with the VTA connecting to the NAcc terminating in the PFC. This pathway is the source of energized mentality, and the experience, perception, and penumbras of pleasure, euphoria, and sexual imagination. Neurologically, this DA loop connects the NAcc of the limbic system *per se* to the VTA of the midbrain *per se* via the medial forebrain bundle (MFB) of the hypothalamus—the major connector of pleasure pathways of the limbic system—forging the brainmark of turbo-charged, rewarding payoffs.

Next door to the VTA in the midbrain is the substantia nigra (meaning: "black substance") a major source of dopamine. It is not hyperbolic to suggest the MLS can quickly become saturated with DA rapid transit to the PFC mesocortical DA regions to become the pathway in charge, taking the brain away from the 5-HT brainmark. A stolen brain is held hostage by DA. This, in fact, is what occurs in addiction.

The Mesocortical DA Pathway

A hijacked brain is the best way to describe the result of the fourth DA pathway, the mesocortical DA pathway—the final nail in the coffin of PFC capture. With both pathways—mesolimbic and mesocortical—illuminated, DA effectively hijacks the entire brain. Does the high-gain dopamine brain enjoy a biological priority over all other brainmarks? It makes sense that it would as survival of the species is obviously its high priority. What on Earth would stop a brain fueled by high-gain DANE as the chemistry of adaptive psychopathy? When sapient brains lead with a sexual and sensual brain, we usually get what we want. At a glance, responding to a beautiful and desirable female, the male brain rapidly transitions to the high-gain DANE brain. Both males and females alike have been known to do desperate things to capture those who stoke the fires within the DA brainmark. So have those with psychopathic criminal minds.

The initial contact point of incoming DA in the frontal lobes is the dorsolateral PFC—the region of brainstorming—a region well connected to the nearby orbitofrontal PFC, which is responsible for behavioral action, and many other cortical regions above and below it. With the MLS saturated with pleasure spikes and DA cascades and the PFC buzzing with dizzying possibilities, the DANE brain is a brain that must be contended with.

Norepinephrine: Focused Sidekick of the DA Brain

In the sympathetic nervous system of the autonomic nervous system, behavior is jazzed by adrenaline cascading in adrenergic neurons (neurons powered by adrenaline), activated by the tiny *locus coeruleus*—literally "blue spot" region of the brainstem. The well-documented fight-or-flight response powered up in the brain because of cascading NE in the brain and adrenaline in the body (via sympathetic nerves) shows how effective our body-wide chemoreceptor networks perform with a dominant high-gain DA brain boosted by NE and adrenaline—the DANE brain—equipped for stress responses, focus, drive, and motivation.

Cascading NE has a pronounced excitatory effect on the brain, mediating arousal, motivation, focus, and attention. Part of our passion in life comes from jazzed chemistry—certainly the laser-sharp focus of the neurotransmitters DE and NE together (the DANE brain) with concomitant firing of adrenergic neurons within the sympathetic branch of the ANS. High-gain NE pathways are known to lead to stress-induced disorders via the fear circuitry of the amygdala, especially post-traumatic stress disorder (PTSD).

The *locus coeruleus* is activated by the perception of stressful stimuli; and in turn, it liberates adrenaline, which increases cognitive focus and attention in prefrontal regions and affect—that is, motivation—via the NAcc in reward pathways of the MLS. Thus, the pathways' stress response is put into play within the cortices of the brain and glands of the body. Adrenaline is secreted from the adrenal glands as hormone blood messengers working double-duty as sympathetic nervous system jazzers. In a powerful network with affinity to DA, NE binds to plentiful adrenergic receptors throughout the brain.

Some highly addictive substances—such as opioids—inhibit firing of neurons in the locus coeruleus. When opioid use is curtailed, locus coeruleus activity is increased as cravings and contributes to symptoms of opiate withdrawal. Pharmacologically, the alpha-2 adrenoceptor agonist clonidine or Catagpres—a synthetic drug used in the treatment of hypertension, prevention of migraine headaches, and management of Tourette's syndrome—is effective in opiate withdrawal.

A moderate to low-gain DANE brainmark needs a boost to acquire attention and focus toward proactivity in life; therefore stimulant medication such as methylphenidate (Ritalin and Concerta), Adderall, and Dexedrine liberate NE to prefrontal regions targeting brains with attention deficit hyperactivity disorder (ADHD), or attention deficit disorder (ADD), in general. It is not known why stimulants work to mitigate hyperactivity in preadolescent (and in some pubescent adolescent) brains but not in adult brains.

Riot Squad: Testosterone

It is easy to see how testosterone is a gonzo sidekick to DANE brain. Moderate to elevated levels of testosterone, of course, enhance DANE's effects on the brain. This fact creates our number two argument—a strong and compelling argument—that testosterone is another chemical transmitters of neuroadaptive psychopathy in the brain.

As the hormone of aggression (even in mild gradations), testosterone is classified as a steroid hormone secreted by the male testes and the female ovaries with ancillary amounts from adrenal glands; it is a sex hormone lying behind *libido*—the sex drive as well as normal sexual functioning. In both males and females, it lies beneath radiant physical and emotional health, such as feeling energetic, and in the body, increasing production of red blood cells, muscle development, and strength, guarding against osteoporosis. Testosterone is an anabolic steroid, a tissue builder, and a stimulator of protein synthesis producing larger muscle mass in males as well as increased size of internal organs, including the brain.

Like all endogenous chemicals, amounts of testosterone reside along the ever-present spectrum—its own strength of gradation—as some individuals register high-gain varieties, some moderate, and other lower gradation, thus influencing a wide range of physical and psychological characteristics. High testosterone paired to agitation from a variety of low-gain brains is known to trigger violence.

What is the one brain mechanism able to prevent low-gain brain dirty tricks of the criminal variety? The answer is a highly developed PFC. If the PFC is immature or not well connected, irresistible emotion and urges are hard to bridle; the brain is overpowered. Imagine how this condition might escalate with an addiction to cocaine or methamphetamine, known to garishly overpopulate DA molecules at synapse. In this case, the brain would be at the mercy of the MLS—clearly a dangerous situation.

Virility Effects and Anabolic Effects of Testosterone

It was not until several large pharmaceutical firms in Europe began full-scale steroid research from the 1930s to 1960—the golden age of testosterone research—that we came to know the potency of circulating testosterone. Testosterone efficacy displays two characteristic effects: (1) *anabolic effects* typify growth in muscle mass, muscular strength, and increased bone maturation and density, while (2) *virility effects* typify maturation of sex organs, especially the penis and scrotum, and at puberty, secondary sex characteristics, such as voice deepening and ancillary body hair. Male brains are hypothesized to masculinize during infancy and early childhood as higher levels of testosterone circulate in the male body versus the female body. Before birth, the enzyme *aromatase* converts testosterone into *estradiol*, the fuse to the early developing male brain.

FORENSIC INVESTIGATIVE SCIENCE AND PATHOLOGICAL PSYCHOPATHY

Thus far, it is not a giant leap in logic to suggest that sexually psychopathic crime involves to one degree or another the following *gradations of circulating cascades of endogenous chemistry as brainmarks*:

- A low-gain dopamine brain would produce anhedonia and dysphoria typically translated into anger and frustration.

- A high-gain testosterone brain typically would produce hyper-masculine behavior with hypersexual libido.
- A low-gain 5-HT brain would produce low self-esteem and a feeling of emptiness.
- A low-gain GABA (gamma amino-butyric acid)—the major inhibitory neurotransmitter in the mammalian central nervous system—typically would produce anxiety and restlessness.
- A high-gain PEA brain, perhaps in specificity, known to lie beneath the "romantic rush" would be initiated by *specific physical traits* (for instance, observed in Ted Bundy's emotional connection to all victims that resembled ex-lover Stephanie Brooks, who wore her long chestnut hair parted down the middle).

The 10 pillars in the modern analysis of psychopathic criminal mind have systematically transformed academic degree plans in progressive institutions of higher education into forward-thinking curricula preparing tomorrow's forensic scientists, technicians, and academicians with never-before available interdisciplinary skills. What an exciting time in history to become a forensic investigative scientist.

Also, we stated plainly and unequivocally that the brain comes equipped with neuroadaptive chemical and cortical dynamics geared toward survival amid fierce competition with characteristics that are required for survival. Additionally, 180 degrees away, these characteristics meet the clinical standards for severe and irreversible PPD. To get a taste of violence and sexuality in extreme psychopathy like Edward Hyde is to go beyond the point of no return.

Extreme examples of violence mixed with sexual sadism—a condition of pornographic psychopathy—and other perversities noted in severe gradations of psychopathy and *possibly* compounded by deleterious effects of *predatory (toxic) parenting* on the developing brain send a clear and compelling message to those preparing for forensics careers: gradations of deception, entitlement, and lying come naturally to the brain. It is not a big leap in logic to posit that violent criminality is a matter of gradations along the spectrum of psychopathy. Sapient brains may rejoice in the maturity of the PFC—the harbinger of cooperation that lies behind peaceful relations in organized societies. In an increasingly permissive society without 21st-century criminal minds analysis, how would we ever rid society of dangerous and violent predators?

Forensic psychology's 21st-century criminal investigative tools and products of capture champion an interdisciplinary investigative science as the most important applied science in modern times. Individual investigators benefit from knowing what colleagues offer in disciplines outside their orbits of expertise. Collectively, this is another way of saying *we must understand the brain and its mental theater* to bridle criminal minds, cold-blooded homicide, and global terrorism. When we pause to consider the wonders of the human brain with all the modern tools of technology and instruments of investigation at our disposal, we indeed are standing on the hallowed ground of cutting-edge knowledge and insights into our collective human condition. I leave readers with a prescient quote to tease brilliant minds into further debates.

At some level all brain cell activity is chemical. Even the conduction of signals along the neuronal membrane, although an electrical transmission, is based upon chemical shifts across the membrane. The replication of the DNA molecular chain is chemically generated and controlled. The synthesis and delivery of neurotransmitters are, of course, chemical events. The hormones generated within the brain, and those delivered to the central nervous system from other organs, all exert chemical effects. Likewise, drugs, licit and illicit act by influencing the brain's chemistry. No crooked thought without a crooked molecule. (Cohen, 1988, p. 1)

REFERENCES

Ackerman, Diane. (2004). *An alchemy of mind: The marvel and mystery of the brain.* New York: Scribner.

Cohen, Sidney. (1988). *The chemical brain: The neurochemistry of addictive disorders.* Minneapolis: Care Institute.

Goldberg, Elkhonon. (2001). *The executive brain: Frontal lobes and the civilized mind.* New York: Oxford University Press.

Komisaruk, B. R., Beyer-Flores, C., & Whipple, B. (2006). *The science of orgasm.* Baltimore: Johns Hopkins University Press.

Larrabee, Glenn J. (2005). *Forensic neuropsychology.* New York: Oxford University Press.

Miller, Bruce, & Cummings, Jeffrey L. (1999). *The human frontal lobes: Functions and disorder.* New York: Guilford Press.

Ramachandran, V. S., & Blakeslee, Sandra. (1999). *Phantoms in the brain.* New York: HarperCollins.

Ratley, John J. *A user's guide to the brain. Perception, attention, and the four theaters of the brain.* New York: Vintage Books.

Read, Cynthia A. (2007). *Cerebrum 2007: Emerging ideas in brain science.* New York: Dana Press.

Restak, Richard. (2003). *The new brain: How the modern age is rewiring your mind.* Emmaus, PA: Rodale.

Rose, Steven. (2005). *The 21st century brain: Explaining, mending, and manipulating the mind*. London: Jonathan Cape.

Wexler, Bruce E. (2006). *Brain and culture: Neurobiology, ideology, and social culture*. Cambridge, MA: MIT Press.

Zeidler, Eberhard. (1995). *Applied functional analysis: Main principles and their applications*. New York: Springer-Verlag.

Chapter 10

Order Becoming Disorder

The brain is the organ of spectrum orders and disorders. This fact alone explains why adaptive neuropsychopathy remained hidden for so long as an evolutionary ordering of the brain; scientists were certain the condition was only a "disorder." In truth, psychopathic characteristics were merely engaging sapient brains in what we do best: the games of deceptive practices thereby misleading the best scientists in the world.

—Don Jacobs (2010), *res ipsa* observation

WEBS OF DECEPTION

"Richard Cory," the epic poem by Edwin Arlington Robinson, depicts a young man deep into deceptive practices. Presenting wealth and a flawless cosmetic appearance—he "glitters when he walks." Hidden below surface appearances in the deep catacombs of a troubled mind masquerade ugly truths that result in his shocking suicide—a violent episode with a bullet through the brain.

Brainmarks weaves the legal doctrine of *res ipsa* into the reality of adaptive neuropsychopathy, which is observed everywhere in children, adolescents, and young adults. It is the evolutionary inoculation that usually but sometimes fails to sustain life. Also, behind our naturally conniving brains, a sobering truth exists: behind every locked door across all communities families have secrets, often ugly truths they shudder to disclose—deep secrets that fester with malignant vengeful jealousies, arrogant pride, and deceit. Do we ever know what really is going on behind the smiling faces and false personas of our neighbors? Examples reach across all points of the compass in every community: from the church-going wife who lies about her age and is clandestinely sleeping with the soccer coach to middle school principals who are pursuing each other in sexual liaisons while their trusting and unsuspecting spouses coach community sports teams with their children as team members. Behind one and all is the crafty and conniving sapient brain deep into deception and dirty tricks.

Take, for instance, the sad news reported recently both locally and nationally of single mom Jayne Peters, once mayor of the affluent community of Coppell, Texas, and her 17-year-old daughter Corrine. The events in this real-life tragedy suggest that nature's protective cocoon of adaptive neuropsychopathy can be so traumatized that death seems the only way out. Left to her own devises after expensive attempts to save her husband from cancer, Jayne had almost lost her home to foreclosure amid mounting debts. She shared none of her emotional, parental, or financial problems with officials at work who might have suggested some way out of her emotional *ennui.* Increasingly desperate she resorted to the illegal use of a credit card issued to her by the city for business-related expenses. Daughter Corrine, apparently oblivious to the dire condition of their financial crisis, believed she was going to the University of Texas, Austin in a few months. Jayne's life was caving in on her from all side. Still, not a word to anyone but the family members who already had loaned her all the money they could. Then, in one violent brushstroke, she shot her daughter in the head and took her own life. Just like that.

The Adolescent Brain Programmed to Survive

The brain and behavior of our beloved and irreplaceable (but nonetheless at times difficult-to-raise) adolescents now make sense in light of how the brain marks behavior via cascading chemistry of neuroadaptive psychopathy within the MLS in childhood and in the developing teenage brain. In the 21st century, augmented by compelling adolescent neurobiological studies, all of the impulsivity, bad choices, sexual shenanigans, drug experimentation, and emotional drama that characterize and forever reverberate through the halls of Hormone High *make sense*. This is boot camp for the rigors of young adult responsibility to come: hard lessons must be learned and incorporated quickly into cortices of the PFC. In truth, it always has made *res ipsa* sense that young brains speak for themselves with turbo-charged neuroadaptive psychopathy, inoculating the mind against sadness and despair with psychological armor, such as the following:

- Superhuman entitlement—doing whatever teenagers thinks they are big enough to do, which is considerable, without thought of consequence; the familiar "leaping before looking"

- Self-absorbed narcissism, emblazoned with self-aggrandizement
- Insatiable curiosity with hedonistic adventure (pleasure-seekers)
- Utter reliance on lying and deception to get what they covet
- A blind trust in "peer tribe" mentality
- Youthful, radiant health, and magnetism (charm) promoting believ-ability in deceptive practices and dirty tricks
- Most dangerous yet most exciting stage of life before further matura-tion afforded the PFC of the young adult brain

BRAINMARKS OF ADAPTIVE NEUROPSYCHOPATHY

The Brainmarks Paradigm of Adaptive Neuropsychopathy offers sketches throughout this volume on how natural selection favors adaptive psychopathy as a brain condition most likely to survive any mil-lennial timeframe. No doubt, academicians and researchers will flesh out an expanded body of knowledge over the bare bones presented by this groundbreaking paradigm. Evidence for this wondrous and beneficial neuroadaptive brain condition is everywhere—from children, to adoles-cents, to young adults who are *born naturals* at all manners of deception in the game of surviving and thriving through dreaming and scheming accomplished by conniving. With teenage lives already overstimulated by iPods, Facebook, texting, and other distractions, teenagers have no idea of the sheer power of their sapient brains in every single activity they pursue. Interestingly, their tribe (peer group affiliation) is acclimated to a rich milieu of tribal psychopathy as a normal condition; lying to each other and on-the-fly cover-ups are daily rituals that inevitably produce the ever-present *teen drama.*

With powerful cascading chemistry—DA, NE (collectively the DANE brain) and turbocharged by testosterone and PEA—circulating through specific regions with connections brain-wide producing well-known and documented conditions—bulletproof entitlement, narcissism, and histri-onicism (drama), amped up with physiological and psychological vitality and virility from testosterone, it is no wonder that the human brain is such a fantastic organ of survival even during some of the most chaotic and dangerous phases of human existence.

Suicide, it now seems, is a failure of adaptive neuropsychopathy as a beneficial brain condition characterized by dreams and "life wishes."

Somehow, bulletproof entitlement and narcissism as cortical endow-ments fail in suicide—evidence of the bleakest outlook on life possible, in which case life is not salvageable and death looms as the only way out. Sapient brains apparently have limits to what a mind can tolerate.

Physical bullying and cyberbullying chip away at this beneficial version of psychopathy in rapid-fire fashion to produce toxic humiliation.

Congenital psychopathy means that we are born naturals at getting what we want and doing whatever it takes to get what we want (or think we want), even surviving really bad choices, humiliation, and embarrassing events.

A few topics sure to be embraced by early research into neuropsychopathy may include the following:

- The neurophysiological basis of low-adaptive neuropsychopathy levels in the brain relative to higher incidences of chronic depression, low self-esteem, and suicide. Almost surely, low 5-HT will factor into this pretzel of affect gradation.
- The specific neurochemical and neurohormonal initiators of the characteristics of "successful psychopathy" versus "unsuccessful psychopathy" across the spectrum.
- The relation between high-gain neuropsychopathy relative to moderate gradations of psychopathy, and how to mitigate its damaging effects with methods to jazz up precociously prefrontal regulatory control. Eventually, maturity of the PFC mitigates whatever is left of adolescent and young adulthood neuropsychopathy.

FORENSIC NEUROPSYCHOLOGY

One of the new tools presented in Chapter 1: Becoming a Forensic Investigative Scientist is *forensic neuropsychology*—the study and analysis of how characteristics of spectrum psychopathy may spill over into moderate gradations and then onward to severe (extreme) psychopathy—a robust engineer of violent, sexual predation producing death at horrific crime scenes. This is the best example of worst-case scenarios of psychopathy moving from order on the dial clear across to disorder with this most dangerous of all personality disorders.

I predict this paradigm will be the most populated by new careers launched by advanced interdisciplinary degrees from cutting-edge graduate schools mixing neurology, the neuroscience of neuropsychopathy, and neurochemistry, and how predatory toxic parenting and toxic social milieu may further degrade mild gradations (of order) into severe gradations producing violent disorder.

Although it has been known for centuries that the human brain is predatory, what was missing was an appreciation of the central roles of deception, entitlement, and narcissism, producing zero empathy and zero conscience by ways and means currently unknown. Living as we do in a postmodern world filled with uncertainties, bitter disappointments, losses, and ambiguities, what we observe as behavior in ourselves and others, through its powerful chemistry, deposits into cortices considerable doses of narcissism and entitlement to counteract a total collapse into ennui. The psychology of ennui and suicide ultimately appears due to lack of neuroadaptive psychopathy within sapient brains. In a worn-out analogy, brains indeed are like snowflakes—we all have highly individualized brains due to nature and nurture.

As we have seen, PPD, the first personality disorder described by psychiatrists, proved to be an accurate summation of extreme gradations of *order becoming disorder*. How and why does this happen? When forensic neuropsychopathy is "fleshed out" over the "bones" of violent brains, we may find the answers.

REFERENCES

Barbaree, Howard E., & Marshall, William L. (Eds.). (2006). *The juvenile sex offender* (2nd ed.). New York: Guilford Press.

Bear, Mark F., Connors, Barry W., & Paradiso, Michael A. (2001). *Neuroscience: Exploring the brain* (2nd ed.). Baltimore: Lippincott, Williams, & Wilkins.

Cooper, Jack R., Bloom, Floyd E., & Roth, Robert H. (1991). *The biochemical basis of neuropharmacology* (6th ed.). New York: Oxford University Press.

Formby, Brandon. (2010). Web of deceptions lay behind mayor's public façade. *Dallas Morning News*, July 20.

Kalachstein, Ari, & Van Grop, Wilfred G. (2007). *Neuropsychology and substance abuse: State of the art and future directions*. New York: Taylor & Francis.

Larrabee, Glenn. (Ed.). (2005). *Forensic neuropsychology*. New York: Oxford University Press.

Millon, Theodore, Simonsen, Erik, Birket-Smith, Morten, & Davis, Roger. (Eds.). (1998). *Psychopathy: Antisocial, criminal, and violent behavior*. New York: Guilford Press.

Ratley, John J. (2001). *A user's guide to the brain*. New York: Vintage Books.

Read, Cynthia A. (2007). *Cerebrum: Emerging ideas in brain science*. New York: Dana Press.

Rose, Steven. (2005). *The future of the brain*. New York: Oxford University Press.

Wexler, Bruce E. (2006). *Brain and culture: Neurobiology, ideology, and social change*. Cambridge, MA: MIT Press.

Autobiography of Lauren's Life: Tortured by Tears

What happens when the only person who can make you stop crying is the person that made you cry in the first place? This is what happened when I was tortured by tears: depression, anger, guilt, and anxiety; can't breathe, can't eat, can't sleep. Add the man who did this to me, and you will find the story that has most influenced my life.

He was my "everything"; he consumed my every thought. He was the answer to my prayers, or so I thought. Before him I could have cared less about a relationship. Now, I can't imagine my life without him, in good ways and bad ways.

Our fateful meeting took place at breakfast near our high school last year. Sitting at the other end of the table talking to my friends, I didn't realize he was even looking at me. I had made up my mind that I wasn't going to be in a relationship the rest of my senior year of high school before I went off to college; it caught me off guard when my best friend wrote me and told me that he wanted my number. Not knowing him, I told her to use her best judgment and give it to him if she wanted to. (I told my adolescent friend to use "her best judgment?" Who was I kidding?)

Minutes later, I received a text from a number that wasn't saved in my phone. I knew it was him. Surprisingly, we talked by text for hours that night. His text messages painted a picture of a charmer—a really nice guy. We even talked that night about going to prom together. Though, being a little skeptical, I contended that we should get to know each other a little better before making that decision.

Unbeknownst to me, *he already had me in his hands*. The second time I ever saw him was at his house with his parents when he invited me to dinner. I knew meeting his parents was quite a big step in our short courtship.

But by this time, I had already figured we were going to date, and I wanted our relationship to be special. By special, I meant deeper and more meaningful; and that's definitely what I got—the deeper, not the more meaningful.

The only date I ever recall going on with him was our first one, but it was amazing, at least to my adolescent sensibilities. We went bowling. I thought he was adorable. We teased each other about beating the other's score and made jokes and laughed the day away. That night we were official, after only a week of knowing each other.

The relationship progressed at the same speed. Spending many days at his house, I became very close to his family. His mom was the nicest person and always fun to talk to, and his brother was the typical little brother who looked up to his big brother. I even took my little cousin over to play with his little brother one day during the summer. Just that fast: they became my second family.

The family did display a few characteristics that were different from what I was used to, though. First, I learned that *everyone* in the family was on medication for depression, even his little brother; my boyfriend himself was also on medication for obsessive-compulsive disorder. Second, I learned his father was an alcoholic. He had been a fighter pilot in the military and received orders to blow up a building that killed many innocent people. This resulted in his dad abusing alcohol; in turn, this caused his entire family and himself to go on anti-depression medication. However, his dad came out of it and became a pilot for a commercial airline and was gone a lot. Because of this, I never really formed a relationship with him.

Anyway, as our relationship speedily progressed, I began noticing other things. I realized we had never gone out on another date besides the first one at the bowling alley—no dinner, no movie, nothing. When I brought up this fact, *he would always have an excuse that he had no money*. However, I saw right through that excuse when always had the money to buy new game stations and X-Box games. He even had the audacity to complain about driving to my house because of gas money, even though it was only 15 minutes away. Nevertheless, I ended up driving to his house 90 percent of the time.

When inquiring about why we would never go to a movie or any sort of outing, he would always send me on a guilt trip: "Why are you being like this? Isn't being with me enough?" Afterword, I would always apologize and attempt to rekindle our relationship, most of the time in tears, afraid of our relationship going to ruins.

However, on the good days, our relationship continued to progress full speed ahead. He always told me he loved me and that I was the best girl he had ever known. He would say that I was all he needed, and that he would do anything for me, and promised he would never leave me. On multiple occasions he would ask me to marry him, and my answer would always be, "someday."

Since college was starting soon for us, we came up with short-term and long-term plans for this contingency. Short-term plans included our different ways to make a long-distance relationship work, where we were going to go to college, and what were going to study. Our long-term plans included getting an apartment after two years, choosing the town we would live in when we would get married, and even as detailed as what our dog's name would be.

I realized I was spending much less time with my friends than in previous summers. In contrast, he didn't have many friends. He had an excuse for this as his family "had moved so much and so recently"; he didn't like being in big groups of people either. At the beginning of summer, right around graduation time, I remember missing most of my friends' graduation parties because he wanted me with him. During my best friend's graduation party I did manage to attend, he constantly texted that he missed me and that he wanted me with him. Even then, I ended up leaving early to spend time with him.

Why didn't I catch on to the toxicity of this relationship early on? I have no clue. I could only relate to what was constantly on my mind—him!

I hadn't realized it yet, but I was very dependent on him. Not having a male around in my single-parent household consisting of mom and me, he was the major male figure in my life. I felt protected when I was with him; vulnerable when I was away. I now know it is one of the differences between male brains and female brains. But, it doesn't have to be that way. He texted me every morning and all throughout the day until late in the evening. When I did see him we were virtually inseparable.

Therefore, on days when he was moody, it was very hard to not have an emotional outlet to share my troubles. So, I would often cry. My thoughts were constantly on him and my emotions were very dependent on him. Completely immersed in codependency, if he was upset, I was upset. If he was happy, I was happy. By the end of our third month of dating, he convinced me that I was depressed; he set me up for an appointment to get medication!

My worst fears came to be reality one night after he had one of his bad days where he wouldn't want to talk to me. *He told me that I was getting too obsessed with him and that it would be best if we broke up.* After getting very upset and crying on the phone questioning why he was doing this all of a sudden, I heard him crying in the background too. All I could hear him say was, "Ok, fine," in short, broken sobs. It never occurred to me until then how deeply and completely I had lost myself.

He took me back that night, but I didn't get a good night's rest. Instead of feeling instant relief, I felt confused and ambivalence in the form of relief, confusion, and anger. The next morning when I wrote him, he still sounded very restrained. When I asked him if he wanted to go to a comedy club because my cousin had gotten free tickets, he asked, "Is *she* going to be there?"—talking about my cousin; when I replied she was he refused to go and said that he *hated* her.

At this point, my anger overcame every other feeling I had toward him. That was my cousin he was talking about—the cousin who was actually more like my sister. I finally stood my ground against him. I told him that if he felt that way toward my family, he could just leave. With this, he said, "Ok," and that was that.

More relief rushed through my system than the night before, but still, half of me was screaming inside, "What did you just do?" Attempting to keep my mind off of him, I went with my cousin to the comedy club. However, as soon as I got home, I broke into tears and cried myself to sleep. This continued for the entire week. Looking back, I still can't believe that only dating him for four months had this much of a negative impact on me. How toxic would my life be now, had I not had the courage finally to end it.

About a week and a half later, he texted me late one night saying he missed me. I actually was fully relieved; I shouldn't have been, but I was. We didn't say much that night, but after what we did say, I had a feeling we would get back together; that was until the next day.

I got a message from an old friend of mine who happened to be the person that he dated before me. She asked why we broke up, and we began to share stories about similar things *he did to both of us*. Shockingly, our stories paralleled and were almost carbon copies to the point of where we went on our first date, even to the extent of using the same "pet names" he called both of us. She said that the weeks before he had broken up with me, he had been writing her and telling her that he missed her. When they broke up, they went out on a date and decided that they were going to try to get back together. However, when she asked her parents, they weren't so sure; they told her that she could only see him in big groups of people. It just so happened that on that night that she told him the news, he wrote me and told me that he missed me. Is this crazy?

Needless to say, we both became angry. The next day sitting next to each other on my couch, we arranged to text him at the same time. All of a sudden I asked him, "Do you still miss me?" When he replied back that he did, she texted him right afterword asking, "Do you miss me too?" Figuring out what we had accomplished, deceptively, we didn't hear from him for a while.

Unfortunately though, this isn't where my story ends. A few weeks after all of that drama, he wrote me and told me that he and his family were moving out of state. I was hesitant to give him back his stuff that he kept at my house, but after learning he was moving, I realized that I needed my things too; ultimately I didn't want him to leave without saying goodbye in person.

When my opportunity finally came, we hugged, and he acted almost as though nothing had happened between us. His mom even called us out in the driveway telling us to come in and have some pizza, as if it were just another day. As we were walking up the driveway, I felt him playfully grab my waist again like he used to, and look at me with his charming smile. It was more than enough to make me temporarily forget every reason that I had been angry. *Just like that, we were friends again.*

Although I will never forget all the things I've been through with him, I still struggle not to desire the type of toxic relationship we once had. *I wonder if there is something wrong with me.* I find myself criticizing all of the other possible boyfriends available that display normal behavior! He is still in the picture. We have remained friends ever since; I hope I am strong-willed enough to let him go.

The things that most importantly get me through these tough times are my friends, my music, and God—Him being the most important. My sadness had overcome me and left me lonely and depressed, but I was made alive again in God. With my friends, I am able to forget about sadness or pain; they encourage me to keep going. My music is a "soother" that allows me to have goals and achievements and escape from reality. In God I find my self-worth, meaning, and guidance for the rest of my life.

LAUREN'S BRAINMARKS

With Lauren, we have an example of adding another self-protective armor or inoculation against sadness and despair with her belief in God. This can be a very good thing. Regardless of the nature and substance of additional layers of protective armor against "giving up on life," life goes on. Why was Lauren so smitten? Is it the nature of the female brain to find completion with a partner who both hurts and soothes? Will females thus marked by their brains "do anything for love?" In contrast, is the male brain marked for "doing anything for sex?"

Although Lauren did not suffer violent abuse and tragic losses like Rachel and Sabrina, she still has experienced emptiness and longing for nurturing and tender affection. Are nurturing traits not entirely possible from high school or college-age students? Are adolescent males only capable of "sexual burglary" in the name of love? By late adolescence and young adulthood, might both males and females eventually find happiness and love due to PFC maturity?

Part IV

Truly, Honestly, Deceptively

troo-lee	accurately, legitimately, and genuinely
on-ist-lee	truthfully, credibly, and sincerely
dih-**sep**-tiv-lee	genuinely false; illegitimate and insincere

Chapter 11

Graduate Seminar

Good looks, a touch of charisma, a flood of words, contrived distractions, a knack of knowing which buttons to press—all these can go a long way toward obscuring the fact that the psychopathic presentation is nothing more than a "line." A good-looking, fast-talking psychopath and a victim who has "weak spots" is a devastating combination.
—Robert Hare (1993, p. 145)

Deception allows everyone the appearance of winning.
—Don Jacobs (2011), *res ipsa* observation

Gender Differences among Psychopathic Serial Murderers

Ashleigh Portales, MFS

Crime Analyst/Crime Scene Investigator, Sheriff's Office Wise County, Texas

Although male psychopathic serial killers are at the forefront of American pop culture and academic research and literature, the female psychopathic serial killer has largely been ignored by both realms of modern society. The existence of a predator about which so little information is known poses a significant threat. Compared with her male counterparts, female psychopathic serial killers tend to be geographically stable, work in traditionally female occupations, choose known victims, employ covert killing methods, and exhibit a myriad of comorbid psychiatric diagnoses, but significant exceptions exist that directly challenge such stereotypes. Additional research, including personal interviews with incarcerated offenders, is needed to fill in the numerous knowledge gaps that exist concerning these elusive killers.

INTRODUCTION

Since Jack the Ripper lurked unseen in the gas-lit London fog, serial murder has captivated the attention not only of law enforcement but also of the media and the general public. Most commonly and correctly defined as the killing of at least three victims in separate events with a cooling-off period between each kill (Jacobs, 2003; Myers, Husted, Safarik, & O'Toole, 2006), the concept of serial killing has become common household knowledge in modern American society. Such familiarity is no doubt aided by the fact that the United States not only boasts the highest global homicide rate but also is home to more serial killers than any other spot on the planet (Schurman-Kauflin, 2000). For homicide, in general, men average a rate of commission nearly six times that of women (Frei, Vollm, Graf, & Dittmann, 2006). As for serial murder in particular, anywhere from 50 to 75 serial killers are believed to be operating at any given time in the United States, of which only seven or eight are female (Schurman-Kauflin, 2000). A relatively rare occurrence, serial killing is estimated to account for just 0.5 to 1.0 percent of all homicides, an amount that translates to between 70 and 140 victims annually (Perri & Lichtenwald, 2010). Of these who fall prey to a serial killer, only about 5 to 10 percent meet their fate at the hands of a female perpetrator (Perri & Lichtenwald, 2010).

Due in part to the fact that women are significantly underrepresented among the population of known serial killers, faulty public perception equates this type of crime primarily with males, resulting in the existence of the female serial killer largely ignored by the public. "Violent aggression is still considered the province of men, one of the pervasive myths of our time" (Perri & Lichtenwald, 2010, p. 52). Historically patriarchal in nature, American society views female assertion and aggression as a threat and thus promotes the belief that such things are "unnatural and atypical" (Perri & Lichtenwald, 2010, p. 52). Rather than confront the seemingly contradictory reality that women can be just as fatal as men, people would rather sweep reality under the rug in favor of those ideals that agree with their picture of how the world should function. A prime example of this was seen in the case of Aileen Wuornos, who was deemed the first female serial killer by the media, an assertion taken as fact by the general public, when in fact the first recorded female serial killer was identified in Roman historical accounts as Locusta the Poisoner, whose list of known victims included the Emperor Claudius and his heir (Newton, 2006). The reluctance of society to truly believe that women are capable of committing the horror that is serial murder can also be seen in the disproportionate application of the death penalty. In January of 2005, 49 U.S. women were

Jack the Ripper captivated the attention of law enforcement, the media, and the general public. (From Furniss, Harold. (1904). *Famous crimes past and present: Jack the Ripper*. London: Caxton House)

on death row, including six serial killers. However, since the reinstatement of capital punishment in 1979, only 10 women have been executed in contrast to 906 men (Newton, 2006).

Furthermore, it appears that this public ignorance has spilled over into the realm of professional research conducted in the world of academia. In a male-dominated society that perceives female aggression as an "anomaly" (Perri & Lichtenwald, 2010, p. 53), the public perspective has guided research, resulting in a bias of studies that equate female violence only with an understandable and excusable retaliatory reaction to victimization. Such a narrow focus on "justifiable and excusable homicide" (Arrigo & Griffin, 2004, p. 375) has resulted in an underestimation of the strength and number of this type of killer and her crimes. And as professional knowledge and discovery operate in a feedback loop with society as a whole, the result is that the phenomenon of female serial predation has remained largely undervalued by society (Arrigo & Griffin, 2004), continuing the vicious cycle of turning a blind eye to a dangerous and mainly undetected predator.

In addition to the erroneous idea that serial killers are always male, media monikers such as "The Night Stalker," "The Killer Clown," "Zodiac," and "BTK" conjure images of blatantly psychotic (not true, however) and evil men who kill without reason or clear motivation. Yet things are not always what they are perceived to be, and serial killing is no exception. A psychotic mental state is the exception when dealing with this type of offender. The rule here is psychopathy; serial killers generally are psychopathic. Present in incarcerated populations at the rate of approximately 16 percent female and 25 percent male (Strand & Belfrage, 2005), the psychological construct of psychopathy is defined as a continuous display of the following affective and behavioral characteristics: glibness and superficial charm, a grandiose sense of self-worth, pathological lying, conning and manipulative behaviors, a lack of remorse or guilt, shallow affect, callousness, lack of empathy, a parasitic lifestyle, promiscuity, childhood conduct issues, poor behavioral controls, a lack of realistic long-term goals, impulsivity, irresponsibility, and a failure to accept responsibility (Arrigo & Griffin, 2004; Cleckley, 1976; Hare & Neumann, 2009; Jacobs, 2003; Weizmann-Henelius, Sailas, Viemero, & Eronen, 2002). The presence of psychopathy significantly predicts violent criminal behavior, parole failure, violent recidivism, and poor response to psychological interventions (Cooke & Michie, 2001; Hare & Neumann, 2009; Hicks, Vaidyanathan, & Patrick, 2010). A key feature of psychopathy that is highly relevant when discussing criminal motivations and responsibility is the fact that psychopaths are not mentally ill or disoriented but rather have intact reality testing and rationally choose their actions (Perri & Lichtenwald, 2010). *Plainly put, psychopaths are not crazy or insane.* Rather, they know what they are doing and select their actions by virtue of will. Psychopaths have been described accurately as "intraspecies predators who . . . cold-bloodedly take what they want and do as they please . . . without the slightest sense of guilt or regret . . . [and use the] external mask of normalcy . . . to shield the true mask of exploitation" (Perri & Lichtenwald, 2010, p. 54–55). The picture painted by these words is that of a psychopathic serial killer. When all the related definitional elements are combined, the psychopathic serial killer emerges as one who commits serial murder for the pleasure it brings. He or she is not psychotic but exceptionally psychopathic (Jacobs, 2003). Taking the life of another brings pleasure and "exhilaration" (Myers et al.,

2006, p. 902), which propels the continuity of the killing career. Others are viewed as objects, mere pawns to be manipulated and overtaken at the whim and for the gratification of the killer.

Although similar in some respects and often comorbid, psychopathy is not to be confused with Antisocial Personality Disorder (APD), the latter of which focuses on blatant antisocial behaviors, whereas the former centers on interpersonal and affective features (Hare & Neumann, 2009). Furthermore, APD correlates to impulsivity, aggression, irresponsibility, child abuse, and comorbid Cluster A personality disorders, whereas psychopathy generally correlates to property crimes, recidivism, and a consistent lack of remorse (Warren & South, 2006). A unique relationship exists between the construct of psychopathy and APD. Most psychopaths meet diagnostic criteria for APD, but most with APD do not meet criteria for psychopathy (Hare & Neumann, 2009). For example, up to 80 percent of those incarcerated meet diagnostic criteria for APD whereas only about 20 percent meet criteria for psychopathy (Warren & South, 2006). Congruently, a general association exists between APD and criminality that is not necessarily seen in psychopathy. Many who are diagnosed with APD are not psychopathic and many who are psychopathic are not violently criminal but rather are highly successful in the professional and political realms (Cooke & Michie, 2001), where cunning, manipulation, a large ego, and the ability to use others without feeling guilty are keys to corporate advancement.

PSYCHOPATHIC SERIAL KILLERS

Regardless of gender, some characteristics and behaviors universally appear across research conducted on serial killers, many of which begin in childhood or early adolescence. The childhoods of serial killers often are characterized by abandonment, instability, and abuse (Jacobs, 2003; Schurman-Kauflin, 2000). Juvenile delinquency, including charges for theft and assault, is considered a significant predictor of adult psychopathy across gender (Ressler, Burgess, & Douglas, 1992; Sevecke, Kosson, & Krischer, 2009). Also included in the deviant adolescent behaviors considered to be highly predictive of psychopathy in general and serial killing in particular are those actions that make up MacDonald's Homicidal Triad, which include fire-setting, enuresis at an inappropriate age, and cruelty to animals or small children (Jacobs, 2003; Keeney & Heide, 2006), all of which are seen in some combination in the history of nearly all psychopathic serial killers (Frei et al., 2006). This triad's behaviors generally are considered to be outward expressions of the developing violent fantasy life of the growing psychopath (Schurman-Kauflin, 2000). Deviant neurocognitive mapping, in which inflicting pain on another becomes equated with power and dominance, lays the groundwork for murder (Jacobs, 2003). Psychopaths begin to plot ways to attain what they have not been able to garner thus far in their real lives and to become the aggressor in the same sorts of scenarios that have been played out against them in their lives. Violence in fantasy increases until fantasy alone is no longer sufficient and when the right victim is unfortunate enough to become paired with the fantasy, murder is the result.

In addition to overt behaviors and private fantasies, several interpersonal and affective traits considered diagnostic criteria for psychopathy typically are evidenced in psychopathic serial killers, thereby supporting the assertion that female versions are significantly more than the myth society would like to believe them to be. Psychopathic serial killers are charming, manipulative, and deceitful (Perri & Lichtenwald, 2010) and consistently display superficiality and a shallowness of emotion that is evident even at the neurological level (Sutton, Vitale, & Newman, 2002). These traits entice victims into the company of the killer; he or she is made to feel at ease by one who, on the surface, gives the appearance of a sincere and genuine human. The psychopathic killer's ability to feel true emotion, however, has been replaced with an insatiable desire for power, the pursuit and ultimate attainment of which brings perverse pleasure that is a replacement for the experience of normal human emotion (Jacobs, 2003; Perri & Lichtenwald, 2010). The psychopathic serial killer is extremely conning and a pathological liar who lacks guilt or remorse for any action (Frei et al., 2006; Perri & Lichtenwald, 2010). In fact, the inability to feel the emotion of guilt frees the serial killer to engage in calculating, predatory aggressive behaviors to satisfy his or her perverse needs (Perri & Lichtenwald, 2010). Beginning as early as age 12 or sometimes even younger (Schurman-Kauflin, 2000), the rapacious behaviors of predatory aggression consist of planned and purposeful violent actions taken against one who poses little or no significant threat without the accompanying experience of emotion to achieve a predetermined goal (Arrigo & Griffin, 2004; Jacobs, 2003). Time is taken to plot the kill to ensure the best possible satisfaction of the goal (Perri & Lichtenwald, 2010). These behaviors are directly akin to those seen in the animal kingdom. The predatory beast stalks the weaker animal prey because he is hungry and in need of satisfaction. He does not rush into the kill but rather takes his time, stalking the unsuspecting prey until the time is right to make a move. When the deed is done and the carcass is left behind, the predator does not feel guilty about what he has done. His needs were met and his desires temporarily quenched. In his mind, he resides at a spot higher on the food chain than the one whose life he has taken and there is no need for remorse over the loss of one whose existence is so trivial. Personal satisfaction is his only care.

In many respects, "psychopathy is well suited to predation" (Ariggo & Griffin, 2004, p. 381). Low autonomic arousal sustains the requisite stalking behaviors because the ability to focus on a singular target of obsession translates to the predator remaining fixed on the goal and the careful execution of a preordained plan (Arrigo & Griffin, 2004). The accompanying lack of emotion and inability to empathize with others allows for the depersonalization of the victim as well as exhilaration during the stalking phase and in the commission of the murder (Arrigo & Griffin, 2004). Pain felt by the victim does not register with the killer because the victim is objectified and dehumanized in the killer's eyes. Additionally, because the victim is something less than human, the killer does not recognize a need to feel remorse for what he or she has done (Perri & Lichtenwald, 2010). Furthermore, the psychopath's grandiose sense of self is fed by media attention given to his or her crimes, simultaneously heightening the killer's sense of self-worth and feeding the desire for fame and recognition (Arrigo & Griffin, 2004). This can only fuel the fires and propel the killer to take further victims.

The psychopathic serial killer also engages in blame externalization (Perri & Lichtenwald, 2010; Weizmann-Henelius et al., 2002) and exerts great effort in the area of impression management. The psychopathy so deeply ingrained in the killer's psyche will not allow him or her to see the self as being at fault for anything that happens. Even when confronted with the fact that they have murdered multiple people, the killer often will shift the blame back to the victim for some behavior or perceived slight directed toward the killer (Jacobs, 2003). Furthermore, the killer constantly engages in impression management by maintaining the false perceptions that those in his or her life have of the killer. Ensuring that others believe in the mask that the psychopath is wearing and continue to mistake it for reality allows this killer to continue in his or her pursuits for personal satisfaction—the taking of more victims. Suspicion must be deflected away from the killer so he or she strives to appear as the best citizen possible so as to be the last person anyone would suspect of such horrific actions. Amazingly, the factors of blame externalization and impression management often continue well after incarceration (Jacobs, 2003). Even in the face of insurmountable evidence, psychopathic serial killers will proclaim their innocence to the grave, often attempting to befriend guards and reporters who speak with them, or if they do admit the commission of murder, they will downplay the circumstances of the crime and attempt to shift as much blame as possible onto the victim or even society as a whole for making the killer into the monster that he or she truly is. Accordingly, psychopathy in serial killers is highly resistant to treatment. Psychopathy is "strongly entrenched" (Hare & Neumann, 2009, p. 798) in the neurological and behavioral systems and directly opposed to change because the psychopath blames others and fails to see fault with him or herself. Treatment is generally sought and successful completion manipulated only when it may serve some personal gain, such as parole (Hare & Neumann, 2009). In short, a psychopath is a psychopath for life (Jacobs, 2003).

MALE PSYCHOPATHIC SERIAL KILLERS

Characteristics and Behaviors

In addition to exhibiting all the behaviors and characteristics discussed above, research has found certain traits that are considered to be unique to male psychopathic serial killers. This type of male killer tends to gravitate toward traditionally masculine occupations (Jacobs, 2003), most likely in an effort to restore and assert the masculinity that has been taken from them in their personal lives and that they aim to recapture via serial murder. Methods of victim selection also set male serial killers apart. Males generally are mobile in their hunt for victims and seek out strangers to kill rather than people they know (Jacobs, 2003). Just any stranger will not do, however. In their mobility, these killers exhibit clear stalking behaviors, such as trolling for victims and actively pursuing the ones they desire, showing clear preference for a specific type of victim above all others (Jacobs, 2003; Keeney & Heide, 2006). Generally, the type of victim selected is believed to correspond to the individual in the killer's own life whom he would like to eliminate but cannot because of the power that person exerts over him (Jacobs, 2003). A prime example of this behavior is seen in the crimes of Theodore Robert "Ted" Bundy, whose female collegiate victims all wore their long dark hair parted down the middle, just as the former lover who had rejected him had done (Jacobs, 2003).

The treatment of their victims is another factor in defining male serial killers. Men generally have superior physical strength and, as such, often choose to render their victim helpless when the time is right (Jacobs, 2003). Once this has been achieved and the victim is under the control of the killer, he typically engages in overt killing methods, utilizing weapons such as guns and knives (Schurman-Kauflin, 2000) and taking an overall "hands-on approach" (Keeney & Heide, 1994) to murder, including such actions as stabbing and strangling the victim. It is often this feeling of literally holding the life of another person, especially one symbolic of the object of the killer's hatred, which brings the empowerment the killer so desperately desires.

Another key factor in distinguishing the gender of serial killers is their motivations for committing their crimes. Males, who tend to score higher on aggression, social dominance, and agency *Psychopathy Checklist–Revised* (PCL-R) scales than women (Hicks et al., 2010; Keeney & Heide, 2006), seek to gain power. The defining element, however, is the way in which males achieve this power: sexualized serial homicides. Although not directly about the act of sex itself, sex is closely associated with power. Tied to strong deviant sexual fantasies that eventually are insufficient to satisfy the killer (Ressler et al., 1992), the perverse and violent sexual actions perpetrated by the killer against the victim both before and after death serve as a medium for the imagined transfer of power from the victim to the killer.

Finally, male psychopathic serial killers are unique in some of the psychological disorders that frequently present comorbidly with their psychopathy. APD is a frequent additional diagnosis, especially when the criteria are met in childhood (Forouzan & Cooke, 2005). Additionally, the deviant sexual aspects of the crimes frequently are explained by the presence of sadism in the personality of the offender (Forouzan & Cooke, 2005).

FEMALE PSYCHOPATHIC SERIAL KILLERS

Characteristics and Behaviors

It has been said of the female psychopath that "she can lie with the straightest face" (Cleckley, 1976, p. 47) while her conscience remains "untouched" (Cleckley, 1976, p. 49). But though the female psychopathic serial killer may resemble her male counterparts in this way, she differs significantly from him in many others. Approximately 15 percent of male offenders meet criteria for psychopathy, while only 10 percent of female offenders do (Hare & Neumann, 2009). Yet, although female rates may be lower than those of males, it is beginning to emerge from the research that males and females may vary in the manners in which they exhibit psychopathic criteria (Weizmann-Henelius, Viemero, & Eronen, 2004). The female serial killer tends to gravitate to traditionally female occupations (Schurman-Kauflin, 2000), sometimes referred to as "pink-collar" jobs (Keeney & Heide, 2006), such as nursing and caregiving roles (Frei et al., 2006; Keeney & Heide, 2006). These women generally come from homes in which traditional male-female roles are perpetuated and caregiving is what they know how and have been socialized to do (Schurman-Kauflin, 2000). Another traditionally female occupation, though arguably not as respectable as nursing, is prostitution, a field that also harbors many female serial killers (Warren & South, 2006; Keeney & Heide, 2006). Higher rates of unemployment, unstable relationships, and use of social welfare programs are seen in female psychopaths when compared with males (Perri & Lichtenwald, 2010). Victim selection for these killers is also directly tied to their job. Unlike male killers, women tend to be geographically stable, living and often working in the same area in which they kill (Frei et al., 2006; Keeney & Heide, 2006; Perri & Lichten-wald, 2010). Accordingly, women generally kill victims with whom they are either acquainted or with whom they have a personal relationship, such as husbands, children, and patients (Frei et al., 2006). In fact, those in the custodial care of female serial killers are most often their victims, nearly 43 percent, with family members coming in second at 37 percent, and strangers, acquaintances, and lovers to whom they are not married constituting the final 20 percent (Frei et al., 2006). Furthermore, female serial killers generally do not express a gender preference when it comes to victim selection, favoring instead the convenience of a helpless victim, such as an elderly individual or a child (Frei et al., 2006). Like the spider on her web, female killers generally lure rather than stalk their victims in ways such as posting ads for boarders, ensnaring husbands and lovers, and engaging in prostitution (Keeney & Heide, 2006). It is likely that this is where the females' mask of psychopathy is prominently displayed—in the seduction and lure of victims (Perri & Lichtenwald, 2010). Interest-ingly, in addition to killing children, both her own biological children as well as those in her care, female psychopaths are highly more likely than males to abandon or neglect their biological children (Warren & South, 2006; Weizmann-Henelius et al., 2004). It is speculated that this happens in part because, during pregnancy, the woman commands the attention of others, which feeds her narcissism, but this attention shifts to the child once it is born. Getting rid of the child may be a way of reconciling this injury to her grandiose self-image (Perri & Lichtenwald, 2010).

Once the victims have been selected, female psychopathic serial killers tend to further divert from the path of the males by engaging in covert killing methods (Perri & Lichtenwald, 2010). Poison often emerges as the weapon of choice (Frei et al., 2006; Keeney & Heide, 2006; Perri & Lichtenwald, 2010; Schurman-Kauflin, 2000) with suffocation and asphyxi-ation also being popular methods for murder (Perri & Lichtenwald, 2010; Schurman-Kauflin, 2000). The choice to use these methods to kill is likely rooted in the reduced physical strength of females when compared with males, but these killers also take advantage of another aspect of these methods in that they are significantly harder to detect than the gunshots, stab wounds, and ligature marks left behind by male serial killers. The implementation of these covert killing methods often results in a failure by law enforcement and others close to the matter to identify the fact that a homicide, or a series of homicides, has actually even occurred (Keeney & Heide, 2006). For this reason, combined with the reluctance of society to suspect a woman of serial murder, female serial killers generally have longer killing careers than males (Perri & Lichtenwald, 2010), averaging 8.4 years before capture compared with the male rate of 4.2 years (Schurman-Kauflin, 2000). The female serial killer's success often is enhanced by the fact that she does not generally engage in pre- and postmortem torture or mutilation of the victim, the completion of which is often key to the satisfaction produced by the killing for male serial killers (Keeney & Heide, 2006) but also makes his crimes significantly more noticeable as such and draws the attention of law enforcement much earlier in his killing career. Such difficulty in the detection of female serial murderers is further compounded by the fact that females express an even higher concern with impression management than males and go even further to maintain their innocent public image (Perri & Lichtenwald, 2010)

Like her male counterpart, the female psychopathic serial killer is motivated primarily by the need for power and control over others. Her need for domination is key (Schurman-Kauflin, 2000). She differs, however, in how she aims to achieve this power. Be it by the acquisition of the victim's money or other valuable assets or simply the authority of deciding who lives and dies at what times, the female serial killer rarely sexualizes her quest for control and authority of another. That is not to say that female sexually psychopathic serial killers do not exist. They simply are an extreme rarity when compared with the number of men who commit similar crimes. Women generally participate in sexual homicide only when working in a male-female serial killing partnership (Perri & Lichtenwald, 2010). Just as in males, paraphilia such as arousal from seeing or touching a corpse can fuel murder in females and is most likely to exist when women kill in female-female teams (Ramsland, 2007). No matter what the method, the female psychopathic serial killer meets or even exceeds her male counterparts' lack of remorse. Females have been shown to exhibit lower feelings of guilt than males, especially when they have committed previous crimes (Weizmann-Henelius et al., 2002).

Concerning psychiatric variables and psychopathy, incarcerated female psychopaths show higher rates and intensity of psychopathology, early environmental deprivation, victimization, and lower levels of functioning than male counterparts (Hicks et al., 2010). Females also score higher on stress reaction, social closeness, and behavioral constraint PCL-R scales than men (Hicks et al., 2010) and are more likely to have a psychiatric history than males (Sevekce, Lehmkuhl, & Krischer, 2009). Furthermore, they display significantly higher levels of anxious, depressive, self-harming, and suicidal behaviors than males (Sevecke, Kosson, & Krischer 2009).

It has been speculated by some researchers that the female display of the psychopathic characteristic of impulsivity, normally seen as the exploitation of others in males, may be seen as self-injurious (Weizmann-Henelius et al., 2004). In terms of diagnoses comorbid with psychopathy, females exhibit some of the same psychological disorders seen in males and others that are unique to the female gender. Female psychopathy is frequently comorbid with APD, especially adult criteria (Forouzan & Cooke, 2005; Weizmann-Henelius et al., 2004), which stands in contrast to the male version in which childhood criteria is the factor of greater significance. Additionally, attention deficit hyperactivity disorder (ADHD) is a significant correlate to female psychopathy, especially the characteristics of callousness, a lack of empathy, and impulsivity and irresponsibility (Sevecke, Lehmkuhl, & Krischer 2009). Also commonly diagnosed are histrionic, borderline, and paranoid personality disorders (Strand & Belfrage, 2005; Weizmann-Henelius et al., 2004).

CASE STUDIES

Aileen Wuornos

Often erroneously identified as the first female serial killer (Newton, 2006), Aileen Wuornos was one of the first women to draw national attention to the fact that women could kill serially with the same aggression as men. Born in 1956 to a teenage mother and a father who would receive a life sentence for the brutal kidnapping and rape of a 17-year-old girl and later committed suicide in prison, Aileen and her brother Keith believed their maternal grandparents were actually their parents until the age of 11 (Arrigo & Griffin, 2004; Newton, 2006). She and her brother suffered sadistic abuse at the hands of their grandfather, Laurie Wuornos, including being tied naked to the bed for beatings with a belt and possible sexual abuse. It was also rumored that incest had occurred between Aileen and Keith (Arrigo & Griffin, 2004). Aileen's adolescence was characterized by unpredictable and violent outbursts of anger, including many fights, sexual favors done for boys in exchange for cigarettes and loose change, shoplifting, drunkenness, and multiple encounters with law enforcement (Arrigo & Griffin, 2004). She gave birth to a baby boy just after her 15th birthday, and neighborhood rumor held that the father was her brother, grandfather, or a neighbor. Whoever the father was, Aileen's grandfather gave up the baby for adoption, and Aileen dropped out of school and was kicked out of her grandparents' home (Arrigo & Griffin, 2004; Newman, 2006). By the age of 16 she was hitchhiking across the country and wound up in Florida. At 20, she married a man in his 70s who filed for divorce and a restraining order one month later, claiming she beat him with his own cane (Arrigo & Griffin, 2004). After the divorce, she continued her life of hitchhiking and prostitution while accumulating numerous legal charges, including assault and battery, disorderly conduct, driving under the influence, and weapons possession, many of which were booked under her many aliases (Arrigo & Griffin, 2004; Newman, 2006).

Aileen always had a "fascination with fame" and often commented that one day a book would be written about her life. She told her friend that she and lesbian lover Tyria Moore were "going to be like Bonnie and Clyde and that they would be doing society a favor" (Arrigo & Griffin, 2004, p. 385). As Aileen became older, she grew to the point that she would seek out confrontation with others and, by November of 1989, she had graduated to the point at which she was ready to kill. Her typical method of operation was to pick up a john, undress herself, and coerce the man into taking off his clothes. While he was undressing, she would exit her side of the car and shoot and kill the man, often with multiple shots, usually screaming something to the effect of "I knew you were going to rape me!" (Arrigo & Griffin, 2004, p. 386). She always stayed to watch the victim before putting her clothes back on and taking his belongings. She would then drive the victim's car to a remote location, abandon it, then drink all the beer she had left before returning to whatever hotel she and Tyria were staying in (Arrigo & Griffin, 2004, Newton, 2006).

Aileen Wuornos was executed at Broward Correctional Institution in Pembroke Pines, Florida, on October 9, 2002, after being convicted of seven murders. To her way of thinking, all of her victims deserved to die. It could be argued that when Aileen killed these men she was symbolically killing her grandfather. As such, she never showed any true remorse for what she had done. She displayed completely unimpaired reality testing and was strongly psychopathic (Arrigo & Griffin, 2004), meeting all classic diagnostic criteria for psychopathy (Frei et al., 2006; Keeney & Heide, 2006; Perri & Lichtenwald, 2010; Schurman-Kauflin, 2000). She lived a life of deceit and showed calculation and restraint by not killing the hundreds of other men she prostituted herself to. She also was charming enough to get her victims to pick her up and make them at ease in her presence. It is unknown why she specifically chose the victims she did, but she did demonstrate the traditionally male characteristic of showing a gender preference in her victim selection (Jacobs, 2003; Keeney & Heide, 2006). Her overt killing methods, mobility, and choice to kill strangers rather than those with whom she was familiar are all additional characteristics more common to male serial killers (Jacobs, 2003; Schurman-Kauflin, 2000).

Colleen Rice

Another equally violent but much less well known female psychopathic serial killer is the now deceased Colleen Rice, whose story, or what is known of it, is best told by Kevin Benton, currently an investigator for the Wise County District Attorney's Office, who pursued Rice through several states (personal communication, 2010). Benton, who has been a law enforcement officer for 23 years and investigated the murders of four serial killers during that time, became involved in Rice's case in February of 1996 when he was working for the Cooke County District Attorney's Office. The body of a nude male with severe head trauma was discovered wrapped in a blanket in a vacant barn off I-30 in Gainesville, Texas, by a couple searching for scrap metal. While conducting a thorough search of the scene, Benton discovered several plastic trash bags containing bloody bedding and towels in the back of the barn. Noticeable on the outside of the trash bags were fingerprints left in what was presumably the victim's blood. Autopsy later confirmed that the victim, identified as 51-year-old James Morrisette, had been shot through the right eye with a 0.22 caliber pistol and had suffered an additional 15 to 20 blows to the back of the head, many of which had punctured his skull. Further investigation revealed that Mr. Morrisette, along with his wife, 57-year-old Joan Marie Morrisette, had been pulling a camper behind his truck while making the cross-country trip to visit his family in California. The pair never arrived. When fingerprint comparison matched the prints found in James Morrisette's blood on the outside of the trash bags to those of his wife, a warrant was issued for her arrest. A database search conducted using her fingerprints also matched those of a woman with outstanding warrants in Georgia and Florida, although under different names. The Georgia warrant was for a weapons charge and the Florida warrant was for a similarly violent offense in which the woman pulled a 0.22 caliber pistol on a storeowner who caught her shoplifting. The storeowner later told Investigator Benton that he had instinctively grabbed the weapon and the two had grappled over it. In fact, the woman had pulled the trigger several times but the hammer of the weapon became hung on the web of his hand and it was unable to fire.

With this information and an arrest warrant for murder in hand, Benton, accompanied by a Texas Ranger, took off in a jet supplied by the Texas Department of Public Safety on a trip that would take them through several states. Much to his dismay, the pair always fell a step behind Mrs. Morrisette, who was moving from one campground to the next and always using drop boxes in adjacent towns for her mail. When renting the boxes, she gave an address of one of the campgrounds she had stayed in two or three moves back, keeping the investigators at bay for a year. Within that time, however, Benton and the Texas Ranger garnered useful information about their murder suspect. She had used several aliases, including "Colleen Rice," "Juanita Sands," "Diane Cordero," and "Joan Fiebig." She had stayed in Tennessee, Georgia, Florida, and Alabama, always taking jobs sitting with the elderly in their homes, an occupation that provided ample opportunity for stealing identifications and social security numbers. At one time, she had undergone treatment for advanced stage cancer at a Georgia clinic, but that was where her trail ran cold and Benton and the Texas Ranger returned home to Texas empty-handed.

It seemed that a break had come in 2000, when Benton got a call from California informing him that the woman he was looking for had been arrested and was in jail in the state. Fingerprints confirmed, however, that it was not in fact the alleged murderess he sought, but rather a woman whose name she had stolen who had been arrested. Yet the mix-up proved not to be a complete loss, as through it, Benton learned that Homicide Investigators in Houston, Texas, also had been notified of the woman's arrest because a woman by that name was wanted in connection with the murder of a man in that city. When Benton contacted the Houston Police Department, he learned that his suspect had been living with a man by the last name of Murphy in an apartment there until she disappeared one day after a neighbor heard a gunshot coming from the unit and reportedly saw her leave the scene. When police arrived, they found Murphy dead in the apartment he shared with her, shot through the left eye. Convinced that the woman he knew as "Morrisette" and the woman in Houston were one and the same, a frustrated Benton filed this information away and prayed that another more promising break would soon come.

His prayers were answered three years later in December 2003 when he, now working as in investigator for the Montague County District Attorney's Office, received a call from his previous boss in Cooke County about the murder nearly eight years before Gainesville. It seemed that the prime suspect was now in jail in Boca Raton, Florida, under the name

"Cordova," and this time her identity as the one who left the bloody fingerprints at the Texas crime scene had been confirmed through fingerprints. Benton boarded a plan to Florida in hopes of getting a confession from the woman he had sought for so long. When he met with the police in Boca Raton he was more than a little shocked by the story they told him. The woman they knew as "Cordova" had been living in the homeless community of the city for quite some time and recently had been taken in by a local real estate agent who made it her hobby to choose a homeless person to bring into her home for rehabilitation. She apparently had gotten a little more than she bargained for with her latest project, however, when "Cordova" became extremely hostile as soon as the woman's husband came home. Her behavior caused several arguments, including one in which she dropped her pants and defecated on the living room floor. At this point, the husband demanded that his wife remove the woman from the home but, rather than comply, she hid her away in the basement and the pair were soon out shopping for a used van, at "Cordova's" request. While shopping, however, "Cordova" confided to the woman that she had killed "a couple of husbands" in her past, including one in Washington State. At the advice of her lawyer, the woman took her charge to the Boca Raton Police, who confirmed the identity of "Cordova" via a Federal Bureau of Investigation (FBI) fingerprint check and placed her under arrest. Yet despite her haggard appearance, the elderly woman did not give up easily. She backed into a corner and began swinging her metal cane like a baseball bat at the officers, managing to bite two of them before being taken into custody.

Accompanied by two Boca Raton detectives, Benton went into the jail to interview "Cordova," whom he could speak to only through glass due to her violent behaviors. When she saw the other detectives, however, she began swearing and refused to cooperate with the interview, saying they had "lied to her." But as she was leaving, Benton uttered the words that would change the course of his case:

> I do this for a living. I hunt people and I've been pretty successful at it. I just wanted to come down here and see you because *you beat me* . . . I lost you. I couldn't find you. I wouldn't be here now if you hadn't decided to come in. I just wanted to tell you that. (personal communication, 2010)

Undeterred, Benton left the jail and traveled to the local homeless shelter, where "Cordova" had been known to stay, to ask the administrator a few questions about her. He was confronted by a man who was angered by the fact that the police had taken so long to respond. The man then informed an obviously confused Benton that he had called the police nearly a year ago about the very same woman and never got a response. Apparently, she had given him details about the murder of a homeless man who had made a pass at her, which she resisted. She told him she had then waited until the man fell asleep and proceeded to cut off his penis. She then said that he woke up, and she stood over him and watched as he bled out and died. The administrator told Benton that he was convinced she had been telling the truth by the level of detail she had provided and further informed him that he had been forced to turn her back out on the streets because of all the trouble she caused at the shelter.

The next day, Benton returned to the Boca Raton jail, this time by himself, and requested to speak with "Cordova" again. She agreed to speak with him because he was "the only cop that has ever been honest with me. . . . You told me yesterday that I was smarter than you and that's the truth." And so her confession began. Benton first asked her about the murder in Gainesville. She said that she and her husband, James Morrisette, had been traveling to California and stopped along the roadside to sleep in the camper. She had been "pissed off" at him for some reason, although she could not remember exactly why, and that she lay awake that night getting madder and madder as he slept beside her. When she could no longer stand it she got out of bed and got her pistol. "I shot him in his eye but he started floppin' around so I picked up a hammer and I started hittin' him in the head with it till he quit movin'." After dumping his body she had sold the truck and trailer to junkyards in two separate states and hitchhiked her way to Florida.

Satisfied with the confession to the murder he had been investigating, Benton then moved the conversation to the state of Washington and the husband she claimed to have killed there. She told him that her name at that time had been Colleen Rice and she had married a homeless man with the last name Davis. It appears that this may have in fact been her real name, as this was the one her children later recounted knowing her by. During the interview, she became enraged when Benton referred to her both as Mrs. Morrisette and Mrs. Cordova, telling him that her name was Colleen Rice and that she would refuse to speak with him unless he referred to her by this name. In 1961, the couple was living outside of Seattle with their four-year-old son in addition to two daughters of Colleen's, ages 9 and 11, from a previous marriage. The 9-year-old was staying over-night in the hospital for a tonsillectomy and the 11-year-old had run away. Colleen remembered that she was getting tired of her husband. That night, after their son went to sleep, she got her 0.32 revolver and "shot him in his eye" while he slept on the couch. When she was sure he was dead, she pushed his body off into the floor and rolled him up in the rug. An unexpected knock on the door announced the arrival of the police who had located her missing daughter. Colleen talked with the police on the porch and sent the daughter, who walked right past the scene in the living room without noticing a thing due to the darkness of the house, to her room. After the police left and the children were asleep, Colleen then dragged her husband's body to her van and drove for four hours. She believed that she had driven all the way to Oregon and, although she could not remember how she arrived there, wound up at a dry creek bed where she dumped the body and then caved in the dirt on the sides of the creek bed to cover him up. On the way home she stopped for ice cream. When she got home the children were awake and they all ate the ice cream, which Colleen remembered as "the best damn ice cream I ever had."

Benton then questioned Rice about the murdered man in Houston. Although she initially denied any knowledge of him, her story changed when he showed her a picture of her and the deceased man together, asking her if she recognized anyone in the photo. She replied, "Well, that's a picture of me. I was a real dish in those days." When he asked about the man in the picture, she spit on the glass and said, "That's what I think of him." She finally admitted to shooting him the eye because he was "pissing [her] off." Autopsy reports confirmed the man had died from a gunshot wound to this location.

At the conclusion of his interview with Rice, Benton asked her a final question: how many had she killed? When she did not appear to like that question, he modified by asking how many husbands she had killed. Rice responded with what Benton described as a "cackly laugh" (personal communication, 2010) and said, "I'll tell you somethin'. You're the detective. You figure it out." She then told him she was tired and was not talking anymore and returned to her cell. That was the last anyone would hear from Colleen Rice, whose advanced cancer brought its own death sentence before she could be extradited to Texas to stand trial for murder. Exactly how many people she killed is a number only she knew, and she took that to the grave. When asked about his impression of Rice as a serial killer and how she compared to males, Benton stated that usually women are "more subtle . . . [they] sit back and wait for it to happen" (personal communication, 2010). Yet that was not the case with Rice, whose overt serial violence was unlike anything the investigator had ever seen in another female suspect. Although no concrete details could be found to confirm either the murder of the homeless man in Florida or of the husband in Washington in 1961, Benton has little doubt that Rice committed these as well. "She had no remorse of any kind" (personal communication, 2010).

Interestingly, Benton was able to track down some of the children of Colleen Rice, who had known her by that name. It soon became apparent that she had a child or children with almost every man she was with and that she gave each of those children away to relatives when they reached the age of 12. The 11-year-old who had run away at the time of the Washington murder refused to cooperate in any way and wanted no mention made of her mother. The girl who had been nine and was in the hospital having her tonsils removed stated that she remembered going to the hospital and that the man she called "Dad" was gone when she returned. Although her mother said he had run off with another woman, the girl found it odd that he had left all his belongings behind. Finally, the boy who had only been four at the time of the murder reportedly turned pale when Benton told him about the case against his mother. The boy, now very much grown, told the investigator that he remembered having a "dream" when he was little in which his mother shot his father and rolled him up in a carpet. The dream had recurred throughout his childhood.

Colleen Rice is a picture of classic psychopathy in many respects (Arrigo & Griffin, 2004; Cleckley, 1976; Hare & Neumann, 2009; Jacobs, 2003; Weizmann-Henelius et al., 2002). She was sufficiently charming enough to woo several men into her grasp. Her entire life was built on one pathological lie after another as she moved from state to state and identity to identity, and her lack of guilt or remorse was blatantly obvious. Her predatory nature and self-centered lack of true emotion are evident in the way she went through men at a whim, keeping them as long as they pleased her and permanently eliminating them when they "pissed her off." Since nothing is known about the years before she began killing her partners, it is impossible to say what her juvenile history consisted of. However, it is a safe assumption that her childhood, especially her relations with the male sex, were far from ideal. In addition to classic psychopathic traits, Rice also exhibited many of the traits found to be unique to women (Perri & Lichtenwald, 2010; Schurman-Kauflin, 2000). When she worked, her jobs tending to the elderly qualify as a traditionally female occupation. Furthermore, she killed victims known to her and systematically abandoned her biological children as they reached the age of 12, giving them away to relatives one at a time. Rice also exhibited characteristics more commonly associated with male psychopathic serial killers (Jacobs, 2003; Keeney & Heide, 2006; Schurman-Kauflin, 2000). She consistently employed overt killing methods in her use of a gun to shoot her victims, a hammer to bludgeon the victim in Texas, and the knife used to mutilate the homeless man in Florida. She also displayed geographic mobility as well as a gender preference for victims, only killing the men she managed to lure into her life. Like Aileen Wuornos, Colleen Rice is proof that female serial killers do not always meet society's stereotypical picture of killing solely for money or out of retaliation for abuse suffered at the hands of her victims. Sometimes, most likely more often than most would like to believe, women kill serially because they desire to do so, needing no further provocation than their own narcissism and psychopathy.

Vickie Jackson

In addition to Colleen Rice, rural north Texas and District Attorney's Investigator Kevin Benton had another run in with a serial killer. This time she was wearing a nurse's uniform and her name was Vickie Dawn Jackson. To the 3,200 residents of Nocona, located in Montague County, Texas, the pudgy nurse with the bleached-blonde hair who worked the night shift at Nocona General hospital was a fixture. Vickie had lived in Nocona since the age of 15 and was a regular at the local Dairy Queen where she usually could be found an hour or so before her shift (Hollandsworth, 2007). She was the quiet wallflower who everyone knew and nobody noticed. In fact, the only trouble she seemed to have since adolescence was that no one else really saw her, but Vickie made sure to change all that on December 11, 2000 (Hollandsworth, 2007). The 34-year-old had dreamed of being Florence Nightingale since she was a little girl, but instead of helping people to live she decided to take their lives in her hands. She would choose who would die and when they would do so by injecting mivacurium chloride, a drug that paralyzes the respiratory system, into their IVs (Hollandsworth, 2007). She killed one patient that first night, but only nine days later she took the lives of two more, injecting the drug into their IVs only 20 minutes apart (Hollandsworth, 2007). In a time span of nine weeks, she killed a confirmed 10 patients, many of whom were in the hospital for minor health issues, attempted to kill another five who survived, and investigators believe she also killed at least another 10. One of her victims was even her husband's grandfather (Hollandsworth, 2007). Vickie never induced a state of distress in her patients to play the hero and deliver lifesaving measures in the nick of time, as one might expect. Rather, in the words of Kevin Benton, "She didn't try to save anyone at all. She wanted people dead. Lots of people" (Hollandsworth, 2007, p. 91). She often comforted the grieving families at the hospital, attended funerals, brought food, and made small talk with them when she saw them in town (Hollandsworth, 2007).

As the killings continued, the Texas Rangers and FBI were called in to aid in the investigation, and Vickie Jackson quickly became their focus. Word travels fast in a small town, and soon everyone knew that she was under investigation. Suddenly heads were turning whenever Vickie entered a room and she enjoyed every minute of it. She continued making her rounds at Dairy Queen and, after her husband left town, she made an appearance at the local country-western dance hall where she danced and smiled as if she had not a care in the world (Hollandsworth, 2007). As a former FBI profiler who was called in for the case told Kevin Benton, who was an investigator with the Montague County District Attorney's Office at the time of the murders, "It's all about power" (personal communication, 2010). Vickie Jackson finally had power over those who had ignored her all of her life. She held them in her sway and she intended to flaunt it. In fact, while the investigation was under way, she obtained a job at a nursing home in the town of Gainesville, located in neighboring Cooke County (Hollandsworth, 2007).

Jackson was arrested in July 2002 and remained in jail until her trial began in October 2006. It was here that her true narcissism began to shine through. Investigator Kevin Benton was having Jackson's mail monitored during her stay in the jail, and what he found confirmed his suspicions that the angelic act Vickie portrayed to the public was precisely that: an act. In letters to her mother and others she bragged about the special diet she was eating and exercises she was doing so she would look good for the television cameras at trial (personal communication, 2010). She also boasted that her bail had been set even higher than that of pop star Michael Jackson, who was also in legal trouble at the time (personal communication, 2010). Yet she maintained her innocence to the public until October 2006, the slated date for her trial, when she unexpectedly entered a plea of no contest (Hollandsworth, 2007).

The public was not the only one shocked by Jackson's alteration in the approach to her case. So one morning over coffee, he asked her defense attorney what had happened. Jackson's attorney told him that he had related to Vickie that the evidence against her was insurmountable and a guilty verdict was certain. She wanted to know what her options were. As the prosecution was not asking for the death penalty, he told her she could either go forward with the trial and await her fate, which would most likely be a life sentence, or she could plead guilty and avoid trial altogether. He told Benton that it was like "a light came on" and she said, "So, what you're saying is that if I were to plead guilty I could still be in control of this? I could do this and still be in charge? . . . That's what I'm gonna do" (personal communication, 2010).

Like all psychopathic serial killers, Vickie Jackson used her charm and deceit to fool the residents of Nocona while stalking the halls of Nocona

General, preying on patients and taking their lives without a hint of true remorse. In the typical manner of a female serial killer, Vickie used drugs to kill covertly in the guise of a caregiving occupation traditionally chosen by females. She also remained in the same small area and killed the towns-people she had known for most of her life, regardless of gender, who were helpless to fight back against her (Frei et al., 2006; Keeney & Heide, 2006; Perri & Lichtenwald, 2010; Schurman-Kauflin, 2000). The striking fact about Jackson, which stands as a testament to her deep-rooted psychopa-thy, is her lack of ability to truly admit that she is at fault for anything that has happened. She still fails to fully realize the kind of monster she is and remains drawn to that position of power she once held. In her final conversation with journalist Skip Hollandsworth of *Texas Monthly,* the two spoke about her recent transfer to state prison and Jackson expressed her excitement about the "nice medical infirmary" at the prison. With a smile on her face, she told Hollandsworth, "Maybe someday they'll let me work there" (Hollandsworth, 2007, p. 189).

CONCLUSION AND FUTURE RESEARCH

The subject of female psychopathic serial murder has long been ignored by the general public, law enforcement, and academia. Empirical evidence exists to strongly support her existence and the danger she poses to those around her. While she exhibits many of the base characteristics and traits of psychopathy of her male counterparts, inherent differences in the expression of psychopathy and victim selection and treatment are vital both to recognizing such behaviors and stopping them as soon as possible. The female serial killer is not the same as the male serial killer, but she is just as dangerous if not more so. As women begin to take on increas-ingly masculine rolls in society, we may begin to see a drastic increase in the amount of violent female predatory serial killing perpetrated in the United States (Forouzan & Cooke, 2005). It is therefore imperative that every effort be made to understand this type of killer in the same manner with which the male version has been studied. A primary gap in need of filling is the absence of personal interviews with incarcerated female serial killers in the same vein as those conducted by the FBI with male serial killers (Keeney & Heide, 2006). Information that only these offenders have is critical to concretely defining female psychopathy, including motives, thoughts, and feelings experienced by these women. Knowledge of these cognitions and emotions can aid in earlier diagnosis and intervention.

Furthermore, it must be recognized that there are dangers associated with the blind application of male psychopathic criteria to females. There are gender differences in the expression of many other personality disorders such as APD, and histrionic, narcissistic, and borderline personalities (Forouzan & Cooke, 2005). Why should psychopathy be any different? It is unknown whether the constructs and diagnostic criteria of male psychopathy apply equally across gender and whether available instruments measure the same construct from males to females (Forouzan & Cooke, 2005). Research has identified three main differences that are emerging between genders in psychopathy: (1) variation in behavioral trait expression, (2) variation in severity of disorder present before symptoms are noticeably expressed, (3) variations in the meanings held by certain behaviors (Forouzan & Cooke, 2005). Further research is needed to facilitate the creation of meaningful constructs to define female psychopathy.

Once these constructs have been established, the next logical step would be the creation of an accurate and adequate measure for female psychopathy and the testing of this measure with various populations to establish baselines. Though the PCL-R is the seminal measure for psychopathy in the 21st century, it was developed using male subjects, and recent studies have shown that some symptoms of psychopathy may not translate directly from males to females with any diagnostic value (Forouzan & Cooke, 2005). For example, the male PCL-R cutoff score is usually 30. However, similar success with females has been found by lowering this number to 27, which produces a "sensitivity and specificity [that is] more comparable to male prisoners" (Hicks et al., 2010, p. 40). This solidifies the need for an instrument that is reliable and valid in its ability to measure the "lethality among female psychopathic offenders" (Arrigo & Griffin, 2004, p. 390).

This area of forensic psychological study is still in its infancy and has far to go, but a handful of researchers are beginning to take steps in the right direction. The best plan is one of action, for something cannot be studied and understood if it is consistently ignored. The task at hand is to challenge the complacency of society and academia regarding the female psychopathic serial killer. She is not the stuff of legend. She is alive in large metropolises and small towns all across America and the greatest weapon against her is knowledge. The face of serial murder is changing. Sometimes the "mask of sanity" also wears lipstick.

REFERENCES

Arrigo, B. A., & Griffin, A. (2004). Serial murder and the case of Aileen Wuornos: Attachment theory, psychopathy, and predatory aggression. *Behavioral Sciences and the Law, 22,* 375–393.
Cleckley, H. (1976). *The mask of sanity* (5th ed.). St. Louis, MO: Mosby.

Cooke, D. J., & Michie, C. (2001). Refining the construct of psychopathy: Towards a hierarchal model. *Psychological Assessment, 13*(2), 171–188.

Forouzan, E., & Cooke, D. J. (2005). Figuring out la femme fatale: Conceptual and assessment issues concerning psychopathy in females. *Behavioral Sciences and the Law, 23,* 765–778.

Frei, A., Vollm, B., Graf, M., & Dittmann, V. (2006). Female serial killing: Review and case report. *Criminal Behaviour and Mental Health, 16,* 167–176.

Hare, R. D. (1993). *Without conscience.* New York: Guilford Press.

Hare, R. D., & Neumann, C. S. (2009). Psychopathy: Assessment and forensic implications. *Canadian Journal of Psychiatry, 54*(12), 791–802.

Hicks, B. M., Vaidyanathan, U., & Patrick, C. J. (2010). Validating female psychopathy subtypes: Differences in personality, antisocial and violent behavior, substance abuse, trauma, and mental health. *Personality Disorders: Theory, Research, and Treatment, 1*(1), 38–57.

Hollandsworth, S. (2007). Angel of death. *Texas Monthly, 35*(7), 88–93, 182–189.

Jacobs, D. (2003). *Sexual predators: Serial killers in the age of neuroscience.* Dubuque, IA: Kendall/Hunt.

Keeney, B. T., & Heide, K. (1994). Gender differences in serial murderers: A preliminary analysis. *Journal of Interpersonal Violence, 9,* 383–398.

Myers, W. C., Husted, D. S., Safarik, M. E., & O'Toole, M. E. (2006). The motivation behind serial sexual homicide: Is it sex, power and control, or anger? *Journal of Forensic Sciences, 51*(4), 900–907.

Newton, M. (2006). *The encyclopedia of serial killers* (2nd ed.). New York: Checkmark Books.

Nicholls, T., Ogloff, J. R. P., Brink, J., & Spidel, A. (2005). Psychopathy in women: A review of its clinical usefulness for assessing risk for aggression and criminality. *Behavioral Sciences and the Law, 23,* 779–802.

Perri, F. S., & Lichtenwald, T. G. (2010). The last frontier: Myths and the female psychopathic killer. *Forensic Examiner, 19*(2), 50–67.

Ramsland, K. (2007). When women kill together. *Forensic Examiner, 16*(1), 64–66.

Ressler, R. K., Burgess, A. W., & Douglas, J. E. (1992). *Sexual homicide: Patterns and motives.* New York: Free Press.

Schurman-Kauflin, D. (2000). *The new predator: Women who kill.* New York: Algora.

Sevecke, K., Kosson, D. S., & Krischer, M. K. (2009). The relationship between attention deficit hyperactivity disorder, conduct disorder, and psychopathy in adolescent male and female detainees. *Behavioral Sciences and the Law, 27,* 557–598.

Sevecke, K., Lehmkuhl, G., & Krischer, M. K. (2009). Examining relations between psychopathology and psychopathy dimensions among adolescent female and male offenders. *European Child and Adolescent Psychiatry, 18*(2), 85–95.

Simon, R. I. (1996). Psychopaths, the predators among us. In R. I. Simon (Ed.), *Bad men do what good men dream* (pp. 21–46). Washington, DC: American Psychiatric Publishing.

Strand, S., & Belfrage, H. (2005). Gender differences in psychopathy in a Swedish offender sample. *Behavioral Sciences and the Law, 23,* 837–850.

Sutton, S. K., Vitale, J. E., & Newman, J. P. (2002). Emotion among women with psychopathy during picture perception. *Journal of Abnormal Psychology,* *111*(4), 610–619.

Turvey, B. (2002). *Criminal profiling: An introduction to behavioral evidence analysis* (2nd ed.). San Diego: Academic Press.

Verona, Patrick E., & Joiner C. J. (2001). Psychopathy, antisocial personality, and suicide risk. *Journal of Abnormal Psychology,* *110*(3): 462–470.

Warren, J. I., & South, S. C. (2006). Comparing the constructs of antisocial personality disorder and psychopathy in a sample of incarcerated women. *Behavioral Sciences and the Law, 24,* 1–20.

Weizmann-Henelius, G., Sailas, E., Viemero, V., & Eronen, M. (2002). Violent women, blame attribution, crime, and personality. *Psychopathology, 35*(6), 335–361.

Weizmann-Henelius, G., Viemero, V., & Eronen, M. (2004). Psychopathy in violent female offenders in Finland. *Psychopathology, 37*(5), 213–221.

The Sexually Motivated Male Serial Killer: An Interdisciplinary Monster

Ashleigh Portales, MFS

Crime Analyst/Crime Scene Investigator, Sheriff's Office Wise County, Texas

In 1888, the gas-lit fog of London's Whitechapel district cloaked the identity of a monster who roamed shadowy alleyways in search of the perfect prey. Time and again, daylight cleared the fog to reveal the bodies of prostitutes, murdered and mutilated by an unseen hand. As the aptly named "Jack the Ripper" kept at his gruesome work, fear and fascination spread like wildfire through the city and around the globe. The modern serial killer was born. Ever since, this enigma has lured the public into its deadly grip and refused to let go. A plethora of books and movies feed society's hunger for entertainment with plots centered around fictional fiends with a thirst for blood and many more books and Web sites exist, giving glimpses of the real thing, spouting information gleaned from trial transcripts and interviews given behind bars. But no matter how many Hollywood horrors are seen or read, the question always left echoing in the public mind is, "Why?"

What makes a man into a murderer who kills multiple victims without any obvious reason or remorse? Who are these men and what is their ultimate motivation? This question has confounded lawmen and laymen alike for more than a hundred years. The historic question between warring disciplines has been that of nature versus nurture; are serial killers born or made? Scholars from various disciplines have put forth explanations for a piece or two of this complex puzzle but have fallen short of interlocking the disjointed pieces into a unified "big picture." What many are lacking is the ability or desire to search for the answer beyond the confines of their own disciplinary boundaries. The interest and knowledge generated by multiple disciplines has failed to comprehensively address and explain this deadly problem looming within society. More than just a weekend blockbuster, serial killers are a genuine threat America, and the world, cannot afford to ignore. It is precisely this situation in which the interdisciplinarian flourishes.

Before the problem can be tackled, it must be clearly defined. While a wealth of information exists on the topic of serial murder, the definition of such can vary greatly between studies. It would be dangerous to apply generalizations made about one type of killer to another, so the range of focus must be narrowed in order to deal appropriately with each individual type of killer. This paper will focus specifically on sexually motivated, male perpetrated serial homicide, which will be defined as the unlawful killing, by a male, of three or more victims with a "cooling-off" period separating each offense. The length of the cooling-off period varies from one offender to the next, and can be as short as a few days or weeks or as long as several months or years.

The sexual aspect of the murders can be seen, either overtly or symbolically, in the condition in which the offender leaves the crime scene. Positioning of the body, sexual assault of the victim, method of killing, and the taking of trophies are all examples that reveal the offender's underlying motivations for the killings (Jacobs, 2003; Myers, Husted, Safarik, & O'Toole, 2006; Salfati & Bateman, 2005). Although serial killers certainly can be female, both their methods and motivations tend to differ greatly from those of their male counterparts. As such, they should be dealt with separately to provide the most accurate analysis and to avoid inaccurate and irrelevant generalizations.

One area in which the gender of the killer does not carry as much weight is in the emotional cores of the public. Whether the killer is male or female, murder is a thing that literally stops us dead in our tracks. Perhaps one reason the word murder resonates so deeply within people is that it takes one from a position of control to one of victimization in which the consequences are most dire: an abrupt, unplanned, and often untimely cessation of existence. For this reason, the most logical approach to sexualized serial murder would be from those disciplines dealing most directly with that same human life and existence in all its various facets, namely, biology, sociology, and psychology. It is the general assumption from this list of academic disciplines that violent predators with no remorse or conscience assemble at the extreme end of spectrum psychopathy.

Psychopathy manifests in emotional detachment, a display of glib superficial charm, lack of guilt, or remorse, and a callous attitude toward others. He is egocentric, manipulative, irresponsible, and lacks behavioral control (Blair, 2007; Dembo, Jainchill, Turner, Fong, Farkas, & Childs, 2007; Jacobs, 2003; Keeney & Heide, 1994; Knight, 2006; Muller et al., 2003; Roberts & Coid, 2007). Psychopaths are cognizant of the legality of their behaviors but fail to grasp moral and ethical acceptability within society. According to Raine and Yang (2006),

> Regarding basic cognitive processes involved in moral decision-making, at a fundamental level there is little question that almost all criminal and psychopathic individuals know right from wrong. . . . Psychopaths show excellent (not poor) moral reasoning ability when discussing hypothetical situations—their real failure comes in applying their excellent moral conceptual formulations to guiding their own behavior. (p. 209)

Therefore, the term *sexual psychopath* is synonymous with sexually motivated serial killer and sexually psychopathic serial killer and the terms will be used interchangeably throughout this text.

Biology is, by its very definition, a "life science." Concerned with the physiological mechanisms of living organisms, the biological discipline explains the inner workings of a killer at the neurological level. Beginning from the base of existence, biology begins with the neuron to address both proper functioning in brain regions as well as the ways in which dysfunction can interfere with normal behaviors. To the biologist, the efficiency of an organism's structural foundations and chemical processes predetermine much of the potential for that life. Biology also attempts to find a genetic link for homicidal behavior. Information in this area is still highly experimental and sketchy, however, and thus will not be covered here.

Sociology, a social science, adds the next layer of understanding by focusing on group dynamics and characteristics. Sociology ascertains the demographics of serial killers based on such factors as socioeconomic status, familial history of abuse and neglect, and the general state of one's environment, to name just a few. To the sociologist, an individual is born as a "blank canvas," the purpose and identity of which is to be defined and influenced by factors largely beyond the individual's control. People are, in a sense, slaves to their environment. Behaviors are geared toward acquisition of social status. For serial killers, this can either be to attain a status he never had, whether within the killer's own family group or a cult-like celebrity media status, or to regain that which he feels was taken from him.

Psychology, a behavioral science, deals with the inner thoughts and feelings, and behavior of individuals. As applied to serial murder, psychology deals with the killer from the inside out. Knowledge is gained by delving into the offenders' deviant thought processes and deciphering how these cognitive deficits explain both predatory and crime scene behaviors. A psychologist sees the killer as an independent individual entity who considers and chooses his behaviors based on personal desires and motivations.

In the interdisciplinary arena, these disciplines will converge on the topic of sexualized serial murder to address the question of "why?" To catch a killer, you must become deeply aware of "who he is" and anticipate his next step before he even knows he is going to take it. This cannot be done without an adequate interdisciplinary comprehension of the male sexually motivated serial killer. This knowledge will be gained through an exploration of current disciplinary literature and expertise addressing serial murder and its perpetrators, resulting in an integration of disciplinary insights to create a deeper and more holistic understanding of these killers and where they come from.

BACKGROUND

Since Cain killed Abel in the book of Genesis, humans have known that murder existed. However, the sexualized serial form of this utmost transgression would be a crime hidden in myth and folklore for many centuries yet. Ancient ancestral legends tell of werewolves, hideous creatures and prowlers of the night who, armed with supernatural power and a thirst for blood, crouched ready to pounce on any unsuspecting victim. To find such a creature, one must simply follow the path of bloody crime scenes and mutilated corpses left in his wake. Documentation of these horrific tales dates back to at least 16th- and 17th-century Europe, where the apex of knowledge lay in religion and superstition. Such murders were attributed to shape-shifting human-wolves, men by day and creatures by night, attacking victims one after the other while most of the town slept blissfully.

In the 21st century, we know these "creatures" were not mythical human-animals and that this tale belief most likely rose out of a combination of a fear of wolves who lived in the woods surrounding the villages as well as a genuine psychiatric condition known in modern times as *lycanthropy*, in which patients actually believe themselves to be wolves. As such, they howl at the moon, run on all fours, and generally engage in wolf-like behaviors (Jacobs, 2003). While the supernatural nature of these killers was only a myth, the killers themselves and their crimes were all too real, and unfortunately not just a historic occurrence.

From Ed Gein (the inspiration for Hitchcock's Norman Bates and the Texas Chainsaw Massacre) to Ted Bundy and Jeffrey Dahmer, modern serial killers are somewhat of a household name as popular culture even assigns catchy monikers like The Night Stalker, The Green River Killer, and BTK (an acronym for this particular killer's method: bind, torture, kill).

Thankfully, not every murder is a serial one and, in the grand scheme of all crimes committed, serial killers actually represent a small fraction. Yet they are by far the most fascinating and, however rare, they have the ability to capture public attention and strike fear in the hearts of millions like no other criminal can. The fact is, they do exist. According to FBI estimates, at any given moment in the United States, an average of 50 serial killers are operating in various stages of their careers (Jacobs, 2003).

While each killer may prefer his own specific type of victim, no one is initially excluded from the possibility of falling prey to one of these modern monsters. Who are these monsters and where do they come from? In search of an informed, intelligent answer void of the superstitious ignorance of the past, we must look to the current disciplinary literature.

DISCIPLINARY PERSPECTIVES, EVIDENCE, AND INSIGHTS

Biology

To function intelligently, living organisms must possess a brain, the advance and complex functioning of which sets humans apart from all other creatures on the planet. Yet just as the power and capacity of the brain places humans at the top of the biological order of life, it may be this very same organ that likens some humans more to the predatory animals above which they are supposed to rank. Mounting biological evidence suggests that parts of the brain, especially the regions of the frontal cortices, located at the front of the brain behind the forehead and eyes, and the amygdala, a more ancient structure lying toward the center and back of the brain, play a significant role in the adaptation of a serial killer. The frontal cortices are divided into several smaller areas, all of which aid in the experience, integration, and expression of emotion (Blair,

2007; Hoaken, Allaby, & Earle, 2007; Vollm, Richardson, McKie, Elliott, Dolan, & Deakin, 2007).

The amygdala helps to associate, through experience and learning, which actions and objects have positive social connotations and which are to be avoided (Blair, 2007). Such roles suggest these areas, relative to normal control subjects, will be significantly dysfunctional in the psychopathic brain. Neuroscientists are testing this theory in two ways: structural MRIs (magnetic resonance imaging) and functional MRIs (fMRIs). Structural MRIs depict the actual anatomy of the brain while fMRIs are able to display activation of specific brain regions in response to stimuli by color-coding blood oxygenation levels and glucose consumption (Vollm et al., 2007). These MRIs create tangible evidence of the psychopathic killer's characteristic deficiency in emotional interpretation and moral reasoning, propensity toward illegal and impulsive actions, and the amount of overkill left behind at their crime scenes.

Biological Dysfunction in Moral Reasoning and Emotional Interpretation

In a study by Kiehl et al. (2004), normal and criminal psychopathic subjects were presented with words of both concrete (for example, legal, illegal, and so on) and abstract (for example, morality, fault, justice, compassion, and so on) content while undergoing fMRI analysis. Criminal psychopaths "fail[ed] to show the appropriate neural differentiation between abstract and concrete stimuli" in the frontal cortices (Kiehl et al., 2004, p. 297). These alarming results explain serial killers' lack of remorse, believing their actions were not wrong (an abstract concept), even though the killer knew at the time that such actions were illegal (a concrete concept). If the processing areas for abstraction are dysfunctional, psychopaths' conceptions of morality are abnormal, and therefore killing for pleasure is not deemed wrong in their minds.

According to Blair (2007), "healthy individuals distinguish conventional and moral transgressions in their judgments from the age of 39 months" (p. 387). However, psychopathic brains are dysfunctional in regions concerned with moral reasoning and measuring others' emotions and distress. This dysfunctionality "disrupts the avoidance of actions leading to emotionally aversive consequences (for example, actively killing another person) shown by healthy individuals in moral reasoning paradigms" (Blair, 2007, p. 391). This dulled response to what is normally considered right or wrong and to the pain inflicted on victims allows the sexual psychopath to murder purely for his pleasure. In another study, participants were asked to identify the emotion being displayed in a photograph of a facial expression. The group of violent offenders tested showed significantly more errors in identifying such emotions than did the normal controls (Hoaken et al., 2007). A serial killer's blunted sense of emotional perception finds victims' emotions irrelevant, allowing him to use victims to satisfy his own sadistic desires. The psychopath's dulled responses to the anxiety and suffering his action cause is precisely why he can murder and enjoy it; his brain never lets him feel bad about it because it fails to register any emotion but his own perverted elation. Additionally, in faces displaying a neutral expression, violent offenders were more likely to incorrectly identify the emotion as disgust (Hoaken et al., 2007).

In retrospect, sexually motivated serial killers often will say that, before killing them, they felt their victims looked down on them or were disgusted by them, furthering the killer's anger. Hoaken's (2007) results suggest these killers may have a neurological basis for the misinterpretation of such facial expressions.

Biological Propensity toward Illegal and Impulsive Actions

A 2005 study by Yang et al. (2005) used a structural MRI to image the brains of "unsuccessful psychopaths" (those who had been caught), successful psychopaths (those who had evaded capture), and normal individuals, focusing on the amount of gray matter in the prefrontal cortex (PFC). The results indicated that unsuccessful psychopaths had significantly less prefrontal gray matter than did their successful counterparts. This lack of prefrontal matter, when combined with "poor decision making [and] reduced autonomic reactivity to cues predictive of punishment [could] render unsuccessful psychopaths less sensitive to environmental cues signaling danger and capture and hence be more prone to conviction" (Yang et al., 2005, pp. 1106–1107). Moreover, the prefrontal gray volume of the successful psychopaths did not differ greatly from that of the normal subjects. This could account for a successful psychopath's "cognitive resources to manipulate and con others successfully, as well as sufficiently good decision-making skills in risky situations to avoid legal detection and capture" (Yang et al., 2005, p. 1107).

It is noteworthy that this study was structural and not functional. While a lack of prefrontal gray matter may explain unsuccessful behaviors, a successful psychopath's gray volume does not imply proper functioning. Instead, the successful sexual psychopath uses this volume to perfect the art of murder and evasion. Frighteningly, such monsters have the neural capacity to be highly intelligent and cunning, sometimes evading capture for decades. Examples of this can be seen in the cases of Dennis Rader, BTK, and Gary Leon Ridgeway, The Green River Killer, both of whom managed to evade police and continue killing victims for multiple decades. Although such serial killers know their actions are illegal, faulty frontal cortices intended to be the brakes of social inhibition allow murderous impulses originating in more primitive brain regions to pass into action.

Impulsivity, a hallmark of psychopathy, causes "individuals [to] focus on the prospect of reward even if environmental cues indicate possible later punishment" (Vollm et al., 2007, p. 152). fMRIs showed no significant response to reward stimuli in the prefrontal cortices of criminally psychopathic individuals. Additionally, a negative correlation existed between one's level of impulsivity and the strength of prefrontal response (Vollm et al., 2007). Dopamine (DA), a chemical neurotransmitter in the brain, produces pleasure when released. Sexual activity, either normal or deviant, is one of the means by which humans experience a flood of DA (Kalat, 2004). Unable to experience pleasure and reward by normal means, the sexually motivated serial killer finds his DA rush in sexualized serial murder.

Biological Underpinnings for Aggression and Overkill

As with all things, sensations reach a saturation point at which pleasurable highs are no longer produced without an increase in the level of the stimulus. In the case of sexually psychopathic serial killers, this creates an ever-increasing need for higher intensity stimuli to produce the desired feelings, resulting in a progression of violence as the killer continues his career. This level of violence is often described as overkill, meaning that much more was done to the victim than was required to end his or her life. In an fMRI study subjecting such psychopathic individuals to positive images (for example, happy couples, puppies) and negative images (for example, heavily wounded people, threatening animals and faces), results indicated "deficient function of the emotion-related brain circuit" (Muller et al., 2003, p. 157). Specifically, negative images activated areas of hyperarousal, suggesting intense focus, and a potential correlation between the psychopathic killer's deviant obsession with creating grotesque and sadistic crime scenes.

Furthermore, positive images evoked responses in areas associated with antagonism, possibly reflecting the intense anger felt toward victims representative of the positive existence the killer cannot attain for himself. This hatred then manifests in overkill. Another reason for overkill is the release of pent-up frustration felt by the killer, which also has been shown to have neurological roots. In an experiment in which rewards for correct responses were delayed and unpredictable, psychopaths showed increased activity in the amygdala, an area linked to feelings of frustration. The same study also revealed a greater overall sensitivity to, and frustration with, loss of an expected reward (Vollm et al., 2007). A key element in serial crime is the offender's frustration in his own life. He seeks the control he has never had by dominating over another in death, a behavior that could be fostered by the amygdala's reaction to his frustrations.

Summary

Overwhelmingly, the evidence suggests that brain regions, especially the frontal cortices and amygdala, are dysfunctional in sexually psychopathic serial killers. "Taken together, the best replicated brain imaging abnormality found to date across a wide variety of antisocial groups, across structure and function and across different imaging methodologies is the PFC" (Raine & Yang, 2006, pp. 205–206). Mounting scientific evidence also suggests widespread structural and functional impairments in the amygdala, hippocampus, temporal cortex, anterior cingulated, and angular gyrus (Raine & Yang, 2006). Yet no one brain region stands alone. Rather, the brain develops in a bottom-up fashion, beginning with the most primitive, reptilian regions and continuing upward to the newer, more sophisticated areas of functioning. Such development creates interdependence among brain regions. For this reason, it is not surprising that multiple areas function abnormally in a killer's brain. In the opinion of Raine and Yang (2006), the likely culprit for the serial killer's development of psychopathy is not one single brain region, but rather in the factor that "the greater the number of neural impairments across different cognitive and affective domains related to an antisocial lifestyle, the higher the likelihood of an antisocial outcome" (p. 206).

The whole brain is engaged in psychopathy. This makes perfect sense, as we know that each brain region is interdependent on others. Once introduced, sexual psychopathy spreads like a disease, finally overtaking its host. By adulthood, psychopathy has infected every part of the dysfunctional brain; it grew there and was perpetuated upward.

SOCIOLOGY

In stark contrast to biologists, who find roots for psychopathy and eventual serial killing in the basic structures and functions of the human brain, "sociologists reject any emphasis on the genetic roots of crime and deviance" (Schaefer, 2008, p. 194). According to Schaefer (2008), sociology defines deviance as behavior that is not necessarily criminal but "that violates the standards of conduct or expectations of a group or society"

(p. 190). Every human is born into a society. It is this society, in all its facets, which shapes who that person will become, how he will think, feel, behave, and perceive himself and others. This shaping is done primarily through the process of socialization, in which members of a particular culture learn what is normal and acceptable in the way of attitudes, values, and behaviors (Schaefer, 2008). Socialization can come in many forms, the most prominent of which is family, followed by school, peer groups, mass media, the workplace, religion, and the government. For any given individual, a list can be developed of the specific influences that made him who he eventually turned out to be.

Sociologists have developed just such a list of environmental factors that perpetuate a breeding ground ripe for male sexualized serial killers. According to sociologists, these unique criminals often are illegitimate children from broken, adopted, or dysfunctional families in which alcoholic or drug-addicted parents subject their children to a life of abuse and neglect. Fathers often are absent, either from a literal or physical standpoint, with the physically present ones generally characterized as harsh and controlling. Mothers tend to swing in one of two directions: either they smother and overpower the child or reject him completely, treating him with hatred and contempt. Many of these killers begin to abuse alcohol and drugs at an early age and ease into a criminal career with early petty crimes. They are commonly of low to average intelligence levels and exhibit behaviors consistent with the MacDonald Homicidal Triad (enuresis at an inappropriate age, fire starting, and cruelty to animals), which will be discussed in further detail later (Knight, 2006; Singer, 2004). Current disciplinary literature focuses on two components of the childhood and adolescent years as principal indicators of later serial killing behavior: a history of childhood abuse or neglect and the early display of criminally deviant behavior.

History of Childhood Abuse and Neglect

There is no debate that murdering innocent victims in a serial fashion is an antisocial behavior. But the answer to where that behavior originates has multiple possibilities. According to a study by Beaver and Wright (2007), "the origins of antisocial behavior are found very early in life—well before adolescence" (p. 656). From the earliest point of life, a child is with his family, an entity that many sociologists contend is a prime factor in the development of sexually motivated serial killers. According to the functionalist view of the family, six integral functions are to be played by this small group: reproduction, protection, socialization, regulation of sexual behavior, affection and companionship, and provision of social status (Schaefer, 2008). In fact, the family is considered the primary agent of socialization and the most important influence in the development of the self. When this primary support system and source of personal identity fails, the results can be long-lasting and devastating.

For a child to develop normally and healthily, the primary caretakers must do two crucial things: take and express joy in the child, which develops self-esteem, and support the child when negative experiences occur, which lays the foundation for healthy coping strategies (Knight, 2006). Knight (2006) further states:

> As a child the serial killer would not have discovered his or her "capacity to light up the mother's face" and thus there would have been no sense of visibility and "recognition in the eyes of the other." These children would have experienced a profound sense of rejection and low self-esteem. (p. 1197)

It would not necessarily take harsh physical abuse to retard normality in these key developmental areas. All that is required is an emotional vacancy on the part of the parent. Physical presence without the companion of love and attentiveness are just as, if not more, devastating to a child than a slap or a punch. This says to the child that he is not important to the parent and therefore has no worth as a person. In the role of the serial killer, this feeling of invisibility and inadequacy remains from childhood. The killer is saying to his victim, "Notice me. Be aware of who I am and what I can do." In essence, the victim is paying for the crimes of all those who failed to give the killer the recognition he feels he deserves (this may be either real or fantastic). The kill is his moment to stand up and be counted, pacification for all the times he was overlooked and unappreciated.

As discussed, sexually motivated serial killers lie at the extreme end of the psychopathological spectrum. Such a continuum also exists for parenting styles and abilities. At the extremely negative end of this spectrum lies antisocial "toxic" parenting, defined by Jacobs (2003) as follows:

> The most damaging and destructive type of loveless and hateful parenting most often observed in the development of sexual psychopathy. Antisocial parenting is characterized by a combination of physical, sexual, and/or verbal abuse, alcoholism, poly-drug abuse, where compulsive viewing of pornography, prostitution, and spousal abuse occur routinely. (p. 234)

Knight (2006) states that "adults who had been physically, sexually and emotionally abused as children were three times more likely than were non-abused adults to act violently as adults" (p. 1199). In the lives of serial killers, violence is a learned behavior that becomes a reaction of distress over what has been unjustly done to them. The killer accomplishes two things through violence: he displays the behavior that has been modeled for him and he attempts to alleviate some of his distress by acting out and displacing some of his pain onto a victim. Further research is emerging to suggest that, of all the horrific factors possibly suffered at the hands of antisocial parents, neglect may be the most detrimental to a child's future and the most likely to gear him toward a future of antisocial behavior and serial killing. This possibly could be because neglect directly affects cognition, with these effects being generally both more pronounced and more permanent than with other types of abuse. (Grogan-Kaylor et al., 2003).

Following in the footsteps of sociologists before them, Singer and Hensley (2004) argue that Social Learning Theory can be applied to the behavior of fire-setting and ultimately to serial murder. In the context of Social Learning Theory, situations in an individual's life translate into either reward or nonreward experiences, the latter of which bring humiliation and frustration and thus is avoided as much as possible. However, the childhood experiences of serial killers consist mainly of nonreward situations, primarily at the hands of the parents, such that the child learns to anticipate humiliation and frustration in all circumstances and loses the ability to accurately differentiate between the positive and negative.

The problem for serial killers further arises in the fact that, as children, they are under the control of the source of their humiliation and frustration: either one or both of their parents. Therefore, they feel helpless to retaliate in their aggression, an act that would serve to permanently alleviate their frustration anxiety.

Summary

Sociology contends that serial murder is a learned behavior, predicated or caused by factors beyond the control of the individual during the formative years of life. Devastating failures within the familial unit to properly socialize and orient children to themselves and the world around them plant the seed of deviance and psychopathy. That seed is then watered by neglectful, antisocial parenting. In the development of a sexually motivated serial killer, red flags are raised. Warning signs exist. Whether or not they are recognized and properly dealt with is the key to the future of this potential offender and his many victims. Unfortunately, the killer in his infancy is already at a disadvantage where this is concerned because, were he in a situation in which abnormal behaviors were noticed and properly treated, then he would not be in the type of environment for the development of those behaviors in the first place.

PSYCHOLOGY

In the 21st century, psychology as a neuroscience is the science of mind via analysis of brain. To professionals in this field, behavior is the result of thought processes and patterns, conditioned by the individual over a period of time, perhaps even years, which converge in an instant to produce action. In psychology, all human behaviors fall on a continuum, a spectrum in which normal lies at the approximate middle. Extremes at both ends are considered abnormal and indicative of various disorders and diagnoses. At the extremely severe end of the spectrum of psychopathy and violent crime lies the sexually psychopathic serial murderer. His crimes are especially callous and committed solely for the purpose of reaching personal highs and goals firmly established within his deviant neurocognitive mapping system. As previously described, psychopathy is the condition in which an individual acts without conscience or remorse such that others exist solely for the purpose of pleasing the individual. Others are viewed, used, and abused as simply a means to a pleasurable end for the psychopath (Blair, 2007; Jacobs, 2003; Knight, 2006; Muller et al., 2003; Roberts et al., 2007). It is the contention of the field of psychology that sexually psychopathic killers are not insane, but rather perfectly cognizant of the legality of their actions; they simply murder because it brings them pleasure (Jacobs, 2003; Raine & Yang, 2006). The "gold standard" for assessing psychopathy is the PCL-R, devised by disciplinary pioneer Robert Hare (Roberts et al., 2007).

Psychologists seek to understand the thoughts and feelings inside the mind of the serial killer by such techniques as personal interviews after incarceration or by a technique known as "criminal" or "psychological profiling." Defined by criminal profiler B. Turvey (2006), the term refers to the "process of inferring distinctive personality characteristics of individuals responsible for committing criminal acts from physical and/or behavioral evidence" (p. 681). In the view of a psychological profiler, the offense of murder is not as important as the way in which the crime is committed (Turvey, 2006; Salfati & Bateman, 2005). In the words of Turvey (2006), "the act of homicide is not a motive. It is a behavior that expresses an offender need. . . . The act of rape is not a motive. It is a behavior that expresses other offender needs beyond those of pure sexual gratification"

(p. 514). These motivations can often be determined through an evaluation of a specific killer's "signature," offender behaviors not necessary for the mechanical completion of the crime but necessary to the offender for the fulfillment of his emotional or psychological needs (Jacobs, 2003; Turvey, 2006, Salfati et al., 2005). A unique signature, although it will most likely continue to develop as the offender grows into his killings, will continue to be left at each of the homicides in a series, if the offender is not hindered in leaving it for some reason. If he does not complete this specific behavior, the killing ultimately will not be fulfilling to him. In these behaviors, the psychology of the sexually psychopathic serial killer is revealed: his motivations and the ways in which he "signs" these motivations on each crime scene he leaves in his wake.

Offender Motivations for Sexualized Serial Murder

Central to the psychological view of serial murder is the idea that sex by itself, just as in rape, is not the major motivation. Rather, sexual gratification has become intertwined in the mind of the killer with power, control, and domination as a result of layer upon layer of deviant cognitive mapping (Jacobs, 2003). A decade ago, Holmes and Holmes (1998) developed a classification system for serial killers that centered on motivation as determined by clues left behind at the crime scenes. These typologies, while insightful, may create so much overlap as to be indistinguishable at times. Further analysis has revealed a central theme of power and control running throughout. "Power and control . . . are not typical of any one type of serial killing but of serial killings in general" (Canter & Wentink, 2007, p. 508). In the killing of another individual, the serial killer is able to claim the power and status he has never been able to grasp in his own life. By becoming the harbinger of life he has elevated himself to god-like status, a position of ultimate power. The sexually psychopathic serial killer derives sexual gratification from the domination of another individual in life and death (Jacobs, 2003). Aside from the visionary killer, who is clinically insane, a serial killer is a sexually psychopathic monster by his very nature. The differences in murder styles, techniques, and behaviors displayed at crime scenes do not necessarily denote a different type of killer but rather a killer whose sexual arousal requires different stimuli than another. The killer does not have to have sex with a victim for the kill to be sexually satisfying to him.

It appears that the specifics of a serial killer's deviant motivation arise early in life. According to Whitman and Akutagawa (2004), "formative events and experience within the backgrounds of the killers culminated in a cognitive structure necessary to commit murder" (p. 694). Like the discipline of sociology, psychology buys into the idea that neglectful antisocial parenting is critical to the emergence of a serial killer. However, psychology focuses on the inner thoughts and feelings produced by this atrocious upbringing. In general, serial killers have failed to experience essential emotional bonding with the mother since the moment of their birth. According to Whitman et al. (2004):

> Extreme deprivation not only causes anxiety, which is countered by destructive urges, but also is a dehumanizing experience in which the child perceives himself as unacceptable, unwanted, and without value. The extent to which a child has been thus dehumanized—as well as through deprivation and physical or sexual abuse—shapes the child's own capacity to value others as individuals of worth. (p. 697)

Thus begins the development of a "deviant egocentric mindset" (Jacobs, 2003, p. 173). Aggression and violence are evident in these killers very early on, even in childhood play (Whitman et al., 2004). MacDonald's Homicidal Triad is also observed. As the child moves into adolescence and early adulthood, larger sensations than those offered by setting fires and torturing small animals are needed to produce an effect. The answer is often found in pornography, which quickly progresses to the hard-core variety (Jacobs, 2003).

Since the sexual psychopath has never been truly loved or taught how to properly reciprocate love, he is incapable of having a normal romantic relationship with a partner. This relegates him to more solitary means, which often are initiated by the viewing of such pornography. Masturbation and paraphilia are essentially self-fulfilling satisfactions. Indulging in these practices does not require the participation or enjoyment of another party for the event to produce the desired result. The offender and his fantasies grow and develop in unison, with each deviant thought further establishing the homicidal cognitive map. He never can get enough. Like any other addiction, his brain cries out for more and he is too far gone to resist. The commission of murder is not a sudden snap in behavior but rather a final destination in the journey from vivid deviant fantasy into reality. Once this bridge has been crossed, there is no return. Murder is forever eroticized in his mind, and he is irreversibly changed by this (Myers et al., 2006).

Many people do things for emotional reasons, for example, overeating, overexercising, and obsessively cleaning. These behaviors are all attempts to fill an emotional void in the life of the person demonstrating the behaviors. In essence, serial killing is a means to the same end, a futile attempt to fill an emotional hole. Just as no amount of food ever creates emotional fulfillment for the obese overeater, no amount of torture, degradation, and murder can do the same for the serial killer. This explains why the violence and overkill often increase with subsequent murders. The fantasy is never made completely real, so the offender tries harder every time to attain perfection in the kill. This would both increase his status and help to attain the ultimate orgasm he seeks. Yet he never can quite make fantasy and reality meet, so he continues the search for perfection.

Anger often has been postulated as a motivation of serial murder. However, Myers et al. (2006) believe that anger may not be a physically possible motivation for these killings as the biological pathways and neurotransmitters, specifically norepinephrine (NE), enacted by feelings of anger are the same ones that are directly antagonistic to the rigid erection response required for sexual arousal and orgasm at a crime scene. Serial sexual murderers indeed may appear angry at interview. This may not be the initial motivation for their crimes, however, but rather a reaction to the normal societal restrictions to their preferred behaviors, which are being forced on the offenders by way of incarceration. The anger may be derived from the very fact that they are not being allowed to hunt and kill freely. When sexually frustrated, even "normal," nonhomicidal men exhibit anger and aggression in their interactions with people. Once again, the issue of an extreme on a behavioral continuum must be considered. Rather than anger as the primary motivation for serial homicide, the cruelty and aggression may be more of a means to an end in that sexual arousal and emotion cannot be attained through any other behaviors. For these killers, anger fuels the fantasy and further perverts the pleasure.

Signature

The signature of a sexually motivated serial killer is just that: a unique behavioral mark left at the crime scene that fulfills some aspect of a specific killer's psychological fantasy and is essential for his emotional gratification (Jacobs, 2003; Salfati et al., 2005; Turvey, 2006). According to Turvey (2006), an Australian criminal profiler, four basic criteria exist for determining whether or not a behavior is signature in nature:

- Takes extra time to complete, beyond more functional modus operandi (MO) behavior—that is, the general operating behaviors necessary to the commission of the crime
- Unnecessary for the completion of the crime
- Involves an expression of emotion
- May involve an expression of fantasy (p. 285)

Some examples of signature behaviors are positioning of the body; the taking of trophies or mementos of the murder, including victim possessions or body parts; or pre- or postmortem acts committed against the victim (Jacobs, 2003). Analysis of a killer's signature provides insight into who the killer is and what he is thinking. "Signature behaviors, therefore, are best understood as a reflection of the underlying personality, lifestyle, and developmental experiences of an offender" (Turvey, 2006, p. 283). It is the "why" behind the "what," the reason sexually psychopathic serial killers feel compelled to commit horrendous acts of murderous violence against unsuspecting innocent victims. The special care taken with the victim, the specific manners in which the killer binds, tortures, mutilates, or assaults, mean more emotionally to the offender than the death itself. Simply killing without the "foreplay" holds little to no value or satisfaction for him. It is the specific process, scripted out by his individual deviant cognitive maps, that must be followed if he is to attain the most possible satisfaction from his killings.

The inner hunger to display signature behaviors and bring deviant fantasy to life drives the killer on to murder after murder.

Summary

Rather than rest with the boundaries of quantifiable, tangible physical evidence found at the crime scene, within the anatomic makeup of the killer, or in his past history, psychology attempts to step into the unseen realm of the mind and what takes place in the thoughts of a sexually motivated serial killer. Power and control become abnormally intertwined with sex and eroticism in the deviant minds of these killers such that one cannot be sufficiently attained and enjoyed without the other. The individual emotional and psychological motivations of the killers are left behind at their crime scenes in the form of signatures. Each offender of this type has one, and it can be found if the psychologist is willing to step inside the minds of such monsters to seek it out.

INTEGRATION AND CONCLUSION

Is it nature or nurture? This great question has plagued mankind since the first werewolf struck in the villages of Europe (Jacobs, 2003). In the 21st century, we are confidently able to say that the answer is "both." The evolution of the sexually motivated serial killer is a complex process begun at birth and spread out over a lifetime. The greatest argument for this reasoning may best be postulated by Knight (2006), who states that "many individuals have negative experiences in childhood and do not become addicts or angry and revengeful serial killers" (p. 1201). This is because sociological milieu alone simply is not enough to create a psychopathic serial killer. Indeed, humans do not enter the world as a blank slate, as champions of this discipline would have us believe. Any mother with more than one child will tell you each of her babies was completely and totally his or her own individual personality from the moment that child entered the world. Personality is dually influenced by the internal makeup of temperament and by the external experiences of the environment (Whitman & Akutagawa, 2004).

Without a doubt, additional biological precursors must exist that are either suppressed or fostered into activity by environmental stimuli. Much like automatic headlights on an automobile turn on when the darkness outside reaches a certain level predetermined by the manufacturer, so too the sexual psychopath comes into the world with preset personality traits that lend themselves to the business of serial killing. Were these individuals to be raised in atmospheres of complete sunshine and harmony it is highly unlikely that such tendencies would ever be triggered to the "on" position. While mild traits of generic, garden-variety psychopathy might develop, the chances are slim that individuals ever would cross over the one-way threshold into homicide. When met with the right atmosphere of toxic circumstances, the darkness around the individual becomes just thick enough to flip the switch and release what always has been stored away in the recesses of the mind. Dysfunctional brain regions are rendered additionally dysfunctional by antisocial, neglectful conditions. This spurs the focus of the individual to sexually deviant fantasies, which in turn add to the dysfunctionality of his already bereft brain. Consequently, the vicious cycle continues revolution after depraved revolution until satisfaction lies only in the transport from fantasy into reality.

That killers display every imaginable criterion for psychopathy is without question. In stark contrast to the crazed killer who has lost his grip on reality, psychopaths are quite sane, a fact which makes them exponentially more frightening. These cold and calculating monsters choose sexualized serial murder because of the emotional reward they feel when their neural pathways are satisfactorily activated through torturing, mutilating, and taking lives. They simply do not operate by the sociological credo that suggests drastic illegal behavior will be avoided because the risk involved outweighs the possibility of reward. They know killing is illegal and are well aware of the stigma capture and conviction bring. They kill because they want to. Sometimes the promise of public infamy even sweetens the pot. For the sexual psychopath, the reward outweighs the cost. Coupled with the grandiose sense of self from the psychological perspective, society is left with a monster who kills for the joy of it and believes his is so superiorly intelligent that he will be able to continue to do so indefinitely without being detected.

This fact is essential when considering incarceration of these criminals. Someone who enjoys murder can never be allowed to return to mainstream society, as he will return to his favorite pastime as quickly as possible. For a criminal to be rehabilitated, they initially must have been habilitated normally. This has never occurred in the life of the sexually motivated serial killer. Therefore, all rehabilitative efforts will be rendered completely futile. False, and dangerous, appearances of success arise only from the fact that the psychopath is clever enough to manipulate the system. He learns what to say to please who he must so that he can be released back into the wild to stalk, hunt, and savagely devour his prey like the predatory beast that he is. Only incapacitation or death can stop him, just as only these two factors can remove a wolf from the hunt. Lifelong incarceration or execution are the only options.

The answer to the mystery of sexually motivated serial crime does not lie in a neatly packaged box. There are many facets, reflecting a myriad of influences in the development of these predators without consciences. Unfortunately, this extreme version of psychopathy is an iceberg whose tip we are only beginning to uncover. An undeniable need exists for further research in this area. Studies similar to the ones referenced here should be replicated, with appropriate updates as needed, to include larger sample sizes and longer serials of homicides. Additionally, personal interviews with incarcerated killers are potentially vast resources of information, if conducted by professionals trained to differentiate between truth and the toying and manipulations of such psychopaths.

While the idea of spending large amounts of time with these killers may be repulsive, these circumstances are prime opportunities to increase our knowledge of serial killers and as such should be tapped for every amount of resource possible. The idea is to arm law enforcement with every weapon available to capture these criminals as early in their careers as possible and save the greatest amount of lives. For this reason, as much background information about these killers should be obtained to further develop our knowledge of the red flags of behavior and circumstances that serve as early warning signs, which, when recognized and properly handled, could avert a serial string of killings before it begins.

The goal is saving lives, and we must never allow the victims in our studies to become so depersonalized that we forget the tragic loss that has occurred with their murder. The victim, not the killer, is the most important reason for studies of this kind. Victims past and future deserve the best efforts of the professional world to combat their killers, ideally before they ever have the chance to victimize. As Myers et al. write, "Human behavior is complex . . . Our scientific knowledge of serial sexual murderers remains limited and the need for ongoing research in this area is crucial in light of the grave societal consequences produced by their crimes" (2006, p. 906).

REFERENCES

Blair, R. J. R. (2007). The amygdala and ventromedial prefrontal cortex in morality and psychopathy. *TRENDS in Cognitive Sciences, 11*(9), 387–392.

Brown, K., & Grunberg, N. (1996). Effects of environmental conditions on food consumption in female and male rats. *Physiology and Behavior, 60*(1), 293–297.

Buss, D. M. (2005). *The murderer next door: Why the mind is designed to kill.* New York: Penguin Press.

Canter, D. V., & Wentink, N. (2004). An empirical test of Holmes and Holmes's serial murder typology. *Criminal Justice and Behavior, 31*(4), 489–515.

Evans, G. W. (1979). Behavioral and psychological consequences of crowding in humans. *Journal of Applied Psychology, 9,* 27–46.

Freedman, J. L., Heshka, S., & Levy, A. (1975). Population density and social pathology: Is there a relationship? *Journal of Experimental Social Psychology, 11,* 539–552.

Gazzaniga, M. S., Ivry, R. B., & Mangun, G. R. (2002). *Cognitive neuroscience: The biology of the mind* (2nd ed.). New York: W.W. Norton.

Hoaken, P. N. S., Allaby, D. B., & Earle, J. (2007). Executive cognitive functioning and the recognition of facial expressions of emotion in incarcerated violent offenders, non-violent offenders, and controls. *Aggressive Behavior, 33,* 412–421.

Holmes, R. M., & Holmes, S. T. (1998). *Serial murder* (2nd ed.). Thousand Oaks, CA: Sage.

Jacobs, D. (2003). *Sexual predators: Serial killers in the age of neuroscience.* Dubuque, IA: Kendall/Hunt.

Kalat, J. W. (2004). *Biological psychology* (8th ed.). Belmont, CA: Wadsworth Thompson Learning.

Kiehl, K. A., Smith, A. M., Mendrek, A., Forster, B. B., Hare, R. D., & Liddle, P. F. (2004). Temporal lobe abnormalities in semantic processing by criminal psychopaths as revealed by functional magnetic resonance imaging. *Psychiatry Research: Neuroimaging, 130,* 297–312.

Kitamura, T., Shima, S., Sugawara, M., & Toda, M. (1996). Clinical and social correlates of antenatal depression: A review. *Psychotherapy and Psychosomatics, 65* (3), 117–123.

Marsden, H. M. (1972). Crowding and animal behavior. In J. F. Wohlhill & D. H. Carson (Eds.), *Environment and the social sciences.* Washington, DC: American Psychological Association.

McCain, G., Cox, V. C., & Paulus, P. B. (1976). The relationship between illness, complaints, and degree of crowding in a prison environment. *Environment and Behavior, 8,* 283–290.

Muller, J. L., Sommer, M., Wagner, V., Lange, K., Taschler, H., Roder, C. H., Schuierer, G., Klein, H. E., & Hajak, G. (2003). Abnormalities in emotion processing within cortical and subcortical regions in criminal psychopaths: Evidence from a functional magnetic resonance imaging study using pictures with emotional content. *Biological Psychiatry, 54,* 152–162.

Myers, W. C., Husted, D. S., Safarik, M. E., & O'Toole, M. E. (2006). The motivation behind serial sexual homicide: Is it sex, power and control, or anger? *Journal of Forensic Sciences, 51*(4), 900–907.

Paydarfar, A. (1996). Effects of multifamily housing on marital fertility in Iran: Population-policy implications. *Social Biology, 42*(3/4), 214–225.

Raine, A., & Yang, Y. (2006). Neural foundations to moral reasoning and antisocial behavior. *SCAN, 1,* 203–213.

Roberts, A. D., & Coid, J. W. (2007). Psychopathy and offending behaviour: Findings from the national survey of prisoners in England and Wales. *Journal of Forensic Psychiatry and Psychology, 18*(1), 23–43.

Salfati, C. G., & Bateman, A. L. (2005). Serial homicide: An investigation of behavioural consistency. *Journal of Investigative Psychology and Offender Profiling, 2,* 121–144.

Turvey, B. (2006). *Criminal profiling: An introduction to behavioral evidence analysis* (2nd ed.). London: Elsevier Academic Press.

Vollm, B., Richardson, P., McKie, S., Elliott, R., Dolan, M., & Deakin, B. (2007). Neuronal correlates of reward and loss in cluster B personality disorders: A functional magnetic resonance imaging study. *Psychiatry Research: Neuroimaging, 156,* 151–167.

Whitman, T. A., & Akutagawa, D. (2004). Riddles in serial murder: A synthesis. *Aggression and Violent Behavior, 9,* 693–703.

Yang, Y., Raine, A., Lencz, T., Bihrle, S., LaCasse, L., & Colletti, P. (2005). Volume reduction in prefrontal gray matter in unsuccessful criminal psychopaths. *Biological Psychiatry, 57,* 1103–1108.

Chapter 12

On Cloud Nine

To elaborate, psychopaths are generally well satisfied with themselves and with their inner landscape, bleak as it may seem to outside observers. They see nothing wrong with themselves, experience little personal distress, and find their behavior rational, rewarding, and satisfying; they never look back with regret or forward with concern. They perceive themselves as superior beings in a dog-eat-dog world in which others are competitors for power and resources. Psychopaths feel it is legitimate to manipulate and deceive others in order to obtain their "rights" and their social interactions are planned to outmaneuver the malevolence they see in others.

—Robert Hare (1993, p. 195)

In the 1950s, the U.S. Weather Bureau launched a typology of cloud study according to the cloud's appearance and texture—Cloud Number Nine described a fluffy cumulonimbus considered the most attractive of all clouds. In the 21st century, the common expression of a person who is blissfully happy ("floating around on cloud nine") pairs happiness with attractiveness and has become a euphemism for a person who is visibly and remarkably happy. A vital tool of forensic investigative neuroscience— neuropsychology—is quick to remind us that DANE brain's chemical cast of powerful excitatory neurotransmitters and jazzing hormones lies behind the emotional bliss of cloud nine as it does for adaptive neuropsychopathy and in a twisted way pathological psychopathy.

Likewise, the same chemistry we hypothesized to lie behind *nature's mood-brightening cocktail of protective and restorative chemistry* is the same chemistry that makes us feel invincible while acting as an inoculation against caving in to life's assaultive and humiliating experiences. How else could our sapient brain at critical times cloak us with resilience to live another day? With narcissistic self-entitled arrogance, wrapped around an engaging and charismatic personality highlighted by an all-encompassing, on-the-fly adaptability to any contingency in the blink of an eye, sapient brains are definitely out to survive.

ADAPTIVE NEUROPSYCHOPATHY

A turtle shell protects and enhances life, as do the quills of the porcupine. The sapient brain is no different. The following are seven noteworthy insights regarding our factory-sealed warranty of cascading chemistry.

The Workhorse of Surviving and Thriving

1. An adaptive, beneficial, and restorative version of psychopathy—a psychopathy in mild gradation—exists by evolutionary necessity in sapient brains as a neuroadaptive chemical inoculation against crushing sadness and despair that threatens to end life. In this paradigm, suicide is the failure of adaptive neuropsychopathy.
2. A maladaptive and detrimental version of psychopathy exists as an irreversible brain condition observed in psychopathic personality disorder. This condition has a long history of peer-review validation and has been quantified for more than 30 years by the PCL-R with scores of 2 in responses to the 20-item checklist that collectively total 30+ required for a clinical diagnosis of PPD.
3. The PCL-R has validated the adaptive version of psychopathy with scores of 1 for collective responses that run in the single and double digits under a total score of 30.
4. It is currently unknown whether psychopathic personality disorder is due to biological dysfunction in the neuroadaptive version, whether or not psychopathic characteristics are exacerbated by moderate versions that developmentally become severe, or whether toxic social influences overpower the slowly developing PFC; most likely, all of the above contribute to varying degrees.
5. Evolution by natural selection is the only known cause-effect process capable of creating adaptive dynamics, including neuropsychopathy for modification and changes necessary for survival. Natural scientists have documented that living is a natural biological process that embraces modification, variation, and change. The epicenter for adaptive dynamics is the sapient brain.
6. Neuroadaptive versions of psychopathy solve problems of living through strategies of survival by deception evidenced in narcissism,

entitlement, manipulation, histrionicism, and lying with cover-up. Ironically, deceptive practices are architects of success through calculating minds engaged in deceptive practices that are congenital to sapient brains. The world is full of monetarily rich individuals and others who are financially secure due to beneficial versions of psychopathy—both adaptive and in moderate gradations. They are the movers and shakers who are engaging in society and perceived as good people to know in business, politics, and all venues that require the marketing of a charming and smiling face often setting atop a "hot" body.

7. Neuroadaptive psychopathy is a workhouse of surviving and thriving long after the PFC has become the last tollbooth to prevent expression of bad ideas, emotional impulsivity, and violent dirty tricks.

Chemistry to the Nines

With the rise in DA's pleasure molecules and by NE's focus and interest, energized by testosterone's sexual and aggressive drives of entitlement, and enhanced by phenylethylamine's (PEA) signaler of attraction to specific sexual cues as hormone and neurotransmitter markers of sapient brains, mediated by serotonin's (5-HT's) "cool and collected confidence," adaptive neuropsychopathy equips species *Homo sapiens* with raw materials of affect not only to survive, but also to thrive, even when All Hell Breaks Loose. The fly in the ointment of adaptive neuropsychopathy's bulletproof entitlement and narcissism is tragic, sudden death because of fatal mistakes caused by impulsivity or unlucky accidents.

It is in the adolescent sapient brain that parents, ironically, can find some peace and hope that their beloved children will survive all the drama and tribulations of adolescent histrionicisms and young adult life as a result of being a member of "peer tribes" during the time span of public school-age experiences. With robust neuroadaptive brain chemistry cascading 24/7, the sapient brain has evolved over millennia as the most powerful force in the universe to shepherd children and adolescents through some of the most dangerous shenanigans and impulsive actions imaginable. Although suicide statistics do increase during adolescence, we believe this occurrence is due in part to the very gradation of neuropsychopathy *per se* in variance of efficacy within individual sapient brains; some have more in gradation, others less. *This fact also corroborates studies that show suicide runs in families, clearly a genetic variant.*

Spanning all development stages and phases relative to brain chemistry, it is what our brain does (not a condition we are necessarily aware of) on a daily basis and how it shields us against emotional traumas and humiliations that truly matters. Adaptive neuropsychopathy provides the chemistry of survivability enhanced by ever vigilant and competent parental supervision until the PFC takes over with reflective second thoughts that truly characterize mature sapient behavior. "In by 10, out by 11" is a sure sign of PFC cognitive dominance over MLS affect shenanigans; just another way of saying "be home by 10 PM and asleep by 11 PM" removes individuals from most of the dangers of criminal randomization in society after dark.

Meanwhile, the march of forensic investigative science and forensic investigative neuroscience in the creation of new tools and improved products to analyze crime scenes and the evolution of the brain behind criminal minds marches on. Our 21st-century understanding and knowledge of pathological psychopathy and what has been hiding in plain sight—*adaptive neuropsychopathy*—has accumulated faster in just 10 years than in all millennia combined.

Forensic investigative science and its cadre of laboratory scientists, investigators, and neuroscientists truly are embarking on the most important applied science of modern times, that is, the reality of arming sapient humans with accurate knowledge of the capabilities and likely possibilities to expect when confronting the one common denominator we bring to every human encounter—*our sapient brains*. It is the same brain that is prone to viciousness and violence that pathological psychopaths bring to victims at horrific crime scenes. Is there no end to this nightmare of violent psychopathy framed by yellow crime scene tape?

In the future, might forensic investigative neuroscientists have a medical procedure that *enhances* adaptive neuropsychopathy while *inoculating* sapient brains against the hyperviolence and hypersexuality of pathological psychopathy? To answer this intriguing question, let's fast-forward and envision 23rd-century forensic investigative neuroscience.

23RD-CENTURY FORENSIC INVESTIGATIVE NEUROSCIENCE

Enter forensic psychopharmacology into 23rd-century forensic investigative neuroscience. In the year 2200 CE, will it be possible to permanently eradicate violence from the cortices of sapient brains? How could this be accomplished? Just like adaptive neuropsychopathy, the answer always has been hiding in plain sight. Maybe the time has come to think differently about what we have always seen, suggested by our friend, the Hungarian chemist who said a mouthful about discovery: "seeing what everyone else has seen and thinking what nobody else has thought."

Enter preventative psychoactive drugs into the landscape of criminal behavior. Drugs that change brain chemistry—*psychoactive drugs*—work naturally in sapient brains and modify affect and behavior; they have been doing so long before the advent of recorded history. Psychedelic mushrooms, and other plants with psychoactive properties such as the *cannabis sativa* version of hemp plants, indigenous to specific ecosystems, have long been associated with hunter-gatherer societies, still commonly observed in tribal cultures around the world. Interestingly, spiritual significance has been routinely attached to the use of psychedelics and hallucinogens alleged to connect humans to the otherworldly.

Modern psychopharmacology does offer an inoculation against hyperviolence and hypersexuality. Evidence for this capability comes by way of the development and marketing of drugs that modify behavior and alleviate symptoms of mental or psychological disorders. In fact, this drug efficacy has become big business in the 21st century. From humble beginnings before the 1950s, for example, one drug alone gave biological psychiatry a backstage pass and the inside track to the fortunes of this new form of non-talk therapy. Thorazine, the brand name of the chemical compound Chlorpromazine, an antipsychotic medication, virtually emptied state hospitals of patients diagnosed with schizophrenia. Chlorpromazine became the prototype for the phenothiazine class of drugs that continues in the 21st century. Introduced in 1950, Thorazine became a breakthrough drug with powerful psychoactive properties that almost overnight curtailed the use of electroconvulsive shock therapy (as it was referred to in those days) and first-time admission to mental hospitals. Prescription medications made physician-prescribed drugs legal; psychoactive medications are here to stay with dominance in biological psychiatry.

Biological psychiatry has been the driving force behind the proliferation of prescription (legal) drugs and, along with the science of psychopharmacology, has produced the mammoth Big Pharma—a collection of pharmaceutical drug companies—that comprise the most successful multi-billion-dollar Wall Street corporations in the world. *The delivery system and science of pharmaceuticals is in place to control brains behind criminal minds.*

Let's now address chemical mechanisms in the brain that are involved in the process of permanently removing violence from criminal minds—the same brains once sent to prisons, but who, in the 23rd century, will be imprisoned in their own minds. No wall of bars required.

Whether synthesized in an illegal lab or in the highly profitable labs of the legal drugs of Big Pharma, or found as growing plants in nature, drugs ingested by mouth, by injection, or by being sniffed, huffed, or absorbed through the skin possess *psychoactive properties* that modify endogenous brain chemistry at receptor sites in neurons (brain cells). By a well-known process, exogenous drugs (such as marijuana or cocaine) mimic endogenous chemistry in sapient brains at receptor sites; or they have no effects. This is critical to understand. Drugs—licit or illicit—do not contain "highs," rather they trigger highs in brain chemistry. When a drug is taken, let's say cocaine, it enters the cells by mimicking the effects of the natural brain chemicals already in residence. Cocaine works psychoactively because it mimics DA and blocks a natural brain process from working known as *reuptake*. This chemical process occurs by the drug blocking the natural reclamation process of the brain's own endogenous chemistry (in this case, DA); by this process, after a chemical message is sent (by absorption in receptors on dendrites), the molecules of the signaler neurotransmitter (DA) is reclaimed by tiny chemical sacs—vesicles—that hold molecules in the axons of brain cells for future use. When the natural process of reuptake is blocked, leftover transmitter chemistry "builds up" in the synapse and in clusters flood through receptors with magnified intensity. Hence, due to liberation, DA produces euphoric pleasure in this process—the drug works *as a high,* from liberated DA overload hitting receptors hard as a result of its accumulation.

This process of blocking reuptake increases and sustains release of endogenous (natural) brain chemicals that can eradicate chemical imbalances as observed in liberating (increasing) low-gain 5-HT in cases of clinical depression by the antidepressant Prozac. Fluoxetine is the drug compound with the brand name of Prozac with efficacy of *selective serotonin reuptake inhibitor* (SSRI) properties. Prozac and related compounds liberate 5-HT selectively into the synapse by the chemical process of blocking reuptake, and thereby more soothing 5-HT is released to balance chemistry. In the process, liberated 5-HT acts as a mood brightener counteracting chronic depression.

Cortical Cell Blocks

Now, let's take an excursion to the 23rd century and the advanced technologies now available for the pharmacological blocking of brain chemistry behind criminal minds. The operative technology in this new age of forensic investigative neuroscience is currently available thanks to what we call "brain chips." Deep brain stimulation devices to modify brain chemistry are accomplished by brain chip technology. Implanted in the torso, batteries provide power to the chips. Implanted brain chips already are available and in use, as evidenced by patients with advanced

Parkinsonism and Alzheimer's disease; most patients show symptom relief. How wide the application will evolve over the coming years is open to conjecture. But in limited use, it is working now.

The New Death Penalty

To permanently control violence, especially brutalizing sexual violence, the leading symptom of pathological psychopathy, chemical modification of their powerful effects must be permanently blunted. The physical, mental, and psychological recipe for hyper-aggression (violence) appended to sexuality is chemically engineered by liberated testosterone—the hormone of aggression and libido (the sex drive). When testosterone is given a free ride in the brain, all sexual hell breaks loose; this condition can worsen with low-gain 5-HT—producing an empty feeling with diminished esteem—resulting in increasing anger and frustration. This condition can spill rapidly over into behavior by a low-performing PFC exacerbated by sexually perverted cognitive mapping—neuronal "wiring" sure to occur with an addiction to violent, hardcore pornography. By creating an internal prison, however, psychopathic personality disorder could be eradicated from human experience. It will be possible.

First, testosterone could be reduced drastically by blocking its efficacy with Depo-Provera-like substances or simply by blocking testosteronergic receptors (receptors activated by testosterone). Physical castration of the genitals and adrenal glands aside, the administration of Depo-Provera has proven successful as a form of *chemical castration* for male sex offenders by reducing the sex drive. Second, DA, the molecule of machismo, could be altered so that "anticipated pleasure" of perverted sensations could be sidetracked. Third, 5-HT can be liberated for uptake by brain cells that produce a calming affect brain-wide. (As we pointed out, low-gain 5-HT is known to exacerbate conditions associated with liberated testosterone in hyper-aggression and hypersexual behavior.)

With 5-HT liberation thus accomplished, the hormone of aggression and sex (testosterone) is dampened in efficacy, while the chemistry that lies behind feeling cool, calm, and collected is enhanced. With a brain closed to the business of brutal sexual urges seeking prey for violent and sexual expression, the mental, psychological, and emotional aspects of the mind are prevented from anticipation of any pleasure to be derived from what now has been blocked chemically. Those who suffer from what we have called "pornographic psychopathy"—the chemical expression of sexually psychopathic violent and rapacious victimization—would have their former mind-set foreclosed by deep brain implantation.

Is it really that simple? No, of course not; but the technology will be advanced by the 23rd century to be completely possible and most likely reliable. And if legal, it would become the new death penalty.

The reasons for not using the deep implantation of brain chips, even though the technology will be available, are every bit as interesting as why they may be used. The number one reason why internal, cortical incarceration will *not* become a reality (at least to our thinking in the first decade of the 21st century) is deceptively simple. *There is no profit to be made.* Suppose the green light would be given by the Food and Drug Administration (FDA) for a division of Big Pharma to develop techno-chemical procedures in brain chip technology for implantation, creating "internal incarceration." Who would get rich by it? Who would be sent the bill to pay for the procedure? Here are more practical reasons:

- Would we trust the technology enough to allow violent prisoners incarcerated in plaster-and- mortar walls and bars to return to free society?
- Would we trust our next-door neighbor, let's say, who used to be a violent pedophile or serial killer, but now with his new technologically altered brain is now our neighbor? How would we ever know of his present condition? Somewhat tongue-in-check, might one of his eyes be in a constant glint of a glowing red beam to alert us to his former condition?

With increasing medical technologies popping up everywhere in the landscape of forensic neuroscience and forensic investigative science, political leaders have a lot to keep them busy over the next 200 years. How does our society want to punish criminal minds? Do we want to prevent violent crime once and for all time? Or, maybe we don't really have that in mind.

It has been my pleasure to present the 10 new products and tools for analysis of psychopathic criminal minds in the 21st century. In an age marked by worldwide terrorism and violence in our own neighborhoods across America, with all we have to offer in forensic investigative science, it is no wonder we feel, by degrees, the world will become a safer place. By embracing adaptive neuropsychopathy as a natural brain condition, we can trust our sapient brains to be competitive by conniving and calculating our way around brains with similar conditions. This is the inbred nature of sapient brains and likely may become the new definition of truth sapient-brained wise. Therefore, we can end the book on a positive note. We will have new tools and new products even more daring at our disposal in 200 years. The big question is this: will we have the courage and presence of mind to control violence expressed in the evolution of criminal minds?

REFERENCES

Cooper, Jack R., Bloom, Floyd E., & Roth, Robert H. (2003). *The biochemical basis of neuropharmacology* (8th ed.). New York: Oxford University Press.

Hancock, Paul, & Skinner, Brian. (Eds.). (2000). *The Oxford companion to the Earth.* New York: Oxford University Press.

Hare, R. D. (1993). *Without conscience.* New York: Guilford Press.

Autobiography of Cassidy's Life: Life Is Bigger Than One Person

People turn out to be what they take from, or don't take from, different experiences. My first memory happens to be of my parents fighting. My sisters and I were sitting along the carpet that led into the kitchen, begging our parents to stop, but that didn't stop the dishes from flying. Nonetheless, they were divorced shortly thereafter. Sadly, this is the only memory I have of my parents being together. I lived with my mom until I was 13. The events leading up to my decision to leave her shaped a huge part of who I am today.

We had shifted from place to place, all around Weatherford. The first apartment I remember was the one where my sisters, my mom, and I were the closest. My mom was helping my oldest sister with her homework when the kitchen caught fire. We got evicted from that place and had to figure out somewhere to live, which ended up being at my grandpa's house. I'm so glad I got to be around him because he was the greatest man alive. Of course, living with him couldn't be permanent, so we soon lived with my mom's boyfriend. Life at the time was perfect in my child's eyes. Then, the boyfriend became controlling and demanding all kinds of things from my mom. She worked nights and we never got to see her. We woke up in the mornings, she wasn't there, so my sister, who could drive at the time, would drive us. She was never there after school for us either, so we would wait after school for an hour while my sister made her way to pick us up. We were always being put off on my aunt and uncle. We never got to be around my mom. She never had any money; turns out, her boyfriend was stealing it from her, including her child support checks. The boyfriend "took us" for all we had, and we were out again on our own. My mom could hardly find and keep a steady job; so again, we saw her coming and going to work.

When we finally did find a steady place to live and my mom found more of a steady job, something always happened. My mom was still always working so we could have clothes and food. Then she lost the job, and we would go nights and days without food. I was the kid who looked forward to school so I could have two meals a day. My mom would get food from somewhere and it would be like Christmas. We would struggle to find money to do laundry so we could have clean clothes to wear to school.

Looking back, I can see how I would become who I am today by what had happened in my life. My childhood wasn't all bad, but I mostly remember the struggles, and the wants. I began to get jealous of the people who had everything. The kids that would come to school, had the good pencils, the pretty clothes, and both parents together; I began to hate them because they had everything, and didn't realize it. I had it a lot better than some kids, and I knew it, but I was still jealous. I could never sign my parents up for career day, or to help with a class party. My dad would take field trips with us, but it still wasn't enough. I was greedy for the attention and possessions that these other kids had.

My sisters and I were never that close. (We are now, but it has taken us a long time to even be able to stand each other.) We would always get in fights. With one of my sisters, it was always going to be a fight. I went to the Emergency Room twice in one summer because she was so physically abusive. She threw me into a glass door and had me up against a brick wall, but never got in trouble herself. Then when she did get in trouble at school, I had to play the parent and comfort her. I grew up fast during childhood and found myself even more jealous of the kids at school because they still had the chance to be kids. They didn't have to worry about where their next meal came from, or what kind of injury they would get at home. I learned to be patient, too, because I was always waiting for my mom to grow up and be a real mom, and I waited to my dad to come to my rescue. That's when I decided to move in with him when I was old enough (at age 12). I was so tired of being around the drugs and smoking that I felt suffocated and trapped. I felt horrible for my mom and I wish she could understand. That was the most selfish thing I had ever done in my life. I didn't think of my mom's feelings too much, or my sisters, just myself and what would be best for me. It was the best thing for all of us though because my sisters started to miss me so we started to get along more and were able to actually be in the same room. My mom even started being my mom.

The teen years, not as full of angst as previously conceived, came with enlightenment. I was never the pretty girl; the boys never had a crush on me. I had the braces, the glasses, and the "I'm too good and young for makeup" attitude. I was more wrapped up in studying and doing stuff around the house than anything. When I did start wearing makeup, it was just base, so it didn't really do much. Entering high school, I wore tons of makeup. I felt like I had to in order to be noticed. My sister always told me that I needed makeup and I never believed her, but then I started to get attention when I wore it. I wore it all the time because I actually felt pretty. I matched it with clothes that screamed attention. I had the patterned pants with the shirts that had weird sayings on then, jewelry that was suggestive, and straightened my hair so people would be intrigued by me. It worked, so I kept doing it. When I did get a boyfriend, he was awful. He was tough, and in a gang in Arlington. I loved the words he would speak to me. It made me feel like I was the only one that mattered to him. I didn't care that he went and jumped someone, or did drugs, because he always made the time to text and call me. Finally, I felt like the special girl I always wanted to be. Little did I know he cheated on me with two girls, at one party! I was devastated, but I stayed with him because he still used the crafty words that kept me around. I still didn't care that he was in a gang or killing people!

That's when the desire to cut myself emerged.

I would slice through my thighs so it would be easy to hide. No one knew what I was doing, and I liked it that way. (People that cut on their arms just do it for attention; they expect to get drugs from the doctor for depression). I got to the point that I liked the way it felt, it didn't hurt, more like feeling relief than anything. *Anytime I would get mad or frustrated I would run for a razor.* I stooped so low as to tear my fingers apart trying to break apart a regular shower razor. That's when I knew I had to get rid of this murderous relationship.

Even after I got rid of the awful boyfriend, I still wanted to cut. I loved it. Then I started going out with a guy I at first had disliked. After going out for a while, I realized things were different. He texted me, he called me, he said things he meant, he had the look in his eyes like I was the only person he loved; it wasn't the look that he was going to get lucky out of this relationship. After a few months, the urge to slice into my own skin was slowing down; I stopped doing it every day. Then it went away for good. I figured that I didn't have to do everything I was doing for attention. There are some guys that make girls feel like that, and it's ridiculous. There is someone out there that will take you for who you are. This is when I realized that *life is bigger than one person.*

I always try to make the best grades I can because I know the only way I can get what I want out of life is to get an education. When I began to fall behind and lose focus, I would look around at others and get jealous. I hated that these people had everything going for them; I wanted to be someone like that, and I was able to regain my focus.

The ungratefulness of my peers irritated me. People would whine that they don't have a cell phone with unlimited texts, or didn't have a brand new car. So what? They whine that their parents want them to have a job, or that they have a curfew of midnight. What do teenagers need to do that late at night anyway? Absolutely nothing is the answer. I often remind myself of the importance of school. I am not afraid of the hard work it takes to do well. In the end, people are completely selfish—those who "have" complain that they don't have enough, while people who "don't have" compulsively want.

Of course, like any other girl, we have our friends. Friends are saviors. There are some friends who are fun to hang out with, and then there are the friends who know absolutely everything and know exactly how to handle things. *Without my best friends, I would have gone insane.* They're my personal therapists, and what they do for me is priceless. From laughing until I cry, to crying until I laugh, they have been there through everything. The level of friendship, love, and support that we have all endured is the most important thing in my life. I don't care if a guy came in and hated my friend, he'd be the one who's gone, not my friends. If not for my friends, I wouldn't have had someone to pick up the pieces when everyone else took them. When I would stress out about my mom not being there, they were helping me get the pieces back. The pieces that the bad boyfriends took were given back to me after my friends helped me find the way back. I could never have felt whole without my friends.

I am "me" because I have taken my experiences, and put them into my developing PFC. I have yet to see the world, but I have seen enough of it that I know that life will be difficult. I am jealous because I don't understand why some people have everything, and some don't. I have yet to figure out why people act like they're the best thing ever to walk on this planet, and some worship everything that makes up this planet. I am independent because I could never count on anyone while I was growing up. I was responsible for finding my own food and for caring for my constantly sick mom. I also had the pleasure of making sure she could get to work on time and making sure she could get me and my sisters to school on time (she often forgot to pick us up after school until it started getting dark).

I am intelligent because I became obsessed with school in order to get out of the rotten place I once called childhood. I am a pacifist because I grew to hate confrontation; it often leads to violence. I would rather talk things through with raised voices than scream with raised fists. I am a lover because I know what it feels like to not feel love. I am a listener because I know what it feels like to not be heard. I am who I am because it's what I chose to be. I decided for myself a long time ago that I can only form my own opinions and decide truth on my own because everyone lies. I am who I am because I learn to be positive rather than negative. I am who I am because of all the lessons I've learned.

Everyone is different because of the things that we have gone through, yet we're all the same. We all yearn to be loved, whether it's from parents, friends, lovers, or anything else, the main goal is to feel cared about on the inside. Everyone has different experiences that make us who we are, but for me the desire to feel loved has put me through abusive relationships and loving relationships and has made me a whole person because of it.

CASSIDY'S BRAINMARKS

Another layer of protection—or soother—on top of our paradigm of adaptive neuropsychopathy can be a substantial bonding to peers. Clearly, Cassidy's brain is marked by peer affiliation and anchored in esteem that gives her the courage to branch off into new endeavors. Also, she realized early on that life is bigger than one person.

The Brainmarks Paradigm maintains that sapient brains surely must have chemical inoculation to prevent self-esteem crashes and cave-ins from life's abuses, abandonments, major disappoints, and deaths, as well as from debilitating, toxic relationships most likely occurring in childhood and adolescence in immature sapient brains. By chemical cascades from DANE brain, 5-HT, testosterone, and PEA, and social bonding from hormones such as oxytocin, what we have come to call psychopathy worldwide can be observed as *res ipsa* evidence of a natural brain condition, as well in pathological versions, by a violent personality disorder. More than 20,000 student autobiographies—represented in the sample autobiographies by Rachel, Sabrina, Loren, and Cassidy—finally have taught me the central importance of an adaptive, beneficial, and restorative version of psychopathy necessary for living. *Ultimately, it was a lesson I learned from my students.* All sapient brains have their stories of surviving fallout from toxic relationships with lovers, bosses, teachers, pastors, pretend friends, or employers with florid psychopathic behavior and the aftermaths they did not see coming. But we have nature's inoculation against devastation and damage, as well as protection *from engaging charms that covers up all the coming harm.*

Eventually, as the PFC powers up, at least by age 30, sapient brains appear to find affinity with expressions of truth and honesty; just such a brain must now get ready to parent progeny. The value of adaptive neuro-psychopathy can now be realized; brainwise, it is nature's way for the owner to survive another day and to produce at least one more brain to carry on for yet another generation.

Bibliography

Ackerman, Diane. (2004). *An alchemy of mind: The marvel and mystery of the brain.* New York: Scribner.

APA (American Psychological Association). (2000). *Diagnostic and statistical manual of mental disorders* (DSM-IV-TR). Washington, DC: American Psychological Association.

Babiak, P. (2007). From darkness into the light: Psychopathy in industrial and organizational psychology. In H. Herve & J. C. Yuille (Eds.), *The psychopath: Theory, research, and practice.* Mahwah, NJ: Lawrence Erlbaum Associates.

Barbaree, Howard E., & Marshall, William L. (Eds.). (2006). *The juvenile sex offender* (2nd ed.). New York: Guilford Press.

Bartol, Curt B., & Bartol, Anne M. (2008). *Criminal behavior: A psychosocial approach* (8th ed.). New York: Pearson.

Bear, Mark F., Connors, Barry W., & Paradiso, Michael A. (2001). *Neuroscience: Exploring the brain* (2nd ed.). Baltimore: Lippincott, Williams, & Wilkins.

Beilin, H. (1992). Piaget's enduring contribution to developmental psychology. *Developmental Psychology, 28,* 191–204.

Beilin, H. (1994). Jean Piaget's enduring contribution to developmental psychology. In *A century of developmental psychology* (pp. 257–290). Washington, DC: American Psychological Association.

Berry-Dee, Christopher. (2003). *Talking with serial killers: The most evil people in the world tell their own stories.* London: John Blake.

Blair, James, Mitchell, Derek, & Blair, Karina. (2005). *The psychopath: Emotion and the brain.* New York: Wiley-Blackwell.

Blum, Deborah. (2002). *Love at Goon Park: Harry Harlow and the science of affection.* New York: Perseus.

Bowler, Peter J. (2003). *Evolution: The history of an idea.* Berkeley: University of California Press.

Brizendine, Louann. (2006). *The female brain.* New York: Morgan Road Books.

Brodsky, Ira S. (2010). *The history and future of medical technology.* St. Louis, MO: Telescope Books.

Brown, Nina. (2006). *Coping with infuriating, mean, critical people: The destructive narcissistic pattern.* Westport, CT: Praeger.

Brussel, James A. (1968). *Casebook of a crime psychiatrist.* New York: Bernard Geis Associates.

Buss, D. M. (Ed.). (2005). *Evolutionary psychology handbook.* Hoboken, NJ: John Wiley & Sons.

Buss, D. M. (2005). *The murderer next door: Why the mind is designed to kill.* New York: Penguin.

Buttafuoco, Mary Jo. (2009). *Getting it through my thick skull.* Deerfield Beach, FL: Health Communications.

Buxton, Richard B. (2002). *An introduction to functional magnetic resonance imaging: Principles and techniques.* Cambridge: Cambridge University Press.

Byrne v. Boadle. (1863). Court of Exchequer. 2 H. & C. 722, 159 Eng. Rep. 299.

Campbell, J., & DeNevi, D. (Eds.). (2004). *Profilers.* New York: Prometheus.

Caspi, A., McClay, J., Moffitt, T. E., Mill, J., Martin, J., Craig, I. W., Taylor, A., & Poulton, R. (2002). Role of genotype in the cycle of violence in maltreated children. *Science, 297* (5582), 851–854.

Changeux, Jean-Pierre. (1985). *Neuronal man: The biology of mind.* New York: Oxford University Press.

Cleckley, Hervey. (1988). *The mask of sanity: An attempt to clarify some issues about the so-called psychopathic personality.* St. Louis, MO: Mosby.

Cohen, Sidney. (1988). *The chemical brain: The neurochemistry of addictive disorders.* Minneapolis: Care Institute.

Cooke, D. J., Forth, A. E., & Hare, R. D. (Eds.). (1998). *Psychopathy: Theory, research, and implications for society.* Dordrecht: Kluwer.

Cooper, Jack R., Bloom, Floyd E., & Roth, Robert H. (1991). *The biochemical basis of neuropharmacology* (6th ed.). New York: Oxford University Press.

Cornwell, Patricia. (2002). *Portrait of a killer: Jack the Ripper case closed.* New York: Penguin Putnam.

Craig, Robert J. (2005). *Personality-guided forensic psychology.* Washington, DC: American Psychological Association.

Cummings, Nicholas A., & O'Donohue, William T. (2008). *Eleven blunders that cripple psychotherapy in America.* New York: Routledge.

Dabney, Dean A. (2004). *Criminal types.* Belmont, CA: Thomson.

Darby, David, & Walsh, Kevin. (2005). *Neuropsychology: A clinical approach* (5th ed.). New York: Elsevier.

Darwin, Charles. (1859). *On the origin of species.* London: John Murray.

De Becker, Gavin. (1997). *The gift of fear.* New York: Dell Books.

Douglas, J. (with Olshaker, Mark). (1995). *Mind hunter: Inside the FBI's elite serial killer crime unit.* New York: Pocket Books.

Douglas, J. (with Olshaker, Mark). (1998). *Obsession.* New York: Pocket Books.

Douglas, J. (with Olshaker, Mark). (1999). *The anatomy of motive.* New York: Pocket Books.

Douglas, J. (with Singular, Stephen). (2003). *Anyone you want me to be: A true story of sex and death on the Internet.* New York: Pocket Books.

Douglas, J., Burgess, A., Burgess, A., & Ressler, R. (1992). *Crime classification manual: A standard system for investigating and classifying violent crimes.* San Francisco: Jossey-Bass.

Esherick, Joan. (2006). *Criminal psychology and personality profiling.* Philadelphia: Mason Crest.

Ewing, C. P., & McCann, J. T. (2006). *Minds on trial: Great cases in law and psychology.* Oxford: Oxford University Press.

Farwell, L. A., & Smith, S. S. (2001). Using brain MERMER testing to detect concealed knowledge despite efforts to conceal. *Journal of Forensic Sciences, 46* (1), 135–143.

Festinger, Leon. (1957). *A theory of cognitive dissonance.* Stanford, CA: Stanford University Press.

Forth, A. E., Newman, J. P., & Hare, R. D. (Eds.). (1996). Issues in criminological and legal psychology: No. 24, *International perspective on psychopathy* (pp. 12–17). Leicester, UK: British Psychological Society.

Gerber, Samuel M., & Saferstein, Richard. (Eds.). (1997). *More chemistry and crime.* Washington, DC: American Chemical Society.

Giedd, Jay. N. (2009). *The teen brain: Primed to learn, primed to take risks.* New York: Dana Foundation.

Girard, James E. (2008). *Criminalistics: Forensic science and crime.* Boston: Jones and Bartlett.

Goldberg, Elkhonon. (2001). *The executive brain: Frontal lobes and the civilized mind.* New York: Oxford University Press.

Granhag, Par, & Stromwall, Leif. (Eds.). (2004). *The detection of deception in forensic contexts.* Cambridge: Cambridge University Press.

Guthrie, Robert V. (2004). *Even the rat was white: A historical view of psychology.* New York: Pearson.

Hare, R. D. (1993). *Without conscience.* New York: Guilford Press.

Hare, R. D. (2003). *Psychopathy checklist-revised technical manual* (2nd ed.). Toronto: Multihealth Systems.

Hare, R. D., & Neumann, C. N. (2006). The PCL-R assessment of psychopathy: Development, structural properties, and new directions. In C. Patrick (Ed.), *Handbook of psychopathy* (pp. 58–88). New York: Guilford Press.

Harlow, H. F. (1962). Development of affection in primates. In E. L. Bliss (Ed.), *Roots of behavior* (pp. 157–166). New York: HarperCollins.

Harris, Thomas. (1988). *The silence of the lambs.* New York: St. Martin's Press.

Hazelwood, Roy, & Michaud, Stephen G. (2001). *Dark dreams.* New York: St. Martin's True Crime.

Heilbronner, Robert L. (Ed.). (2005). *Forensic neuropsychology casebook.* New York: Guilford Press.

Heilman, Kenneth M. (2005). *Creativity and the brain.* New York: Psychology Press.

Herman, Gabor. T. (2009). *Fundamentals of computerized tomography: Image reconstruction from projections* (2nd ed.). New York: Springer.

Hickey, Eric W. (2006). *Serial murderers and their victims* (4th ed.). Belmont, CA: Thomson.

Hindle, Maurice. (1818/1992). Introduction to *Frankenstein* by Mary Shelley. New York: Penguin Books.

Holmes, R. M., & Holmes, S. T. (2002). *Profiling violent crimes: An investigative tool* (3rd ed.). Thousand Oaks, CA: Sage.

Jacobs, Don. (2003). *Sexual predators: Serial killers in the age of neuroscience.* Dubuque, IA: Kendall/Hunt.

Jacobs, Don. (2007). *Mind candy: Who's minding the adolescent brain?* Plymouth, MI: Hayden-McNeil.

Jacobs, Don. (2008). *The psychology of deception: Sexual predators and forensic psychology.* Plymouth, MI: Hayden-McNeil.

Jacobs, Don. (2009). *Brainmarks: Headquarters for things that go bump in the night.* Dubuque, IA: Kendall Hunt.

Jacobs, Don. (2009). *Psychology of deception: Analysis of sexually psychopathic serial crime.* Dubuque, IA: Kendall Hunt.

Jeeves, Malcom. (1994). *Mind fields: Reflections on the science of mind and brain.* Grand Rapids, MI: Baker Books.

Johnson, Steven. (2004). *Mind wide open: Your brain and the neuroscience of everyday life.* New York: Scribner.

Kalechstein, Ari, & Van Gorp, Wilfred G. (Eds.). (2007). *Neuropsychology and substance use.* New York: Taylor & Francis.

Kantor, Martin. (2006). *The psychopathy of everyday life.* Westport, CT: Praeger.

Keppel, Robert D. (1997). *Signature killers: Interpreting the calling cards of serial murder.* New York: Pocket Books.

Kirschner, Marc, & Gerhart, John. (2005). *The plausibility of life: Resolving Darwin's dilemma.* New Haven, CT: Yale University Press.

Langer, Walter. (1972). *The mind of Adolf Hitler.* New York: Basic Books.

Larrabee, Glenn, J. (Ed.). (2005). *Forensic neuropsychology: A scientific approach.* New York: Oxford University Press.

Lynch, Zach. (2009). *The neuro revolution: How brain science is changing our world.* New York: St. Martin's Press.

Masson, Jeffrey Moussaieff. (2003). *The assault on truth: Freud's suppression of the seduction theory.* New York: Ballantine Books.

Mattson, James, & Simon, Merrill. (1996). *The pioneers of NMR and magnetic resonance in medicine.* Jericho, NY: Dean Books.

McCrary, Gregg O. (with Ramsland, Katherine). (2003). *The unknown darkness: A former FBI profiler examines his most fascinating—and haunting—cases.* New York: HarperCollins.

McDonald, J. M. (1963). The threat to kill. *American Journal of Psychiatry, 120,* 125–130.

Meloy, J. Reid. (2002). The "polymorphously perverse" psychopath: Understanding a strong empirical relationship. *The Menninger Foundation Journal, 66* (3).

Michaud, Stephen J., & Hazelwood, Roy. (1999). *The evil that men do.* New York: St. Martin's True Crime.

Miller, Bruce E., & Cummings, Jeffrey L. (1999). *The human frontal lobes: Functions and disorders.* New York: Guilford Press.

Miller, Kenneth. (2007). *Finding Darwin's god.* New York: Harper Perennial.

Millon, Theodore, Simonsen, Erik, Birket-Smith, Morten, & Davis, Roger D. (Eds.). (1998). *Psychopathy: Antisocial, criminal, and violent behavior.* New York: Guilford Press.

Mladinich, Robert. (2001). *From the mouth of the monster: The Joel Rifkin story.* New York: Simon and Schuster.

Morrison, Helen. (2004). *My life among the serial killers.* New York: HarperCollins.

Nasar, Sylvia. (1998). *A beautiful mind: The life of mathematical genius and Nobel laureate John Nash.* New York: Touchstone.

Neufeld, Gordon, & Mate, Gabor. (2004). *Hold on to your kids.* New York: Ballantine Books.

Norris, Joel. (1989). *Serial killers.* New York: Anchor Books.

Owen, David. (2004). *Criminal minds: The science and psychology of profiling.* New York: Barnes and Noble Books.

Patrick, Christopher J. (Ed.). (2006). *Handbook of Psychopathy.* New York: Guilford Press.

Pron, Nick. (1995). *Lethal marriage: The uncensored truth behind the crimes of Karla Homolka and Paul Bernardo.* Toronto: Seal Books.

Purcell, Catherine E., & Arrigo, Bruce A. (2006). *The psychology of lust murder: Paraphilia, sexual killing, and serial homicide.* New York: Academic Press.

Raine, Adrian. (1993). *The psychopathology of crime: Criminal behavior as a clinical disorder.* New York: Academic Press.

Raine, Adrian, & Sanmartin, Jose. (Eds.). (2001). *Violence and psychopathy.* New York: Kluwer Academic.

Ramachandran, V. S., & Blakeslee, Sandra. (1999). *Phantoms in the brain.* New York: HarperCollins.

Ramsland, Katherine. (2002). *The criminal mind: A writer's guide to forensic psychology.* Cincinnati: Writer's Digest.

Ramsland, Katherine. (2006). *Inside the minds of serial killers: Why they kill.* Westport, CT: Praeger.

Ratley, John J. (2002). *A user's guide to the brain. Perception, attention, and the four theaters of the brain.* New York: Vintage Books.

Read, Cynthia A. (2007). *Cerebrum 2007: Emerging ideas in brain science.* New York: Dana Press.

Ressler, Robert K. (1992). *Whoever fights monsters.* New York: St. Martin's Press.

Ressler, Robert K., Burgess, Ann W., & Douglas, John E. (1992). *Sexual homicide: Patterns and motives.* New York: Free Press.

Restak, Richard. (2003). *The new brain: How the modern age is rewiring your mind.* Emmaus, PA: Rodale.

Reynolds, Cecil, & Fletcher-Janzen, Elaine. (Eds.). (2006). Brain SPECT imaging. In *Encyclopedia of Special Education.* Hoboken, NJ: John Wiley & Sons.

Rose, Steven. (2005). *The 21st Century Brain: Explaining, Mending, & Manipulating the Mind.* London: Jonathan Cape.

Rosen, Jeffrey. (2007). The brain on the stand. *New York Times* magazine. Available at: http://www.nytimes.com/2007/03/11/magazine/11Neurolaw.t.html?_r=1.

Salekin, R. T., Rogers, R., Ustad, K. L., & Sewell, K. W. (1998). Psychopathy and recidivism among female inmates. *Law and Human Behavior, 22,* 219–239.

Samaha, Joel. (1999). *Criminal law* (6th ed.). Belmont, CA: Wadsworth.

Samenow, Stanton E. (1984). *Inside the criminal mind.* New York: Crown.

Samenow, S., & Yochelson, S. (1976–1986). *The criminal personality* (3 vols.). New York: J. Aronson.

Schweitzer, N. J., & Saks, Michael J. (2007). The CSI effect: Popular fiction about forensic science affects public expectations about real forensic science. *Jurimetrics, 47,* 357.

Siegal, Larry. (2000). *Criminology* (7th ed.). Belmont, CA: Wadsworth.

Simon, R. I. (1996). Psychopaths, the predators among us. In R. I. Simon (Ed.), *Bad men do what good men dream* (pp. 21–46). Washington, DC: American Psychiatric Publishing.

Simon, Rita James, & Mahan, Linda. (1971). Quantifying burdens of proof—A view from the bench, the jury, and the classroom. *Law and Society Review, 5,* 319–330.

Stevens, Dennis J. (2001). *Inside the mind of sexual offenders: Predatory rapists, pedophiles, and criminal profiles.* San Jose, CA: Authors Choice Press.

Stevenson, Robert Lewis. (1995). *The strange case of Dr. Jekyll and Mr. Hyde.* New York: Barnes & Noble.

Stirling, John. (2002). *Introducing neuropsychology: Psychology focus.* New York: Taylor & Francis.

Turvey, Brent E. (2002). *Criminal profiling: An introduction to behavioral evidence analysis* (2nd ed.). San Diego: Academic Press.

Verona, E., Patrick, C. J., & Joiner, T. E. (2001). Psychopathy, antisocial personality, and suicide risk. *Journal of Abnormal Psychology, 110* (3), 462–470.

Voplagel, Russell. (1998). *Profiles in murder.* New York: Dell.

Walsh, David. (2004). *Why do they act that way? A survival guide to the adolescent brain for you and your teen.* New York: Free Press.

Weiner, Irving B., et al. (Eds.). (2006). *The handbook of forensic psychology* (3rd ed.). Hoboken, NJ: John Wiley & Sons.

Wexler, Bruce E. (2006). *Brain and culture: Neurobiology, ideology, and social culture.* Cambridge, MA: MIT Press.

White, Theodore H. (1975). *Breach of faith: The fall of Richard Nixon.* New York: Atheneum Publishers.

Wilson, Colin. (2004). *A criminal history of mankind.* London: Mercury Books.

Wrightsman, Lawrence. (2001). *Forensic psychology.* Belmont, CA: Wadsworth.

Zimmer, Carl. (2009). The ever evolving theories of Darwin. *Time,* February 12.

Zimmer, Carl. (2009). *The tangled bank: An introduction to evolution.* Greenfield Village, CO: Roberts and Company.

Index

modification, evolutionary
development and, 134–135, 139
Moniz, Egas, 44
moral depravity: biological
dysfunction and, 266–267;
psychopathy and, 116–117
Morrisette, James, 250–256
Morrisette, Joan Marie, 250–256
Moss, Michael, 160
mothering: antisocial behavior and
role of, 199–200; surrogate
mothers, 196
Mullany, Patrick, 23, 27–28, 164

narcissism, 118; orgasm and
psychopathy and, 205–206
Narcissistic Personality Disorder
(NPD), 118
Nash, John, 108–109
National Center for the Analysis of
Violent Crime (NCAVC),
163–165
natural science, criminal psychology
and, 28
natural selection: adaptive
neuropsychopathy and,
143–144; evolutionary
development and, 135, 138–139
Naval Criminal Investigative Service
(NCIS), Cold Case Unit, 9–10
Neufeld, Peter, 11
neuroadaptive psychopathy. *See*
adaptive neuropsychopathy
neurochemistry: cortical brainmark
regions, 126–127; criminality
and, 167–171; forensic
investigative science and,
218–220; parenting-in and
parenting-out strategies and,
188–190
neurocognitive mapping: cognitive-
behavior psychology, 61; *res
ipsa* evidence and, 150–151; of
serial killers, 242–244

neurolaw: brain on trial in, 70–72;
emergence of, 12; neuroscans
and, 73–75
neuroplasticity, 127–128
neuropsychology: adolescent
neurobiology and, 38–40;
brain fingerprinting and,
33–34; brain imaging
techniques, 44–48; Brainmarks
Paradigm and, 41–43; clinical
forensic neuropsychology,
13; compelled *vs.* choice
behavior, 62–65; criminal mind
analysis and, 11–12; forensic
investigative science training
and, 9, 36–38; Histrionic
Personality Disorder and,
121–126; memory- and
encoding-related multifaceted
EEG response, 35–36;
neuroscan imaging, 40–41;
pathological psychopathy and,
43–44; qualitative differences
in personality disorders and,
166–167. *See also* adaptive
neuropsychopathy
neuroscan techniques: criminal mind
analysis and, 11–12; evolution
of, 40–41; neurolaw and, 73–75;
pathological psychopathy and,
43–44
neurosis, abuse and, 26–27
neurotransmitter, adaptive
psychopathy and, 111–113
Newton, Isaac, 140–141
nigrostriatal pathway, dopamine
chemistry, 214
Nixon, Richard, 113–115, 159–161
norepinephrine (NE) chemistry:
adaptive neuropsychopathy
and, 285–286; anhedonia and,
213–214; Brainmarks Paradigm
and, 109–111; criminal brain
analysis and, 13–14; DANE

About the Author

An educator by choice and writer by passion, DON JACOBS has been an innovator in higher education for 25 years. In 2004, Professor Jacobs was the architect of the FORS rubric of academic transfer courses preparing students to major in forensic science. As forensic psychology represents one of the most important applied sciences of the 21st century, Professor Jacobs has been a driving force behind new textbooks, cutting-edge conference presentations, and the interdisciplinary preparation of today's forensic investigative scientists. In this volume, he presents in detail 10 new tools and improved products that have been highly effective in analyzing and capturing criminal minds. Likewise, insight into the adolescent phase of development has been one of his intellectual curiosities and is reflected in a long-running essay assignment—Who are you? Why?—required for introductory psychology students. Across three decades, the content of the essays remained consistent with themes of deception and entitlement that helped to shape his ground-breaking paradigm of adaptive neuropsychopathy documented in this volume.

About the Series Editor

PATRICK MCNAMARA, PhD, is Associate Professor of Neurology and Psychiatry at Boston University School of Medicine (BUSM) and is Director of the Evolutionary Neurobehavior Laboratory in the Department of Neurology at the BUSM and the VA New England Healthcare System. Upon graduating from the Behavioral Neuroscience Program at Boston University in 1991, he trained at the Aphasia Research Center at the Boston VA Medical Center in neurolinguistics and brain-cognitive correlation techniques. He then began developing an evolutionary approach to problems of brain and behavior and currently is studying the evolution of the frontal lobes, the evolution of the two mammalian sleep states (REM and NREM), and the evolution of religion in human cultures.

DATE DUE
